DEBACLE

Michael Ledeen
& William Lewis

VINTAGE BOOKS A DIVISION OF RANDOM HOUSE · NEW YORK

DEBACLE
The American Failure in Iran

FIRST VINTAGE BOOKS EDITION, APRIL 1982
COPYRIGHT © 1980, 1981 BY MICHAEL LEDEEN AND WILLIAM LEWIS
ALL RIGHTS RESERVED UNDER INTERNATIONAL AND PAN-AMERICAN
COPYRIGHT CONVENTIONS. PUBLISHED IN THE UNITED STATES BY
RANDOM HOUSE, INC., NEW YORK, AND SIMULTANEOUSLY IN
CANADA BY RANDOM HOUSE OF CANADA LIMITED, TORONTO.
ORIGINALLY PUBLISHED BY ALFRED A. KNOPF, INC., NEW YORK,
IN APRIL 1981.

LIBRARY OF CONGRESS CATALOGING IN PUBLICATION DATA
LEDEEN, MICHAEL ARTHUR, 1941-
DEBACLE, THE AMERICAN FAILURE IN IRAN.
INCLUDES BIBLIOGRAPHICAL REFERENCES AND INDEX.
1. UNITED STATES—FOREIGN RELATIONS—IRAN.
2. IRAN—FOREIGN RELATIONS—UNITED STATES.
I. LEWIS, WILLIAM HUBERT, 1928-
II. TITLE.
E183.8.I55L42 1982   327.73055   81-52262
ISBN 0-394-75182-5 (PBK.)   AACR2

MANUFACTURED IN THE UNITED STATES OF AMERICA

To Kathleen and Barbara

Contents

Foreword to
the Vintage Edition

SINCE WE WROTE this book, there has been a change in the White House. Thus far, the Reagan administration has tried to follow a more traditional foreign policy than that of its predecessor. Geopolitical problems have once again been given priority over an abstract human-rights doctrine. More attention—and money—is now devoted to the reconstruction of American military power, and the East-West conflict once again occupies central stage.

All of this is encouraging for those, like ourselves, who believe that the national interest, while requiring a moral dimension, is first and foremost a geopolitical concept. However, many of the problems that we analyze in *Debacle* still remain. It would be surprising if it were otherwise, since a change in administration does not produce a sudden change in the thousands of persons who participate in the formulation of national policy. For example, the debate over Saudi Arabia this past spring bears a striking similarity to earlier discussions involving Iran. To what extent should the United States arm Saudia Arabia? How many Americans should be sent to that country? Should Americans insist on control of the advanced weapons systems sold to Saudi Arabia? At what point does our support of the royal family risk provoking violent anti-American and anti-Western sentiments among the populace?

Moreover, as we write in *Debacle*, our failure in Iran was a symptom of a more profound crisis in the very nature of American foreign policy, and it is unlikely that a few changes in personnel can resolve such a question in a short time. A country like the United States can only conduct an effective foreign policy if there is a substantial consensus among those who make policy and in the body politic as a whole. Unfortunately, in the first months of the Reagan administration there were conflicting views among its principals and sharp clashes among leaders of the Republican party.

Finally, many of the problems faced by the new administration stemmed directly from the disaster that befell our foreign policy in Iran, which we tried to examine in this work. The urgent necessity of strengthening our ties with Saudi Arabia is a result of the fall of the Shah and the ruination of Iran by Khomeini's clerical fascism. If the West depends more than ever on Saudi oil, that is due in large part to the virtual disappearance of Iran from the petroleum market. And if the strategic menace of Russia and its satellites on the Persian Gulf is also stronger than ever, that is due in large part to the fact that Iranian military power no longer counts on the international chessboard. One cannot totally exclude the possibility of a Khomeini-like revolution, with a different style and different actors, to be sure, in the future of Saudi Arabia.

Introduction

THIS BOOK BEGAN when the editors of the *Washington Quarterly*—David Abshire, Walter Laqueur, and Michael Ledeen—felt it was important to investigate the nature of American policy during the Iranian crisis of 1978–79. It was the kind of subject that a foreign-policy quarterly is well suited to, for the daily press lacks the resources to devote weeks and even months to probing the details of policymaking. It was also a subject that seemed likely to remain at the center of American policy debates for a long time, precisely because the geopolitical consequences of Ayatollah Khomeini's successful assault on the Pahlavi dynasty were so serious.

The first choice of the editors was William Lewis, a former foreign service officer with considerable experience in the Middle East and intimate knowledge of the workings of the Washington bureaucracy. Having only recently left the State Department for a position at the George Washington University's Sino-Soviet Institute, Lewis knew most of the major actors in the Iranian drama at first hand, and seemed ideally qualified to write such an article for the *Quarterly*. But after several weeks of research, Lewis concluded that he could not accomplish the entire project by himself: some crucial sources were either unavailable to him or actually outside the country, and some matters lay outside his own field. He suggested, therefore, that the subject warranted a group effort. Michael Ledeen thereupon became Lewis's collaborator, and the result was an article, "Carter and the Fall of the Shah: The Inside Story," published in the spring of 1980.

In the course of producing the article, there were several themes that were necessarily dropped without adequate investigation, and because of the inevitable requirement of (relative) brevity, a paragraph was often used where the authors would have preferred to write several pages. But to compose a full-length book required considerable additional research, both inside and outside the United States. This problem was solved when we received encouragement from Alfred Knopf, and *Debacle* was essentially completed within four months of our agreement.

Our aim has been to write the story of an historic failure of American policymaking, and we thought it important to attempt a first approximation while people's memories were still fresh and their passions hot. Some of those wounded by their participation in the affair will develop explanations and self-deceptions regarding their own roles, while others may forget some of the crucial details. We have tried to give a sense of the strong passions that moved many of our policymakers. Americans felt very strongly about the shah, and about the "revolution" that toppled him, and their passions were central to the way in which American policy was made.

On the other hand, in trying to capture quickly the mood within the government, we may have overlooked some elements of the story that will only emerge with time and the more sustained research of others. And of course, we had only limited access to the documentary records of the past few years, and while government officials have put less and less on paper of late—preferring verbal communication for some sensitive operations—there is undoubtedly much to be learned from a careful study of the documents.

Our account is thus one of both scholarship and journalism. Our search for all available sources, cross-examination of some of the participants, and insistence on having multiple sources for major claims, all make this a journalistic undertaking. The information thus obtained was integrated into an overall context that rests to a considerable extent on the works of other scholars, and on those occasions when we have been able to consult a substantial body of documentation, our approach has been a traditional one. Both of us are scholars by training.

Despite our natural inclination to provide detailed footnotes for our evidence, there are not many notes in the text. A great deal of information—much of it crucial to our analysis—came from individuals who requested, and were promised, anonymity. In many cases, the request for anonymity was understandable and proper: some who spoke to us fear for their security and well-being if their identities should be revealed. Other sources were anxious to help us understand the problems, but were concerned about possible adverse effects on their careers. One may wish to have such persons speak "on the record," but they will not. The practical choice before us was whether to listen to them talk "off the record" or to do without.

From our standpoint, there was little difference between having sources who spoke for the record or anonymously, for in each case we had to evaluate their testimony. We have worked hard to check our sources' claims, and there is no major element of this analysis that rests upon the unconfirmed testimony of a single anonymous source. Much of what we were told turned out to be false, and in several cases the sources thanked us for helping them correct their own misimpressions. We were encouraged by the international reaction to our *Washington Quarterly* article; no one challenged the overall analysis, or any of the basic facts we presented. We have since discovered some minor errors, and have changed emphasis here and there, but the main outlines of our analysis remain intact.

If we have made mistakes, they are of course ours, whether they stem from attempts at deception by some of the participants or failures in research or analysis on our part.

This book was written with a political purpose: we wanted to produce a case study of a major event that would help explain why we currently find ourselves in such grave difficulties. While the government that failed to cope with the Iranian crisis was Democratic, the causes for the failure are not unique to the Carter administration. The Iranian debacle points to a general crisis of American policymakers of both parties, and of those elements of the professional bureaucracy involved in the process.

We are indebted to the editors and staff of the *Washington Quarterly*, who made this project a smooth and enjoyable one. Special thanks are due to our employers at the George Washington University and Georgetown University's Center for Strategic and International Studies, for their patience and encouragement. Our research was assisted by two talented persons: Barbara Ledeen and Robert Abeshouse. Finally, our thanks to Ashbel Green of Knopf, who dispassionately and rigorously kept us on track, and saved us from several traps of our own devising.

MICHAEL LEDEEN
WILLIAM LEWIS
Washington D.C.
November 3, 1980

DEBACLE

ONE

The King of Kings

THE HISTORY OF PERSIA is rich with the tales of strong and weak rulers who sought and achieved power only momentarily. Some squandered it on foolish adventures or passed into history after briefly indulging their passion for riches or grandeur. Others, like Cyrus the Great, who proclaimed himself king of Persia in 546 B.C., enlarged and even sustained impressive empires. But for millennia, the Persian kings—shahs—based their claim to legitimacy less on their lineage than upon their real personal power, and this in turn rested both upon their military strength and upon their force of character.

The lack of a stable dynastic tradition in Persia meant that few shahs were able to devote their energies to long-term programs. Rather than attempting to lay the groundwork for generations of stable prosperity and grandeur, Persian monarchs by and large survived by establishing firm working alliances with local chieftains, military leaders, and other powerful individuals at the expense of the populace. In the words of two eminent historians, the Persian monarchical heritage is a fairly dismal one: "A significant part of that heritage has been a relatively centralized, authoritarian monarchy that used agricultural surpluses to maintain its army and bureaucracy, leaving the majority of people powerless, illiterate, and poor."[1]

Nonetheless, the Persian monarchy served for a very long time as the linchpin of Iranian society, and its importance for the stability of the country must be measured in both institutional and psychological terms. The whole of Iranian institutional life eventually came to depend upon the shah himself; the country was structured vertically, with each separate compartment communicating directly with the shah at the top. Even in the most recent periods Iran retained the distinctive outlines of medieval autocracy. At the end of the days of the monarchy, Iran was a nation with an increasingly modern class structure and industrial apparatus but an outmoded governmental system. For those who believe in "models of revolution," Iran in the post–World War II period had a classical prerevolutionary structure.

The shah's psychological role was perhaps even more important than his purely institutional power. In order to appreciate the emotional bonds between ruler and ruled in Persia, one must experience the impact of the eleventh-century *Shah Namah*—the *Book of Kings*. Perhaps the finest work of Iranian literature, this epic poem by Firdausi chronicles the lives of legendary Iranian kings who led the people against "the wicked enemies of the realm." Even isolated and illiterate modern Iranian peasants were apt to be familiar with various passages of this epic, for the *Shah Namah* was part of the country's rich oral tradition. The work added to the legitimacy of the monarchy and of Persian nationalism that provided the bedrock of rule by Reza Shah Pahlavi and his son, Mohammed Reza. For the overwhelming majority of peasants, bazaari merchants, students, and aspiring intellectuals, the shah was far more than a mere person; he was a living legend, the embodiment of the nation.

This quasi-mystical charisma was a source of considerable political power for Persian rulers, particularly in the countryside, where the oral tradition was not often subjected to critical reappraisals; but such a tradition can obviously cut two ways, and a shah who attempted to break with tradition might well find himself accused of violating the precepts of the *Shah Namah*. In fact, the epic is full of tales of resistance by the Persian people to rulers of despotic inclination. And the chronicles of the real Iranian kings show the importance of this theme: many shahs were removed from the throne by violence from below.

In short, the ruler of Iran drew upon a body of legitimizing legend that encouraged him to exercise power in a direct and colorful way.

But this same fund of legitimacy could be used against the shahs who were seen to violate its precepts. The decisive factor was the ruler's personality: a shah who was believed to act vigorously was generally hailed (unless of course his actions led clearly to disaster), while weak and indecisive rulers were scorned with an abrupt fickleness that itself represents a constant theme of Iranian history. With such a background, it is hardly surprising that most shahs ruled through a highly centralized system, and were very suspicious of any new power centers. They dared not offend either the military caste or the entrenched local and regional officials, who exercised their bureaucratic power with little regard for the general welfare or the occasionally enlightened interests of the monarchy. These local officials were more often than not religious leaders in their own right, drawing their authority from the Islamic vision, which admitted no separation of "church" and "state," holding, on the contrary, that the man of religion was the only one endowed with sufficient wisdom to govern according to Allah's light. Thus any shah who would change the basic structures of Iranian society would of necessity be forced to bring the Islamic mullahs to heel. Until the twentieth century, no Persian ruler was able to carry off such an operation—even if he had wanted to.

Before this century, then, the Persians were ruled by men who were generally disinclined to attempt any basic restructuring of the institutions of the country (the occasional nineteenth-century reformer either died young or was blocked in his efforts), and this meant that there was little in the way of real participation for the great masses of the people. It also meant that the small coterie of rulers—in the court and in the mosques—greatly enriched themselves. Whatever wealth was available rarely trickled down below the level of the dominant caste, and corruption was so widespread that enlightened westerners familiar with Persia at first hand despaired of any change in the languid stasis of the country. Arthur Arnold, a nineteenth-century British adventurer, wrote the still definitive observation in his book, *Through Persia by Caravan:*

> One can imagine a good man killing himself in the effort to reform the Government of Persia. But success would seem impossible and endurance must lead to compromise with evil and corruption of every sort. A violent death would be the likely end of a good man in such

a position, and wealth that of one who would accept the place and
swim in the stream of corruption.[2]

In many cases, Persian monarchs achieved great wealth first, and
a violent death somewhat later. In the two hundred years before the
reign of Mohammed Reza Shah, only three shahs died of natural
causes. With few exceptions, this unhappy pattern remained the rule
in Iran until 1925, when the Peacock Throne was vacated by the last
Qajar dynastic ruler, and was ascended by an aggressive young Cossack Brigade officer, Reza Khan, the father of Mohammed Reza
Shah. Reza Khan had joined the brigade at fourteen, and quickly
established a reputation for forcefulness, daring, and courage. He
had a brilliant military career, and a remarkable stroke of luck
opened the door to power at the end of the Great War, when Great
Britain occupied Iran in an effort to contain the spread of the Bol-
shevik Revolution. As part of their anti-Communist program, the
British removed all Russian officers from the Iranian Cossack Brigade and replaced them with Iranian nationals. Reza Khan soon
came to the attention of the area commander of the British troops,
Major General Sir Edmund Ironside, and he was selected to lead the
brigade when the British began their withdrawal from the country.
He quickly made his presence known, presenting the ruling monarch
with an ultimatum: Reorganize the government or abdicate. Not
surprisingly, the first option was adopted in early 1921, and Sultan
Ahmad Shah ruled fitfully for four more years under the stern surveillance of Reza Khan and his military colleagues. In the end, the
government was brought down by a simple parliamentary vote under
the terms of the 1906 Constitution, and Reza Shah—the prime minister of the moment—had himself crowned king on April 25, 1925,
taking the title Reza Shah Pahlavi. The designation "Pahlavi" was
significant, for Pahlavi was the language of the ancient Parthians
who ruled Persia after Alexander the Great. The Pahlavi language
was the forerunner of modern Farsi, and Reza Shah's choice of name
significantly linked him—and later his son—to the ancient traditions
of the country rather than to the more recent, Islamic patterns of
Persian life and faith.

Reza Shah thus initiated a conflict with the religious forces of Iran
that ended with the triumph of the mullahs in 1979. It is to be
doubted that he undertook this campaign against the Islamic leaders

out of any desire to transform the structures of Iranian society. Although he frequently indicated a wish to emulate Kemal Atatürk's modernization of Turkey, Reza Shah lacked the culture to appreciate the vastness of the task before him. He was a simple, even crude man, who slept on the floor of the Palace rather than accede to the wishes of those royal counsellors who urged that he retire to a canopied bed. He preferred the food of the officers' mess to the cuisine of the Palace, and had a distinct taste for military uniforms rather than civilian attire.

Yet this simple man began what would later be termed the "White Revolution." Reza Shah delivered several telling blows to the mullahs: He opened the schools and even the University of Tehran to women, and abolished the requirement that all females wear the chador. He carried out a modest reform program that removed land from the religious leaders and put it under royal control. Moreover, he provided for a secular judiciary, thus further weakening the power of the mullahs, and even demonstrated that his religious opponents could not take sanctuary inside the mosques in order to escape his wrath. In 1936, he sent his troops into the Shrine of Imam Reza in Meshed to murder the religious protesters who were challenging his reforms. In May 1979, the forces of the Islamic revolution took their vengeance by destroying his mausoleum at Rey, just outside the capital city.[3]

With all that, Reza Shah never really tried to eliminate the religious clergy from effective power, nor was he interested in thoroughly secularizing Iran. It was essential to limit the power of the mullahs, but he knew that they represented both a stabilizing force and a potential adversary of enormous power. He never directed a systematic challenge to the mullahs; that would be the work of his son. Reza Shah's accomplishments were nonetheless decisive in laying the groundwork for a modern nation-state, breaking the power of tribal chieftains, and strengthening ties between the peasantry and the central government; reorganizing the military and starting a modern bureaucracy; revitalizing Persian nationalism and identifying the monarchy with the historic grandeur of the country. Perhaps most important of all, Reza Shah created a modern army, which made a thoroughly centralized government possible for the first time in recent Iranian history. The monarchy could finally have its orders enforced throughout the land.

This remarkable personality was removed from power by Great Britain and the Soviet Union in the fall of 1941, when Reza Shah's outspoken sympathies for the Axis—he was convinced that the Germans would prove the victors—made him unacceptable to Churchill and Stalin. A British ship sailed into Bandar Abbas and carried him to exile. Reza Shah had done wonders for his own country, but he failed to understand that Iran was part of a larger pattern:

> In the end Reza Shah was destroyed by events bigger than himself. His country and its oilfields had become of major significance to Britain. He rarely travelled outside Iran and failed to appreciate the extent to which his pro-German sympathies antagonized the British and the Soviets. . . . Or if he appreciated this, he failed to realize that both Britain and the Soviet Union were capable of riding roughshod over Iranian sovereignty if they felt their vital interests were at stake.[4]

Reza Shah died in Johannesburg in July 1944. His body was embalmed in Egypt and brought back to Iran after the war was over.

MOHAMMED REZA PAHLAVI and his twin sister Ashraf were born as commoners on October 26, 1919. The future shah received a superb education at Le Rosey school in Switzerland.* In keeping with his father's tastes, Mohammed Reza then underwent a period of training at the Iranian Military Academy. From Europe he gained an appreciation of international affairs, and of the material rewards offered by the West; from the Military Academy he learned concepts of strategy and discipline. In addition, the military training strengthened him physically, for he had been a weak and sickly child.

Although the shah ultimately came to hold great power, it took him many years to acquire it, and there were times when it seemed unlikely he would ever master his fate. He had first to endure three distinct periods when power was in other hands: 1941 to 1946, when Iran was dominated by the Allies; 1946 to 1953, when the shah was forced to play second fiddle to strong prime ministers, influential parliaments, and hyperactive nationalists; and 1954 to 1955, when the

---

*He was permitted to take one Iranian friend, and he chose Hossein Fardoust, who later remained at the imperial court as the shah's lifelong close friend and associate. Fardoust is now the head of SAVAMA, the successor to SAVAK, the internal security and intelligence organization.

country was under military rule by a strong prime minister who also controlled Iran's security forces. It was not until 1955 that the shah selected his own prime minister. From that period onward, Mohammed Reza Shah consolidated his power.

The first years of his rule left a profound imprint on his attitudes and political outlook. Early on, he found himself regarded with deep suspicion by his own people. The national disgrace of occupation lay heavily on Iranian pride, and the Peacock Throne appeared to be represented by the offspring of a discredited dynasty, reflecting a national humiliation. According to the diaries of a principal court adviser of the time, the British gave the current prime minister (Mohammed Ali Foroughi) the choice of becoming the president of a new Persian republic or remaining prime minister under the existing constitutional monarchy. Fortunately for the young shah, Foroughi opted for the latter course. He resigned for reasons of ill health six months after assuming office. There followed an extended period of revolving-door prime ministers, the large majority being selected by the British overlords. The young shah was regarded by London as a weak and pliable figure.

The continual change of prime ministers, often carried out at Russian insistence, was a reflection of the impotence of the Iranian leaders to determine the policies of the nation. The Majlis (parliament), for example, was made up of deputies selected and approved on political grounds by the occupying powers. This is not to say that the period was a tranquil one, for Iran was torn by intense domestic turmoil, some of it stemming from indigenous sources, some as the result of Soviet efforts to destabilize and subvert the country. One source of trouble that was to last for some time was the small nationalist liberal group led by Dr. Mohammed Mossadeq, a pajama-clad grandee of eloquent speech and fiery temperament. Passionate in his hatred of Great Britain and the United States, Mossadeq was one of the first Iranians to mobilize public sentiment on behalf of an intensely xenophobic nationalism. At the same time that Mossadeq made his appearance, there were other centrifugal forces on the Iranian scene: The Tudeh (Communist) Party, nationalism in Azerbaijan Province (which led to the brief proclamation of the "Azerbaijan Democratic Republic" with Soviet backing), and constant scheming among the various elements in the country all made the wartime and immediate postwar periods particularly volatile.

The question of Communist subversion was faced by both Pahlavis, and two major events demonstrated the seriousness of this
phenomenon. In the 1930s, Reza Shah discovered that the Soviet
intelligence service, the OGPU, had recruited several Iranian officials as espionage agents, and had effectively infiltrated both the
separatist movements in the northwest and northeast (including the
Kurds) and the embryonic trade union movement. Two decades
later, in 1954, Mohammed Reza Shah learned that massive Soviet
penetration of the Iranian armed forces had taken place, and he was
forced to approve a purge of the military. In the words of one of the
best-informed observers of the phenomenon:

> More than 450 officers were arrested, some as high-ranking as colo-
> nel, including a deputy to the army's Judge Advocate General, a
> deputy police chief responsible for the Shah's security and for the
> security of Vice President Nixon during his 1953 trip to Iran, and the
> chief of the police cryptography branch in Tabriz. The officers' organi-
> zation had been responsible for the 1950 escape of Tudeh Party leaders
> from prison, had engineered the sabotage of Iranian Air Force planes,
> had robbed banks to replenish party coffers and had served as an
> execution squad murdering party defectors.[5]

Mohammed Reza was greatly impressed by the Communist effort
at subversion, and it remained an obsession for his internal security
organization, known as SAVAK.* Indeed, the concern about Soviet
attempts to bring Iran under Communist influence undoubtedly
made it more difficult for the shah to appreciate the gravity of the
threat from his religious opponents in the seventies, for he was
constantly watching for threats from the far Left.

In the early period, Mohammed Reza Shah had little if any influence over the principal institutions of government; within the parliament his voice was rarely heard, and little attention was devoted to
his views. His political influence among his own people, let alone the
British and the Russians, was negligible. This was a testing period
that the shah later recalled with a combination of bitterness and
outrage.

After World War II and the British and Soviet military withdrawal from Iran, nationalist forces came to the fore, and Qavam

---

*The name was derived from the Persian title, *Sazeman-e Eltala'at va Amniyate Khasvar*,
meaning State Organization for Intelligence and Security.

es-Saltanah was named prime minister to appease nationalist sentiment. However, pressures from the Soviet Union compelled Qavam
to appoint three representatives from the Tudeh Party to his cabinet.
Through a combination of subtle maneuvering, exceedingly good
luck in the political arena, and discreet backing from the British,
Qavam managed to survive in office for more than eighteen months.
He skillfully conducted the Iranian campaign to remove Soviet influence from Azerbaijan Province, and in 1947, Qavam's Iran Democratic Party easily swept local contests. But, typical of Iranian politics, Qavam was not reappointed to the premiership. Jealous aspiring
politicians in the Majlis led the majority to revolt against Qavam.
The shah, although less instrumental than the Majlis in eliminating
Qavam, was delighted to witness his departure, for Qavam es-Saltanah represented a threat to the Pahlavi dynasty, a threat that could
mobilize antimonarchist forces to press for the creation of a republican government.

U.S. Ambassador George Allen assessed the basic strengths and
weaknesses of the shah's position in the wake of the Qavam removal
in prescient terms:

> Despite the fact that the shah is by far the most powerful figure in
> Iran today, his power is largely negative in that he can prevent almost
> any action he does not like, and is unable to do very much of a positive
> nature. Hardly anyone could drive the Iranians into doing very much
> to improve their country except a dictator, and the present shah shows
> apparent dislike for that role, and realizing that he is not cut out for
> it, I hope he continues to do so, for I prefer the painfully slow progress
> of democratic Iran to the meteoric but lopsided accomplishments of
> his father.[6]

The years following the elimination of Qavam remained difficult
ones for the shah. In short order, the issue of British control over
Iranian oil was raised, the Tudeh Party banned (although it remained far from inactive), the first of many attempts was made on
the shah's life, and the National Front appeared for the first time.
The vigor with which the shah could pursue policies and programs
of his own in this volatile environment was minimal; in the period
after 1947, it became readily apparent that tides were flowing in Iran
that once again threatened the monarchy. In 1949, former Prime
Minister Assad Hajir, a friend of the sovereign and at the time

minister of the imperial court, was assassinated by fanatical *Fe-day'i* nationalists*—thought by a number of observers to have been goaded into action by supporters of General Haji Ali Razmara, who made clear his wish to tame the Palace. In 1950, the elections for the Majlis brought new shocks to the young ruler: the National Front was gaining strength, and debates in the lower chamber made it clear that the Front intended to subordinate monarchical powers to the national legislature.

During this period, the potential for political mischief on the part of the military also became apparent. The military exerted its influence for the first time when General Razmara was brought to power as premier in June 1950. He immediately began to play off the British against the Russians to the growing advantage of those Iranian officers who were personally loyal to him. In due course, he was disposing of more political power than any other Iranian prime minister since World War II. Extortion, threats, and terror were the general's principal weapons. They proved exceedingly effective as increasing numbers of Iranian politicians were cowed and impelled to align themselves behind the military. Even the life of the shah appeared endangered, particularly after the assassination of court minister Hajir.

Oil was a central issue of the period. Shortly before he was himself killed by the *Feday'i,* Razmara negotiated an oil settlement favorable to Iran that even the most extreme of Iranian nationalists would have endorsed. Yet for some unexplained reason Razmara failed to notify the Majlis of the fruits of his negotiations or to otherwise publicize his success with the British. Observers at the time speculated that the general had been eliminated by supporters of Mohammed Reza Shah, who wished to frustrate Razmara's widely rumored plans to remove the monarch in favor of his half-brother, Abdol Reza—a scheme that completely alienated the shah from his brother.

The turbulent period that followed the assassination of Prime Minister Razmara brought Dr. Mohammed Mossadeq's radical nationalists to power. Mossadeq was carried to the premiership in April

*The *Feday'i*—the Zealots of Islam—were "opposed to democratic and parliamentary institutions, to female emancipation, to religious equality, to secular law—in fact to all forms of Western influence, and to all forms of association with the West." Cf. Bernard Lewis, "Bag Omvoeltingen i Persien" in *Nationaltidende,* 27 August 1953.

1951 on a wave of nationalist frenzy and agitation against the British and the throne. With his ascendancy began another painful, personally humiliating period for the young shah, then barely into his thirties. During this time there were more assassination attempts; eventually, Mossadeq stripped the shah of all power and even drove him to leave the country. Mossadeq's strength reposed in his lengthy record of government service, his nationalist credentials, his support from the clandestine Communist apparatus, and his ability to take advantage of the average Iranian's mistrust of foreigners (a xenophobia only too evident today). What also made Mossadeq a particularly dangerous adversary for Mohammed Reza Shah was his implacable hatred of the Pahlavi family itself—it appears that Mossadeq's mother traced her lineage to the Qajar dynasty, which had been overthrown by Reza Shah.

In the months preceding the Mossadeq-Palace confrontation, Mossadeq proved adept at eroding Palace authority, both symbolically and concretely. The shah's twin sister, Princess Ashraf, was sent abroad, thus isolating the monarch from one of his personal confidants and advisers. In rapid succession, Mossadeq retired senior army officers suspected of harboring royalist loyalties; the distribution of crown lands was halted on the grounds that these possessions were acquired illegally and therefore not to be treated as part of the royal patronage; and the royal fiat within the Majlis was circumscribed. Isolated politically and rightly concerned about the safety of his family, the shah fled Iran, initially to Baghdad and then to Rome. Three days after his flight, the fortunes of the throne improved dramatically: a combination of American covert intervention under the redoubtable CIA officer Kermit Roosevelt, a mutiny by loyal army officers, and agitation by leading bazaari merchants produced sufficient street mobs and demonstrators to ensure the resignation of Mossadeq as prime minister and the return of Mohammed Reza Shah to the Peacock Throne. Mossadeq was arrested and placed on trial for treason in November 1953. He was convicted and sentenced to three years' imprisonment, later to live out his years in a country home outside Tehran under virtual house arrest until his death in 1967.

The shah learned that he could not permit aspiring politicians to share the royal "charisma" or to serve as a hyphen between the Palace and the Iranian population at large. Henceforth he would keep aspiring leaders under control. Further, he had discovered a new source of guidance and support: the United States of America. The Americans had saved and flattered Mohammed Reza, and Washington's decision to restore him demonstrated that he was considered a valuable asset and a source of stability. While the British government of the day also opposed Mossadeq's machinations, it was the Americans, concerned by the rising power of the Tudeh Party (and Moscow's potential influence over the Iranian Communists), who took effective action to bring back the shah. From that moment, the interests of the United States and the fate of the monarchy were inevitably linked. The United States had a friend and client in the Middle East, head of a strategically situated nation—albeit one that was looking for internal stability and international acceptability. With the urging and consent of successive American administrations, the shah determined in the aftermath of the Mossadeq period that he should become the true son of his enterprising father. Mohammed Reza certainly had the intellectual equipment; it remained to be seen if he had sufficient strength of character.

Following the overthrow of Mossadeq, General Fazlollah Zahedi, chief of staff of the Imperial Iranian Army, was chosen as prime minister. The nine months in which Zahedi presided over cabinet deliberations were characterized by stern and repressive military rule. The Tudeh Party was crushed and driven underground, and many of its leaders fled abroad. Zahedi was supported in these efforts by General Teimur Bakhtiar, later the head of SAVAK. The Eighteenth Majlis, elected during Zahedi's tenure as premier, was composed largely of pro-Palace landlords, conservative merchants, and deputies who had supported the shah during his confrontation with Mossadeq. The shah did not yet completely control the military, but he had achieved substantial sway over parliament, and his prime minister, however powerful, could be "managed" through blandishments and other means.

With a judicious use of honors, pensions, and other rewards, the shah was able to secure the graceful exit of General Zahedi from office. The American government played a considerable part in the effort, having determined that its interests would be best served by ensuring that no new strongman should come to the fore in Iran.

After the removal of Zahedi, the U.S. Embassy at Tehran evaluated the rising power of the shah in the following terms:

> The shah himself is now presiding once a week over meetings of the Cabinet. . . . Although [he] presided at times over meetings of the Zahedi Cabinet, this had never been a weekly practice. The shah is reported to be enjoying his current role, and, for example, was reported to be greatly pleased at a foreign newspaper report to the effect that he intended now to rule, as well as to reign.
>
> The emergence of the shah into the realm of practical day-to-day administration, which had been growing in intermittent fashion during the life of the Zahedi government, appears to be the most important single element in the present internal political scene in Iran. Reactions are varied: many political leaders appear overjoyed that the hand of the shah can now be looked upon as a stabilizing influence that will result in a quick improvement of general conditions. Others express a real or pretended fear that the shah is not capable of effecting a genuine reformation, or that he will not continue to make the effort required, and that failure will damage the power and prestige of the Monarchy irrevocably.[7]

For the moment there was little need for worry, since the security situation, so uncertain for so long, had been stabilized. This permitted the shah to appoint Hossein Ala—formerly Iran's minister to Washington—as prime minister in April 1955, together with a group of other distinguished reformers. Men of remarkable talent and integrity, they were directed by the Palace to launch programs to rebuild the national economy and to develop an integrated political system. Within the cabinet team were two particularly able officials, Ali Amini and Abol Hassan Ebtehaj. The latter was a distinguished banker who assumed responsibility in the national economic sector as managing director of the Plan Organization (the body charged with responsibility for economic development). With massive American economic assistance, a sudden growth in oil revenues, and able administrative direction by key Iranian cabinet officials, Iran began in 1955 and 1956 to evidence clear signs of growth and development.

By April 1957, Ala was succeeded by Dr. Manuchehr Eqbal as premier, a position he held for almost four years. The Eqbal period is important because for perhaps the first time the shah had at his disposal a prime minister who was completely subservient to the will

and direction of the Palace. Through much of this period, the cabinet
acceded to the shah's directives, and the successes and failures of the
government could be attributed to the Pahlavi monarchy once again.

The Nineteenth Majlis, whose term expired in June 1960, was
unique for two additional reasons. It was the first parliament in
Iranian history to serve a full term, and it was perhaps the most
impassive and politically static as well. As plans proceeded for new
national elections, the Palace again intervened, prevailing upon two
national figures to form separate political parties and to engage in
mock competition. The Mardom and Melliyun parties were created
by Assadollah Alam (the shah's close associate and court minister)
and Dr. Eqbal respectively, and participated in the public charade
with the benevolent endorsement of the shah. The campaign proceeded with considerable public fanfare, but the overwhelming majority of Iranians were little deceived. Public indignation mounted,
and after it became apparent that a continuation of the staged competition would produce an explosive situation, the elections were canceled. Dr. Eqbal resigned the premiership, as well as his leadership
of the phantom "Melliyun Party." A second election to the Twentieth Majlis was duly held; despite public protests over "irregulari-
ties," the results were confirmed by the Palace, and the deputies
seated. However, it was clear that social and economic changes in the
country at large had produced a more informed and politically active
citizenry—one that would express its indignation when the Palace
engaged in outrageous practices. To retain and to broaden his power
successfully, the shah now had to take actions that would intensify
his ties with the mass of Iranians and to create in the popular
imagination a positive impression of their sovereign. During the
1960s, he felt compelled to strengthen his control over the instruments of government even further, as well as to attempt to establish
a more durable charismatic bond between himself and the majority
of Iranians whose fortunes and whose destiny he had to guide. The
shah now assumed direct responsibility for the performance of his
ministers, the excesses of the royal family, the abuses of the security
services, the rising and falling fortunes of workers, peasants, students, and politicians.

Yet it was one thing to embark upon a new course; it was quite
another matter to carry off an ambitious program. The shah, for all
his dreams and intentions, was not able to assume such vast respon-

sibilities without considerable assistance. He had to have help on two
levels: at home, he required guidance in political matters, for he
lacked the ruthless instincts necessary for effective rule. And internationally, he needed both technical and strategic advice, for he understood neither the specific requirements for the construction of a
modern military force nor the detailed planning necessary for its use.
At this crucial turning point in his reign, the shah was blessed with
outstanding assistance: at home from court minister Alam and a
coterie of lesser-known individuals; internationally from a handful of
talented Iranian generals, and above all from enthusiastic American
advisers.

The question of the American-Iranian connection will be dealt
with in the next chapter, but it is important to recognize that the U.S.
government took an active role in Iranian affairs throughout the
post-Mossadeq period. This American role extended over the full
range of Iranian decisionmaking, and thus was a constant influence
on Mohammed Reza Shah himself. In the period under consideration—the early sixties—the Kennedy administration was concerned
about the shah's rising appetite for military weaponry. The Kennedy
liberals were not impressed with the shah, and they did not take
kindly to his requests for steadily increasing military grant assistance. In a later period, when the shah again dismayed an American
government with his demands for armaments, the situation would be
somewhat different: in the early sixties Iran was in essence asking for
aid, whereas later the shah would be merely asking permission to buy
what he wanted. It was far easier to exert leverage in the former case,
and the Americans weighed in to limit the requests. At the same time
they suggested that it might be best if Mohammed Reza chose as
prime minister a man with the understanding necessary to deal with
modern economic and military problems. The result of these American pressures was the appointment, in 1961, of Ali Amini.

The Kennedy administration thought very highly of Amini, and
the President made an obvious reference to the Americans' favorite
minister in a toast to the shah in Washington in April 1962:

> We are quite aware that were it not for the leadership that [the shah]
> has given, in identifying himself with the best aspirations of his people
> —whom he is bringing out of an entirely different historic period into
> today, of surrounding himself with able and dedicated Ministers—we
> are quite aware that this vital area of the world, which has been, as

Mr. Molotov made clear, a vital matter of concern to the Soviet Union, for many, many years, would long ago have collapsed.[8]

Amini was indeed a genuine political talent, respected for his ability, his devotion to country, and his independence from monarchical "guidance." In announcing Amini's appointment, the Palace stressed that the shah would retain control over both the security forces and foreign relations. Amini, for his part, made clear his determination to launch a far-reaching land reform program for the country, to fight the corruption that was becoming widespread, and to reorganize and strengthen the administrative machinery of government. However, it soon became apparent that Amini was not in control, a development noted with evident unhappiness by officers from the Political Section of the U.S. Embassy:

> . . . the shah continues to think of himself as the ultimate political power in Iran and considers any power which Amini may have a delegation of authority rather than a transfer of power. Amini's now [July 1961] pessimistic, now optimistic view of the subject of the extent of his authority suggests that this is a matter for practically daily negotiations with the shah. The evidence would seem to point to the following conclusion: While the shah, out of fear, gave Amini wide authority at the time of his appointment, he has since regained his equilibrium and is eager to show that final authority rests with him, although Amini continues to have considerable latitude. Amini apparently either understands or senses this, but is ready to gloss over such a state of affairs since an admission of it on his part would put him precisely in the category of his subservient predecessors. In this connection, Amini can, however, cite actions such as the arrests for corruption which his predecessors never would have taken.[9]

At the outset of his appointment, Amini had made a mistake of a tactical nature that proved his undoing: he chose to accept appointment as prime minister without calling for new Majlis elections, as required by law. He did so for what seemed at the time an excellent reason—free and unfettered elections could not be assured. Moreover, should the elections confirm the Palace in its power, he would be hampered in his efforts to institute reforms. But Amini's calculations were clearly misplaced; the shah consistently undercut his efforts, popular opposition to the prime minister increased (due largely to the failure to hold elections), economic hardships resulted from his reform program, and his refusal to delegate authority antagonized large numbers of people. Amini became a spent force; in July 1962, he resigned.

After the fall of Ali Amini came the appointment of the shah's personal friend and confidant, Assadollah Alam, which was followed by the resignation of the more independent-minded government planners, a tightening of internal security control, and transformation of the reforms begun by Amini and his associates into the much-publicized and vaunted "White Revolution." Although there was little in this excellent reform program that originated with the shah, he took full credit for it. Mohammed Reza had finally become a shah, and he was fully prepared to take advantage of the opportunity that fate, good fortune, political skill, and American backing had created for him. The "White Revolution" was under way. The shah grasped the initiative in reaching for popular support, and was able to do so without having to confront any effective opposition. Religiously inspired demonstrations were methodically suppressed. In foreign affairs, by working toward what was called "a normalization of relations between East and West," the shah also asserted more independence than at any time during the previous two decades.

By mid-1965, the shah held virtually absolute control. He had uncontested command over most of the country's levers of power: the security services and the armed forces, the prime minister and the cabinet, the parliament and the bureaucracy. However, in a society undergoing rapid social and economic change, Mohammed Reza Shah lacked the unqualified support of old-line National Front politicians, the remnants of the Tudeh Party, intellectuals of the Left, students, the Shi'ite clergy, and the new proletariat that was burgeoning in Iran's major cities and towns. This last consisted of an unskilled and underutilized urban peasantry, an unemployed mass that had moved from the countryside to the cities in search of jobs and new opportunities for itself and its children. As in so many parts of the Third World, the proletariat found that they were the disinherited members of Iran's new society, without employment security or hope of self-betterment. It was from their ranks that many of the initial recruits of the crisis of 1978 were to come. Elsewhere, the Palace appeared to have neutralized its opposition, both existing and potential.

The most dangerous of the shah's enemies were undoubtedly the religious leaders, the mullahs. It is a commonplace in the literature

of social science that the religious caste becomes less and less powerful as a society embarks on "modernization," and that religious
leaders count for relatively little in a modern society. Yet in Iran, the
rule had not held true in the first half of the twentieth century. Until
the advent of Reza Shah, the mullahs—or, to use the more technical
term for the leading men of the faith, the ulama—had actually
become more powerful, forcing Reza Shah to undertake an intense
campaign to limit their influence early in his reign. And after the
downfall of Reza Shah they returned to the fore, on occasion allying
with secular opponents of the monarchy to present Mohammed Reza
with his most enduring challenge.

That this challenge was a grave one was demonstrated clearly in
1963, when an alliance of the ulama and secular enemies of the shah
produced a major outburst, leading to the exile of the Ayatollah
Ruhollah Khomeini to Iraq. Yet to all observers the outburst was
more a desperate last gasp of religious fervor than an indication that
the shah faced a continuing struggle for power. In 1971, one of the
most distinguished American scholars of Iranian history and society
observed that:

> There has been no repetition of the 1963 events. This may be largely
> explicable on the basis of the demonstrated military power of the
> government to quell disturbances, but one may also surmise that the
> leadership position of the ulama has been eroded. The position of the
> ulama seems bound to continue in general decline as literacy, secular
> schools, and scientific education spread; as Islamic practices regarding
> the relations of the sexes and other matters are increasingly ignored;
> and insofar as some of the ulama can be identified with a self-seeking
> opposition to reform.[10]

Moreover, with the explosion of oil wealth in the seventies, the
shah was able to funnel substantial funds to the mullahs, thus giving
them a direct stake in the success of his efforts to lead Iran into the
modern world. Yet precedent was against the shah. His father had
triumphed temporarily but had certainly not brought the ulama or
mullahs to heel. The shah's own success in 1963 had been due more
to the determination of his top advisers—above all, Alam—than to
his personal resolve and courage. While most Western observers
were convinced that the course of history and the models of social
science were on the shah's side, his task remained a perilous one.

MOHAMMED REZA SHAH embarked on a course of reformation and
change well aware of the fate of his ambitious predecessors. According to many of those who knew him best, he did so because of a
certain mystical confidence that his efforts would be guided and
supported by divine providence. He found ample evidence that he
was operating under a special dispensation in the fact that he had
survived one air crash and at least six assassination attempts. The
1949 attempt by a university student was felt to be the most significant: five bullets had been fired and had entered his body.

The shah was convinced that his own survival was miraculous,
and that his special destiny was to lead Iran into a period of grandeur
similar to that of the ancient Persian Empire. Could one believe that
the long succession of escapes from failure and death was mere
happenstance? Mohammed Reza did not, and he seemed drawn to
religious concepts that themselves came from the pre-Islamic period.
Many of his closest associates never believed that the shah was a
truly devout Muslim. Certainly there was some good evidence for
their skepticism: the introduction of the ancient Persian calendar; the
increasingly explicit references to the days of Cyrus the Great; and
finally the vast celebration at Persepolis in 1971, an event that perhaps
more than any other single act antagonized the religious leaders of
Iran and drove the wedge between the shah and the pious masses of
the country.

On a dusty, windswept plain next to the ruins of Persepolis—the
city of Darius the Great—the shah gave orders to build a city cover-
ing 160 acres, studded with three huge royal tents and fifty-nine lesser
ones arranged in a star-shaped design. No expense was spared to
make this one of the most lavish events of modern times. Food was
catered by Maxim's of Paris, the buildings were decorated by Jen-
sen's (the same firm that helped Jacqueline Kennedy redecorate the
White House), the guests ate off Ceraline Limoges china and drank
from Baccarat crystal glasses. The electric power station constructed
especially for the occasion would later provide energy to fifty villages. Indeed, the cost was sufficiently impressive that the shah for-
bade his associates to discuss the actual figures, and foreign press
criticism of the extravagance was enough to provoke Mohammed
Reza into an uncharacteristic outburst: "Why are we reproached for

serving dinner to 50 heads of state? What am I supposed to do—serve them bread and radishes?"

Many of the world's leaders attended: nine kings, five queens, and twenty-one princes and princesses, along with such luminaries as American Vice President Spiro Agnew and Emperor Haile Selassie of Ethiopia. Protocol was dictated by the principles laid down at the 1815 Congress of Vienna. It was a great spectacle, both because of the opulence of the festivities and because the shah was explicitly attempting to tie his own monarchy to that of the ancient Persian kings, several of whom—Darius, Xerxes, Artaxerxes I, and Darius II—were entombed nearby.

The Persepolis ceremonies antagonized many of the Iranian people, for the contrast between the dazzling elegance of Persepolis and the misery of the nearby villages was so dramatic that no one could ignore it. The shah's enemies made great capital out of the event. On the same day as the state dinner at Persepolis, the Iranian consulate was bombed in San Francisco, and the Confederation of Iranian Students at Berkeley, claiming responsibility for the explosion, demonstrated near the consulate, shouting: "Death to the shah!" In retrospect, Persepolis was a turning point in the anti-shah movement, alike for secular and religious opponents of Mohammed Reza. The shah might have survived the wrath of the mullahs, but in a way that would become typical of the last years of his reign, he managed to get the worst of both worlds: his intense and in many ways admirable pursuit of modernization alienated the traditional sectors of society; while his inability to create new political institutions at first frustrated, then antagonized the newly emerging groups and classes.

Mohammed Reza was a modernizer, but not a man capable of radically transforming the political structures of Iran. His was a traditional approach to kingship, and he never extended the elitism of the court to the technocrats and intellectuals who emerged from Iranian and Western universities. Indeed, the shah's system provoked the new classes, for they were excluded from effective participation in real power. Those already in possession of power, position, and prestige were in charge of the distribution of rewards from the Palace, resources from the government, and contracts from foreign corporations. Occasionally a new face was brought into the inner circle, but this was done on an individual basis, not systematically according to training and merit. Power was based on the calculus of personal relationships; in the words of Manfred Halpern, "upon the intimidation of one prominent man, the purchase of another, upon the expectation of future favors by a third, and upon the fear of losing privileges not earned on grounds of talent or skill." Unwilling to touch this ageless way of conducting national affairs, the shah fell victim to the limitation of what Halpern calls transitional authoritarian rulers, those who "are barred by the very nature of the ties that created their power from engaging in reforms that might harm existing relationships—not only between those who count and those who do not, but any reforms that would destroy the very system in which politics remains synonymous with the calculus of personal relations."[11]

As Mohammed Reza grew in age and maturity, he tended increasingly to resemble his father in outlook, political attitudes, and political preferences, although he rarely evinced the cruel streak of his father, nor was he capable of facing crises alone. Throughout his reign, he exhibited a disinclination to face problems unsupported by advisers, both internal and external. Yet, like his father, throughout the last two decades of his reign Mohammed Reza systematically discarded from power all men who might have developed a popular base of support. While his methods were not nearly as ruthless as those of Reza Shah, he made it clear that he did not wish to have strong-minded men in the position of prime minister, and that he disapproved the appointment of such men in other, even if lesser, positions of authority.

The shah's failure to provide for the integration of new classes into the political structure left him personally isolated. Eventually, this would become a psychological fact of great importance. The situation was duly noted as early as 1964 by the distinguished American ambassador Julius Holmes:

> All Chiefs of State are lonely people, but the Shah of Iran is lonelier than most. He bears a very heavy personal burden for the stability, security, and progress of the nation. He is not well served by advisers, either in the government or outside it. This is partially because of his innate suspicions of the ambitions of others and the lack of highly-qualified persons to assist him. Even those who are qualified are loath to give negative advice and follow the Persian tradition of telling the Monarch what they think he wants to hear. This often takes the form

of exaggerated flattery, to which the Shah is surprisingly susceptible. He is a vain man and those around him know it.[12]

The shah had few, if any, real friends, and even his closest associates rarely had the strength of character and the intellectual acumen to give him good advice. To be sure, there were some notable exceptions, foremost among whom was court minister Alam. The death of Assadollah Alam in 1977 was to be one of the most significant events in the second half of the seventies, for it deprived the shah of his one constant source of strength and integrity at the court. Mohammed Reza first had to deal with a challenge from the Ayatollah Ruhollah Khomeini in 1963. At that time Alam took matters into his own hands, ordered a swift and uncompromising reaction to the rebellious mullahs, then presented the shah with a *fait accompli.* Alam told the shah that if he disagreed with the actions, he could remove Alam and take different measures. Mohammed Reza approved the decisions. But when Khomeini struck again in the late seventies, there was no Alam to take the necessary steps.

In the end, the shah's greatest support came from his wife Farah Diba, his sister, and his ambassador to Washington, Ardeshir Zahedi —the son of the general who had consolidated the shah's power after the Mossadeq explosion in the fifties.

Of these three, the shah was perhaps closest to his sister, Princess Ashraf. She was subtle of thought, unflinching where challenges confronted them, quick-witted and tough-minded, a confidant with spirit, wisdom, and confidence well beyond her years. Without Ashraf, the shah probably would not have survived the eternal crises of his first twenty years on the throne.

By the early 1970s, almost fifteen years after he had introduced the White Revolution of agrarian reform in Iran, the shah was the focus of all authority and decisionmaking. His agents were everywhere, and he exhibited an unflagging capacity for absorbing their written reports. He directly received ministers, governors, internal security officials, military commanders, development bankers, foreign diplomats, press representatives, and assorted businessmen. He occasionally despaired of his taxing workload, having told the National Press Club during one of his frequent visits to Washington: "This king business gives me nothing but headaches." But the king business, as Mohammed Reza Shah conducted it, was distinctive for the modern age. He was potentate, grandee, monarch, tribal chieftain, and secular deity all encapsulated in one small "father figure."

Mohammed Reza Shah was convinced that there was no other conceivable path for moving Iran into the twentieth century. He had watched other potential strongmen assume responsibility for Iran's affairs, falter, and ultimately fail—whether because of the envy of other ministers or officers, of personal deficiencies, the disinclination of parliament to support their policies or actions, confusions within the ministries and operating agencies of government, or a host of other reasons, all signifying the incapacity of key components within the body politic to subordinate their parochial interests and to work in harmony for any appreciable period of time. As a result, the shah became convinced that his personal intercession and direction were essential for the unity of the country and for its effective development.

In pursuit of these goals, he used three effective devices to sustain him. The first might best be described as the fragmentary system of governing. Under this system, Mohammed Reza Shah refused to delegate ultimate authority in a given sector to any one government agency or agency head. Instead, he created parallel organizations, to cross-check and to monitor one another's activities. Thus there was the public or constitutional face of government, with its cabinet, its parliament, and its local councils. Elections were held, political parties were formed under the watchful eye of the Palace, and opposition "factions" permitted to express their views on occasion. But this reflected a gigantic deception or masquerade, designed to hide from public view the informal activities of the less well known agencies. Sometimes the two sets of bureaucracies would converge in their activities, but their performance and the loyalties of officials would always be under the scrutiny of the Palace, of the shah's Special Bureau, of various intelligence agencies, and of courtiers within the Palace. In the 1974 edition of his book *My Mission for My Country,* the shah explained his "system" in the following terms:

> I am a great believer in a plurality of administrative channels and in having alternate channels always available. If through ignorance, laziness or self-interest one official refuses to bestir himself to vigorous action, then I turn to somebody else. . . . I do not employ advisers in the usual sense of the term. To do this is, I think, dangerous for any

head of state. One of the few mistakes my father made was to rely on a narrowing circle of advisers. Fearing Reza Shah, they flattered him rather than telling him the truth; and I am sorry to say that they were by no means incorruptible. My system is entirely different. I know that advisers, no matter how technically competent they may be, sometimes make the national interest subservient to their own. Furthermore, they are prone to funnel all information through themselves and to seal off independent intelligence channels. So in lieu of advisers I obtain information from many quarters and then try to strike a balance sincerely and solely in the light of the public interest.[13]

Increasingly, Mohammed Reza turned to "alternative channels," particularly in the seventies. His sense of insecurity mounted with each assassination attempt, so that finally he was convinced he could trust few professed friends and allies, foreign or domestic. The actions he took to seal off, isolate, or eliminate potential sources of danger were wide-ranging. Exile was not a rare occurrence for public figures who could not work within the system; in other instances, handsome pensions and subtle threats sufficed. In the end, however, the system destroyed itself through mistrust and paralysis. One example of its fatal immobilism at times of crisis could be detected in the military establishment, where the shah, after previous experiences with such emerging military strongmen such as Generals Razmara and Bakhtiar, refused to delegate authority, create a tightly knit command structure, or integrate the various services. Thus, the commander of the imperial guard was frequently played off against the commander of the army; the latter, in turn, had no influence or span of control over the commander of the imperial air force or the commander of the imperial navy.

The second device utilized by the shah to sustain himself in power was closely related to the first: to establish a special, near-mystical relationship with "the people," brooking no intermediaries or intercessions by avowed "representatives of the people" with the Palace. As practiced by the shah, the linkage was less a modern form of populism than an expression of a traditional variant of the now familiar "cult of personality." In the words of a U.S. Embassy dispatch:

The shah's picture is everywhere. The beginning of all film showings in public theatres presents the shah in various regal poses accompanied by the strains of the national anthem. The birthday of the shah, the queen, and the crown prince are occasions for fireworks, parades, and demonstrations. The monarch also actively extends his influence to all phases of social affairs . . . there is hardly an activity or vocation in which the shah or members of his family or his closest friends do not have a direct or at least a symbolic involvement. Much effort is made to stress the 2,500 year continuity of the Iranian monarchy. All the resources of the mass media have been exploited to stress the idea that loyalty to the monarchy and national patriotism are identical.[14]

Such trappings were typical of traditional monarchies throughout the world, although Mohammed Reza's own insecurity undoubtedly drove him to overdramatize his majesty. His deification proved a truly herculean task, not least because of the reticent personality of the monarch. Described by his contemporaries as "dry" and "desiccated" in his public speeches, he failed to project an image of tough decisiveness or firm command; rather, it was the traditional image of a remote ruler preferring to operate in subtle and unfathomable ways that came across. This image paradoxically aided Mohammed Reza Shah, for it reinforced his reputation for inscrutability and deviousness. In addition, rumors of his involvement in the assassination of rivals, or his approval of machinations of SAVAK, created a degree of uncertainty and anxiety on the part of potential adversaries, as well as actual critics, that proved a tactical advantage. Terror was regarded as an excellent tonic for disloyalty.

The third device was the cooptation of the ideas of others. At this the shah proved to be a master, using it both as a tactic of control and manipulation and as a form of channeling creativity to the advantage of the Palace. For example, the much-vaunted White Revolution of the early 1960s represented a projection of the views of Prime Minister Amini and his able agriculture minister, Hassan Arsanjani, both of whom were defenestrated prior to the full implementation of the reform program. Given the rising discontent in the countryside over inflation and low market prices for Iranian crops, the shah used this disaffection to terminate parliamentary democracy in Iran and to assume supreme power personally. His moves were sanctioned in a popular referendum reflecting widespread backing for the reform program, which he also interpreted to mean support for the elimination of an independent legislative branch. The six points contained in the referendum of January 26,

1963, were: (1) The abolition of the landlord-serf relationship; (2) nationalization of forest lands throughout the country; (3) sale of government industrial plants to compensate landholders for land reform; (4) amendment of the election laws to permit the enfranchisement of women; (5) approval of workers sharing company profits; and (6) formation of a literacy corps to strengthen efforts at mass compulsory education. These were commendable initiatives in the abstract; but their application left much to be desired, adding to the popular frustration with the Pahlavis as the years passed.

So a chain reaction was produced, which promised a profound social transformation of Iran while also pointing toward the severe limitation or even destruction of the monarchy. It is beyond our purpose or intent to analyze these forces, but their main characteristics can be identified relatively easily.

Demographic dislocation: A massive, virtually uninterrupted flow of peasant population from the agricultural to the urban areas had begun in the late 1950s, increasing dramatically with the shah's land reform programs in the next decade. Thus one of the most "progressive" measures of the White Revolution produced a force that lent itself to a revolution of quite a different color. By the seventies, the flow from countryside to city had reached 100,000 per year. The urban population of Iran doubled in a decade (5 million in 1956, 10 million a decade later), and was predicted to reach 20 million by 1980. The situation was further exacerbated by the extremely high percentage of young people involved in the dislocation: one half of the population was younger than twenty by the time of the revolution.

Lack of adequate social services: Both civil and military services became bloated by the late seventies: 800,000 in the former, 700,000 in the latter. Yet despite the large numbers, the performance of the civil service was highly unsatisfactory, often failing to provide the most elementary requirements for the rapidly expanding urban masses. There was nothing unique in these developments; indeed, they are familiar to students of developing countries in all corners of the world. But they were particularly explosive against the background of the shah's rhetoric, the high expectations raised in the populace (especially after Persepolis), and the relentless attacks from the clergy. Under these circumstances, the failure to provide for attractive living in the exploding cities of Iran took on greater importance. In fact, the mullahs—and Khomeini himself—not only condemned the shah for undermining the traditional existence of the people, but constantly reminded the Iranians that the shah could not make the system work properly.

The growth of a hostile middle class: The shah's modernization programs required a Westernized middle class, and this was produced both at Iranian and foreign schools and universities. The United States and France were the two most popular foreign centers; Iranian students flowed to American and French universities in the tens of thousands. They were trained in modern scientific, military, and business methods, and also came into contact with some of the explosive political ideologies of the period. Upon their return to Iran, they were generally frustrated, for the country did not offer positions commensurate with the expectations of the new class. Many were unemployed, and many others were compelled to accept positions far below their level of training. Their resentment against the shah was heightened by the farce of the creation of the *Rastakhiz* (Renaissance) Party in 1975. The shah had presented this as a political breakthrough that would give the literate and politically charged middle classes greater weight in the government, and some of them believed that it was indeed the first step toward a general democratization of the political system. Yet by the end of the following summer, evidently worried that the party might actually challenge some of his own prerogatives, the shah had imposed stringent limitations on independent political action, including the *Rastakhiz* Party. This was a flagrant provocation to those students, intellectuals, and businessmen who had enthusiastically participated in party activities. As in the case of the new urban classes, the background of high expectations made the shah's failure to deliver acceptable rewards all the more galling.

At the same time, there were those among the new class who would have called for the downfall of the shah no matter how successful the White Revolution had been. Some of these, in fact, were sent abroad precisely because of their outspoken hostility to Mohammed Reza. Just as the colonial powers used to send their "problem cases" abroad in the nineteenth century, so the shah dispatched many of Iran's dissidents to foreign universities, hoping that they would learn the virtues of moderation in a different environment. This was not always a successful operation. In fact, Khomeini's three closest associates during the revolutionary period all returned to Iran from foreign universities: Ibrahim Yazdi from Texas, Abol Hassan Bani Sadr from Paris, and Sadeq Ghotbzadeh from Georgetown University in Washington, D.C. Even college graduates—or dropouts, as in the case of Ghotbzadeh—could retain the intense faith of the Shi'ites.*

Concentration of strength in the hands of the religious leaders: While Khomeini had been exiled in the early 1960s (first to Turkey, then to the city of Najaf in Iraq), the shah never took decisive action against the mullahs, who bitterly resented his programs. Like Reza Shah, Mohammed Reza provided for civil judges (thus depriving the mullahs of financial and political opportunities) and greatly enhanced civil rights for the populace at large, particularly for women and minorities. These measures flew in the teeth of the Shi'ite leaders' convictions that women should be unseen and unheard outside the home, and that the governance of the country should remain in purely Shi'ite hands. Perhaps the most provocative of the shah's actions was to appoint several Baha'is (followers of a nineteenth-century religious movement considered heretical by Islamic leaders) to cabinet-level positions.

Beginning in 1976, there were large-scale demonstrations demanding greater adherence to fundamentalist Islamic practices. Rather than meeting the Shi'ite challenge head on, the shah alternated between harsh measures and attempts at appeasement (as, for example, his return to the use of the Arab calendar in the autumn of 1978). This was only understandable, for the struggle with the Shi'ites would have been enormously difficult even under the most favorable circumstances, and in the second half of the 1970s the shah found himself on the defensive in many areas. As one of the best analysts

---

*Shi'ism has its roots in the disputes that erupted after the death of the Prophet Mohammed as to who should wear his mantle as leader of the religious community *(Umma)*. The Shi'ites are those who remained loyal to Ali in the line of succession. Widely distributed throughout Iraq and Iran, as well as the Persian Gulf and Pakistan, the Shi'ites proclaimed the legitimacy of the Caliphate within the family of Ali. In time, however, various schools of interpretation evolved, reducing the homogeneity of the Shi'ite religious community. The various schools include the Qarmats, the Ismai'ilians, the Nusayris, and so on.

of the revolution has observed, "the clergy was the only group in Iran equipped to engage in oppositional activities. It possessed a functioning system of communication; local facilities in the form of mosques and related buildings . . . close daily contact with the masses and the possibility of including political themes in the Friday sermons. With all this, the high-ranking clergy enjoyed a certain degree of immunity from the shah's grip."[15]

While the shah challenged the mullahs indirectly—by enactment of the legislation that made up the White Revolution—he had no stomach for the kind of unholy war that would have been necessary to bring the Shi'ites to heel. His father had been far more forceful, and there were many around him who urged Mohammed Reza to emulate Reza Shah. Yet paradoxically, the greater the shah's authority (and authoritarianism) in secular matters, the less he seemed inclined to challenge the mullahs.

The hostility of the bazaaris: The bazaar merchants, who made up a traditional merchant class of considerable power, had long resented the shah's modernization program. His introduction of the Western banking system threatened the bazaaris' income from moneylending (at rates much higher than those permitted by the banks), and his plans for the creation of cooperatives also menaced their traditional activities. Worse yet, the shah proposed the construction of a new commercial and shopping area precisely on the site of the traditional bazaar, thus threatening the bazaaris with physical removal from their business places. Along with these hated steps, he periodically called for crackdowns on price-gouging. It was thus not surprising that many bazaaris supported the revolution, both for their own self-interest (often of a highly avaricious sort) and to a certain extent out of religious conviction. Lastly, there was an unpleasant "ethnic" component to the bazaaris' anti-shah activities: they hoped to remove their Jewish and Armenian competitors by supporting Khomeini—hopes that were to be fully realized after the revolution.

The physical presence of a foreign community: If any Iranian needed a physical symbol of the changes the shah had wrought upon the country, it was readily at hand in the large foreign ghettos in Tehran, and to some extent other cities as well. The most obvious of these groups was the American community, composed of business persons and their families, along with the sizable contingent of military personnel. This visible presence acted as an irritant in many ways. First of all, the Americans and other foreigners clearly benefited from the oil wealth of Iran in ways most Persians could never dream of. The American enclaves were lavish, Tehran's active nightlife—another challenge to the mullahs' stern moralism—was frequented in large part by non-Iranians, and foreigners were often seen in the most luxurious automobiles, dressed in the finest European styles. Second, the mere presence of such a large foreign community indicated to many hypernationalists that the shah was a captive of foreign powers. Most Iranians were convinced that their country was the object of endless foreign intrigues, and they would have believed this even if there had been very few foreigners in the streets. But with so many Americans present—ranging from embassy personnel to businessmen, from scholars to Peace Corps volunteers, from journalists to military officers—the fanciful paranoia so typical of the Iranian world view received apparent justification. Oddly, the American inclination to mix with "the locals" rather than staying quietly in their own areas heightened suspicion, although more withdrawn behavior might have served the same purpose in the end. Third, the mores of the foreigners offended religious sensibilities, especially in the area of women's dress and behavior. (One of the first demands of the revolution was that women should wear the chador and that coeducational facilities should be terminated.) In the shah's day, girls in modern dress—including jeans and short skirts—attended school with boys. This was viewed as a foreign-inspired violation of the Shi'ite code.

Like so many of the errors of the seventies, the presence of such a large number of Americans was pinpointed as a potential problem in the early 1950s, when there were only one thousand Americans in the country. At that time the CIA suggested the construction of "listening posts" in the northeastern part of Iran, in order to surveil Soviet military tests, intercept Soviet telecommunications, and increase American intelligence-gathering capabilities in other areas. While these programs were obviously of immense value to the intelligence community, some senior members of the embassy staff warned against them, on the grounds that any increase in the number of Americans in Iran would only add to the already visible anti-Americanism in the country. At the time of the shah's fall, there were 45,000 Americans in Iran.

The vacillation of the shah himself: When the Iranian crisis reached fission stage in late 1978, the American national security adviser Zbigniew Brzezinski used to lecture his associates on the anatomy of revolution. One of his basic themes was the relationship between the growing strength of the revolutionary tide and the firmness of will of the ruling classes. Drawing upon the works of the Harvard historian William Langer, Brzezinski observed that in nineteenth-century Europe revolutionary movements succeeded in those countries where the rulers made concession after concession and never stood firm against their enemies. Where the rulers acted to put down revolutionary opposition, the revolution failed. He suggested that the same methods might work in Iran.

Whatever the accuracy of this assessment, the shah behaved like those rulers who were swept away in the European revolutions. Rather than assert his authority and demand obedience from his subjects, the shah backed and filled, alternating concessions with tough-sounding statements that were never enforced by action. This was fatal, especially because the proximate cause of the civil disturbances in the mid- and late seventies was the shah's own reform program. The enormous influx of money following the oil price increases in the early and mid-seventies, for example, encouraged Mohammed Reza to undertake an ambitious program of wealth distribution. In 1976, inexpensive public housing was made available, low-interest loans were offered to bazaar merchants and industrialists, and other subsidies were introduced. This program failed when inflation outran the subsidy rate, and the shah changed both the program and his prime minister in 1977, when stringent anti-inflationary measures were passed. But just a year later there was yet another about-face, when the government of Sharif-Emami was brought in, public sector spending reintroduced, wages raised, and subsidies on food staples restored. Each of these turnabouts came in response to popular demonstrations.

One may sympathize with the shah's specific decisions, but the result of the overall pattern was to convince the public that he did not know what to do. In the context of the turbulent social change introduced in the seventies, this heightened the impression that the country was out of control. Faced with a tempo of change never before experienced, a government that seemed to lack the will and the competence to manage the crisis, and a ruler who seemed less the master of Iranian destiny than the fragile object of forces greater than himself, the people turned to those who held that the national crisis could only be resolved by leaders who preached the old sermons, albeit with some new wrinkles.

The shah, then, was not a great oppressor. Had he been such, the revolution in all probability could never have triumphed. For all the notorious excesses of SAVAK, the shah did not permit the full force of the security organization to be brought to bear on his enemies. Khomeini was exiled, not killed, and there was no attempt to eliminate him, either in Iraq or later in Paris. Mohammed Reza wished to be loved, not feared; his methods were accordingly quite benign in the context of Middle East politics. As one commentator put it: "Compared with most of its neighbors, the shah's Iran was freer than either the socialist military dictatorships or the conservative religious monarchies."[16]

But the shah was no great modernizer, for he lacked the political wisdom to make the structural reforms in the polity that his industrial and educational innovations required. Thus his failure was two-fold: he was unable either to make the accommodations to social change that might have absorbed the explosive forces of the seventies, or to ruthlessly contain the explosion until the transformation of Iran was complete. The product of forces greater than he could comprehend, Mohammed Reza left as he had arrived, following the footsteps of his father into exile. And just as Reza Shah had been carried abroad to die on a British vessel, so Mohammed Reza Shah, armed with American guarantees, flew an American-built airplane to Egypt. Reza Shah was embalmed in Egypt; his son went to await his death in the same land.

TWO

The Washington-
Tehran Axis

THE AMERICAN FOREIGN POLICY establishment was rarely unified in its support of Iran and the shah. Divisions over policy surfaced from time to time, with the basic lines of cleavage running through a wide range of differing outlooks and assessments. Early in the reign of Mohammed Reza Shah there was little reason for any American administration to commit itself totally to this untested, youthful figure. Indeed, there was little in his record to suggest that he had the qualities to survive the intrigues and challenges that eddied around him.

In the 1940s, moreover, there was little need for the United States to play a leading role in guiding Iran's domestic and foreign policies. Iran was regarded in Washington as an integral part of the British sphere of influence—an extension of the Persian Gulf—where British advisers served as proconsuls to Arab sheikhs. Furthermore, the British Raj was paramount in India, and the influence of Whitehall remained potent in much of the remainder of the subcontinent despite the rise of local nationalisms. To be sure, the United States had established a modest presence in Iran during World War II, to supply arms and ancillary equipment to the Soviet Union—the other great regional power. But as soon as the war ended, the United States Persian Gulf Command was speedily dismantled.

Nevertheless, the United States did meddle in Iranian affairs. In 1943 (and even earlier) Americans began to assume responsibility for the administration of that country's internal finances. Subsequently, Washington provided advisory services in the area of internal security. Colonel Norman Schwarzkopf was in charge of a military mission whose assignment was to reorganize, train, and arm the Iranian gendarmerie (the equivalent of a rural police force). These were exceedingly modest initiatives, in no way intended to contest or undermine the prevailing British authority. The British themselves had no great sympathies for the Pahlavis: London had, after all, forced the abdication of Reza Shah. Both during and after the war the British continued to keep the Palace under close scrutiny. Mohammed Reza Shah himself was treated with little public deference, the British preferring to work through "cooperative" Persian prime ministers and cabinet-level officials. The principal preoccupation of Britain was how to diminish Soviet influence while at the same time maintaining the appearance of Allied unity in Iran.

The British government exercised a deftness and flexibility throughout the war that reduced tensions and acrimony between London and Moscow to the minimum, and the United States generally acquiesced in this approach in the interest of the overall wartime effort. But such acquiescence dissolved during the Azerbaijan crisis of 1945–46, when dissident groups acting with Soviet connivance declared the independence of the region. Washington registered vigorous protests with Moscow against its venturesome policies in Iran, as elsewhere. In due course, the Azerbaijan secessionists were crushed by Iranian forces, and the Soviet Union withdrew its military from the country. But the battle lines had been drawn, and Iran was held to be a front-line country in the struggle to contain Soviet expansionism. In 1948, the United States and Iran concluded an agreement that launched a major American military assistance effort. The agreement was fully authorized the following year under the Mutual Defense Assistance Act, a principal instrument of U.S. foreign policy during the cold war.

Despite the mounting level of activity, the Truman administration continued to support London as the primary Western presence in Iran. As has been seen, the British had earlier offered Prime Minister Mohammed Ali Foroughi the choice of becoming president of a new republic—an action that would have spelled the end of the monarchy. After the war the burgeoning of nationalist sentiment led to the appointment of strong prime ministers, a number of whom could easily have toppled Mohammed Reza Shah. However, British economic interests dictated a more prudent approach to internal Iranian politics, and Whitehall counseled against precipitous action. Indeed, by 1950 the British government was deeply worried over the mounting organizational skills and power manifested by the Iranian nationalists, particularly in the wake of the assassination of General Razmara.

These concerns were justified. In 1951, Mohammed Mossadeq came to office dedicated to the destruction of both British influence and the monarchy. He succeeded in his first objective by nationalizing British oil investments in Iran and forcing the withdrawal of British businessmen and advisers. He almost succeeded in the second; but like so many foreign leaders in the twentieth century, Mossadeq underestimated the desire and ability of the United States to take rapid and decisive action:

> From the start Mossadegh made one important miscalculation. He believed the Americans, who had no stake in the Anglo-Iranian Oil Company, would support nationalization. This belief was based on American resentment of Britain's role in the region and the influence flowing from British involvement in AIOC. His misreading of the scene was not entirely his fault as the American ambassador in Tehran, Henry Grady, encouraged this view. In the event the Americans sided with the British, at first merely to ensure that nationalization did not work. Then, as they feared that the Soviet Union might exploit the situation and the outlawed Tudeh Party gain ground in Iran, they considered the more drastic solution of overthrowing Mossadegh. This was preferred to direct military intervention, although at one stage British paratroops were on standby in Cyprus.[1]

The removal of Mossadeq provided an opportunity for the shah to consolidate his own political power and for the United States to extend its influence. At the time, American foreign policy was presided over by John Foster Dulles, a man of singular purpose and dedication in defense of what he took to be American interests. Dulles embarked on a crusade of salvation for the so-called free nations of the world, intended to contain Soviet ambitions within a well-defined European perimeter. Dulles welcomed the challenge to American leadership of an unsettled world: his sense of "realism" dictated the formation of alliances with all manner of non-Communist nations, and the provision of whatever weaponry might be required to frustrate Moscow's expansionist ambitions.

The supply of American economic assistance and military equipment for Iran rose prodigiously in the wake of the Mossadeq crisis. With the shah's reinvestiture in 1953, President Eisenhower approved the provision of $45 million in economic aid, even though the oil nationalization question had not been fully resolved—an action that produced deep distress in London. There was a spectacular increase in the military supply field as well. Provided on a grant (i.e., nonreimbursable) basis, American support almost quadrupled. Between 1949 and 1952, the United States had extended a mere $33 million in economic and military aid; but between 1953 and 1957, a total of $500 million in assistance was proffered, of which $125 million was directed to the Iranian armed forces.

By 1954–55, the United States had clearly supplanted the British as the principal Western influence in Iran, and Washington—like London earlier—was not fully convinced of Mohammed Reza's talents. Eisenhower, a military man of modest foreign affairs background, was not dazzled by the wealth and pomp of court life in Tehran. His instincts and preferences were more attuned to republican regimes and less pretentious leadership. Dulles, on the other hand, was inclined to support the shah on the basis of the time-tested theorem, "The enemy of my enemy is my friend." Yet even Dulles was far from impressed by the early performance of the shah. After all, it was the Iranian military under General Fazlollah Zahedi that had demonstrated a capacity for determined action, not the shah himself.

Washington embarked on a two-track Iranian policy in 1954, a policy that was to be continued and amplified by successive American administrations over the next quarter of a century. The first track was to reinforce ties with the Palace, through a combination of flattery and symbolic acts intended to demonstrate American backing for the shah. The decision did not entail blind support for his absolutist impulses, which the Americans tried periodically to moderate. At the same time, the evolving situation required that the Americans underscore their support in tangible ways. This was accomplished by various devices, ranging from military and economic help to support of the notorious security agency SAVAK in 1957.

The Central Intelligence Agency provided the initial inspiration, training, and guidance for SAVAK. Later, Israeli and Turkish intelligence agencies joined the American intelligence community in bolstering SAVAK's capabilities.

The second track of American policy concentrated on the Iranian armed services. In a sense, the Iranian military was to serve as a "safety net" for the Palace were it to be threatened once again. The Americans may have concluded that the Iranian military, properly armed, trained, and indoctrinated, could act as a stabilizing force with or without the monarchy. As Robert Pranger and Dale Tahtinen noted, the Iranian military became the object of a major campaign: "In fiscal years 1953 through 1961 our total military assistance to Iran was about half the assistance we gave all countries in the 1953–1969 period, and all of it was in the form of outright grants."[2] Many Iranian military officers were trained at academies and schools in the United States and Europe. More than 25,000 Iranian officers and enlisted men learned English, familiarized themselves with modern American military equipment, absorbed American military doctrine, strategy, and tactics, and in the process became familiar with American institutions and principles of government. There were added dividends for the United States in this budding relationship: Iran was a strong supporter of the ill-starred Baghdad Pact which, following Iraq's 1958 revolution and subsequent withdrawal from the alliance, was transformed into CENTO (the Central Treaty Organization), whose members included Turkey, Pakistan, and Iran, as well as the United Kingdom. To support CENTO, the United States entered into identical bilateral agreements with Iran, Turkey, and Pakistan, the provisions of which included the following paragraph:

> The Government of [Iran] is determined to resist aggression. In case of aggression against [Iran] the government of the United States of America, in accordance with the Constitution of the United States of America, will take such appropriate action, including the use of armed forces, as may be mutually agreed upon and as envisaged in the Joint Resolution to Promote Peace and Stability in the Middle East, in order to assist the Government of [Iran] at its request.[3]

The agreements were not concluded in treaty form and hence were not binding on the U.S. Congress, even though they were tied to a joint resolution of Congress on the Middle East of 1957 (amended in 1961), the so-called Eisenhower Doctrine.

From the perspective of the shah and the Iranian military, these were relatively minor inconveniences. The Iranian military was obviously benefiting from the American connection, both in terms of morale and promises of enhanced combat efficiency. In due course, this would accord Iran greater weight in its search for an expanded role in the Persian Gulf and adjacent regions. Moreover, American assistance helped the shah to tame his own military through a combination of blandishments, close continual supervision, and adoption of a divide-and-rule approach to the military "high command." Whenever a potential strongman appeared on the horizon, he was most frequently deflected from his ambitions by assignment abroad, indirect coercion by SAVAK or some other suitable security service, or early retirement. Whatever the device employed, the Iranian armed services never became a cohesive or integrated military system, despite the best American intentions. The armed forces were structured vertically, with no umbrella command structure at the top; each branch reported directly to the shah. While they remained among the world's largest forces numerically, and accumulated increasingly sophisticated weaponry, they were not to be tested in war (with the exception of the minor Oman campaign in the mid-seventies), and had virtually no experience in the area of combined arms.

Thus, although the organization, structure, and staffing of the military benefited the Palace, it portended serious difficulties should either an internal or external crisis arise. It was difficult to imagine the armed forces acting as a coherent unit. Furthermore, the military was in a state of near-constant turmoil from 1969 onward, when the American grant military assistance program was terminated. Beginning in 1970, Iran assumed primary responsibility for decisions on the size and structure of its armed forces, and on equipment to be procured from abroad. The Iranian graduation from grant military assistance status stemmed from an American decision predicated on Iran's mounting oil revenues, and the desire to demonstrate to the American Congress and people that traditional "forward defense" countries were increasingly capable of "standing on their own two feet."

The altered status of Iran coincided with two other international events that were to have serious implications for the shah. First, the

British government announced in 1968 the intention to withdraw virtually all its forces based east of Suez by 1971. This decision threatened to create a military vacuum in the Persian Gulf region, one that either Iranian or radical Arab forces might hope to fill. (Egyptian forces, at the direction of President Gamal Abdel Nasser, were deeply involved in the Arabian Peninsula on behalf of the Yemen "civil war.") Mohammed Reza Shah was convinced that the British withdrawal represented a "call to destiny" for himself and the Iranian military. The second event involved radical Arab efforts to form a political coalition against moderate countries in the Middle East. Here again, Nasser was viewed by the shah as the principal architect of the coalition, and Iraq was seen as the main Persian Gulf state that would enter into the coalition and challenge Iranian claims to primacy as the British withdrew.

Accordingly, the shah determined that a full-scale program of equipment modernization was required by his armed forces. This entailed replacement of F-86 aircraft with F-5s and F-4s, to be followed by F-14s; on the ground side, the M-47 tank was to be superseded by (upgraded) M-48s, M-60s, Chieftains, and other hardware; the naval component was to dispense with World War II–class frigates and coastal craft in favor of Spruance Class destroyers and related ships, all intended to transform the Imperial Iranian Navy into a "blue ocean" force as rapidly as possible. The resultant strains on the Iranian military became intolerable. Fighter pilots (and mechanics) who had familiarized themselves with the F-5 were soon "transitioned" to the vastly more complex F-4s and F-14s. Confusion began to develop in the maintenance and logistics commands as systems became overloaded, and maintenance grew haphazard. The choices narrowed—enlargement of the armed forces by recruitment of skilled specialists in the Iranian labor market, or hiring of foreign (inevitably, American) experts to manage and sustain an increasingly overburdened "system." Typically, the shah opted for both solutions.

The American decision to graduate Iran from the ranks of grant aid recipient had other consequences that would fatefully shape the response of the military to the revolution ten years later. No longer could the United States dictate the type and quantity of equipment to be made available to Iran. The choices and options now reposed with the purchasing country; and since Iran had the funds to buy and the marketplace was populated by a substantial number of quite eager sellers, Washington's influence on decisionmaking in Tehran was markedly diminished. The shah, who evinced a growing interest in military matters, determined that he alone should make the major decisions on weapons purchases and training requirements. In due course he became a frequent peruser of catalogues, a fancier of armaments, even an amateur strategist. He left few meaningful choices in these fields to his generals and admirals; yet the shah had neither the formal training nor the experience necessary for completing the task successfully. His choices were not simply the result of detached strategic analysis. He knew that military power also serves to heighten the apparent grandeur of a monarchy and to enhance the political prestige of a nation. His calculations proved correct, for Iran's prestige increased along with its arsenal, not least in the eyes of American leaders.

Successive American administrations perceived in the Iranian complex a bastion of strength, a stable country, and a source of support. American and Iranian interests became progressively entangled, and the choices available to Washington seemed to narrow with the growing self-assurance of the shah and the prepossessing military inventory of his armed forces:

> In the fifteen years after Mossadegh's departure, American involvement in Iran became the key external factor in the shah's ambitious plans for the development of Iran and the solidification of his personal power. By fiscal year 1969, the last year the United States would supply significant amounts of military equipment to Iranian armed forces through outright grants or defense department credits, it was clear that American interests in the Persian Gulf were closely linked not only with Iran but also with the shah's regime. This close identity was a feature of the decade between 1968 and 1978 as well. Because of this closeness, it was becoming increasingly difficult to disentangle American interests from those of the shah, a problem which affected not only policy perceptions but our intelligence analysis as well. This entanglement was to have serious repercussions on U.S. policies in 1978. . . .[4]

THE PERIOD 1969–72 represented a watershed in American relations with Iran. It was one that produced new couplings and linkages with the Palace; it was also one in which the United States was party to the transformation of Iran into a virtual dictatorship.

With the arrival of the Nixon administration, Mohammed Reza Shah had grown considerably in stature and now demanded a wider field of engagement—one that would permit him to exercise what were becoming considerable powers of statesmanship. Like so many leaders, Mohammed Reza found international affairs far more exciting than domestic politics, and he had developed a strategic overview of what was occurring in the Middle East, as well as a grand design for countering the forces of "radicalism," with himself and Iran in the vanguard. The shah had been grooming himself for the role of statesman for some time. He had served as a mediator in the Pakistan-Afghan dispute of 1962–63 (a role acknowledged and applauded by the United States). Earlier, he had lent his name to the notion of an "Aryan Union," which envisaged a loose political federation of Iran, Pakistan, Afghanistan, and Turkey; and later he sought leadership responsibility in CENTO, encouraging the notion that he should be designated supreme commander for CENTO forces.

In 1971 the U.S. Embassy in Tehran had observed the extent to which the shah's ambitions had come to embrace more than the precincts of Persia:

> . . . He had on other occasions sent up trial balloons to test his acceptability as a mediator for the Kashmir dispute. Lately he has shown signs of trying to take a few pages out of General de Gaulle's book, searching for a way to assert his "independent nationalism" in foreign affairs. (He told a recent visitor that he had developed a real personal friendship and serious basis of cooperation with De Gaulle.) This recent disposition has not, however, as yet taken on any important substance. He continues to consult closely in the first instance with the U.S. . . . and continues to be susceptible to our counsel in all important matters of global policy.[5]

There had been stormy moments in the relationship, however, especially when the aspirations of the shah exceeded both his own capabilities and the willingness of the United States to cater to all of his presumed "needs." Thus, during the Kennedy administration, Mohammed Reza Shah constantly begged the President and Secretary of State Dean Rusk for urgent deliveries of sophisticated weapons. When these petitions went unheeded, he delivered a storm of

abuse and threats on Washington, which responded with calm stern-
ness. Kennedy personally indicated that neither he nor his administration would yield to such pressure, urging the shah to "reconsider"
his position, which the latter did with some private peevishness.

As in any relationship between two parties of greatly unequal
strength, the shah chafed at his dependence on the United States. He
was sometimes perplexed by America's slowness in responding to his
wishes, by its efforts simultaneously to resist Soviet aggression and
yet search for bases for mutual accommodation, and by its seeming
to offer less than full-scale support for Israel and "other friends and
allies." Above all, the shah was confused by the democratic processes
that afflicted American leadership, by the insistent voice of Congress
in foreign affairs, and by the importance of public opinion in shaping
American foreign policy.

The shah's frustration with American democratic processes is only
one example of a general problem facing Washington policymakers.
Like most people outside the West—including the best educated and
most powerful—he simply did not understand the sloppy and uneven
processes that characterize a democratic society. Baffled by the presence of so many centers of real and potential power, confused by the
constant outpouring of discordant views, frustrated by the slow
march of legislation and even executive decisionmaking, the shah
inevitably conjured up an unseen logic behind the chaotic appearance of events. He searched for hidden conspiracies and Machiavel-
lian cunning, where often there were none to be found. Since
Mohammed Reza made full use of all instruments of power in maintaining his own position and advancing the interests of his country,
he presumed that the United States did likewise. He was not the only
foreign leader to view the American government in such a way. To
take a recent example, when the Carter administration withheld
support and technical assistance from West European governments
threatened by terrorism, the heads of those governments presumed
that Carter favored their political opponents. In reality, the government's hands were tied by legislation from a previous period, permitting assistance only in the case of "international terrorism," and not
when the terrorist movement in question was believed to be domestic. But even close allies found it hard to believe this was the only
explanation. For leaders outside the Western tradition, misunderstandings were far more frequent and far more profound.

So it was with the shah. Since he dealt with domestic opponents in summary fashion, he found it hard to believe that the American President could not always prevail on matters the shah believed important. If an American President failed to "deliver," the shah saw it as purposeful, even when it was simply a matter of domestic political opposition. And at the very end, the shah attributed greater political power to Western democracies than actually existed: His repeated request to the French that the Ayatollah Khomeini be kept in Paris was based in large part on the unstated conviction that President Valéry Giscard d'Estaing could and would manage the situation so as to keep Khomeini relatively quiet. The shah had failed to understand that once public interest in Khomeini had been aroused, no democratic country could subdue the turmoil.

There were other misunderstandings as well. It was difficult for the shah to appreciate the importance to Americans of the internal politics of his own monarchy. In part this was due to his own cultural limitations, but in part it was the result of American inconstancy in the conduct of foreign policy. Paradoxically, those American administrations in the recent past that considered themselves most "progressive" often tended to take an extremely active role in suggesting the best conduct for their allies in their own countries; while those administrations generally considered conservative or even "reactionary" often deferred to foreign leaders in such matters. Thus the Kennedy–Johnson period was characterized by the use of American power to effect basic social and political change, whether through organizations like the Peace Corps (a revivified American cultural and information program) or overt and covert military intervention.

So the shah generally had more trouble with Democratic presidents than with Republicans. Kennedy, Johnson, and then Carter called for internal changes in Iran, for greater liberalization, for less torture and censorship. On most occasions the shah attempted to comply with such American requests, even though the periods of liberalization alarmed his security advisers, and even though he himself took pains to observe to his American interlocutors that Iran was not a European country, and that his people were not "mature" enough for the responsibilities of democracy.

Aside from such general considerations, the shah had some more specific problems whenever the Americans attempted to impose their social and political standards on Iran. Above all, he had to avoid loss of face before the Iranian public—he could not permit it to be believed that he was a mere "puppet" of Washington. This was a serious problem even when American prestige was at its highest, both in the immediate post–World War II period and in the early enthusiasm of Kennedy's New Frontier; it became of critical importance in the Carter period, when American prestige was at low ebb and the perception of American power and resolve was dropping with each passing year.

On the other side of the relationship, American governments have always had a problem when they found themselves allied with undemocratic countries. The American public is uncomfortable about supporting authoritarian or totalitarian regimes, and the longer the alliance lasts, the more difficult it becomes to maintain public approval. There are several ways to make such an alliance more attractive to the public. One, and by far the most successful, is to justify the relationship by appeal to a genuine international crisis: thus Roosevelt had little difficulty in justifying support of Stalinist Russia during World War II. A second method is to suggest that the ally in question is slowly moving toward more democratic forms and/or greater social justice: thus various American governments have argued that countries ranging from Francoist Spain to South Korea or post-Maoist China were in the process of "modernization" or "democratization," or at least en route to a higher standard of living. A third, distinctly less successful, method is that of arguing that the United States derives tangible benefits from an alliance even when the ally is morally unattractive. This works only when the ally is only moderately unpalatable to the general public—and then only for limited periods. In short, while *realpolitik* may be good policy, it is bad politics. And since most countries are undemocratic, American presidents and secretaries of state must constantly attempt to cope with public criticism and allied outrage at that criticism.

The increasingly close relationship with Iran was a classic case of the general problem, and it was exacerbated in the late 1960s and early 1970s by the growth of Soviet strength and the decline in real American power, both military and economic. Suffering from incipient military defeat in Vietnam and from a national economy in disrepair, the Nixon and Ford administrations had to find new methods for dealing with international challenges. These new methods had not only to accommodate the changed global balance of power but also to deal with a disgruntled public opinion that had lost considerable enthusiasm for an activist foreign policy. The consensus of the 1950s and much of the 1960s had dissolved; Americans no longer were willing to man the barricades against communism, insurgency, and terrorism, as was the case in the days of Kennedy. The sense of "manifest destiny," of a nation set aside from others and therefore bound to exercise leadership in the world community of nations, had been weakened. Nixon, along with his national security adviser Henry Kissinger, attempted to design what they called a "stable structure of peace." These code words meant: (a) preservation of American primacy in the "free world" while exploring new avenues of normalization and accommodation with the Soviet Union and the People's Republic of China (the newly evolving triangular relationship in which the United States would serve as the fulcrum); (b) maintenance of rough parity with the Soviet Union in the strategic arms field while launching efforts at arms control (under the newly evolving Strategic Arms Limitation Talks—SALT); (c) reduction of American forces abroad while maintaining American security commitments and obligations (the newly evolving security/business relationship that was officially designated the Nixon Doctrine, first enunciated at Guam in 1969).

In dealing with past adversaries, the Nixon administration hoped to replace "containment through confrontation" with "containment through negotiation." The centerpieces would be negotiations of the disposition of Soviet and Allied forces in Europe under the heading of Mutual and Balanced Force Reductions, the Strategic Arms Limitation Talks, and agreements that entailed joint efforts to reduce the likelihood that crises and upheavals in the third world would produce a "big power confrontation." The last encompassed a Moscow-Washington early warning system to alert both capitals to impending upheavals or conflict situations. At the same time, Dr. Kissinger evolved the detente theory, which suggested that while competition between the superpowers could not be brought under full or early control (and on occasion would inevitably require the direct use of American military power), networks of interdependence in the areas of economic exchange, technology transfers, fishing rights, joint efforts at space exploration, and the like would serve to tame the Soviet "impulse to competition." Detente would hopefully end many of the dangers attributed to vertical politics. A horizontal layering of relationships would reduce the risks of big power confrontation and at the same time diminish opportunities for client states to ensnare the powers in their local "games of chance." And it would help to reduce the virulent anti-Americanism at home and abroad.

In the Third World, the Nixon-Kissinger strategy appeared to offer a number of attractive advantages. It could permit the United States to withdraw from Vietnam, with some assurance that the Soviet Union and China would exercise sufficient pressure on Hanoi to make the retreat honorable and without serious incident. At the same time, Washington could hedge its bets by maintaining ties with such "stable regimes" as existed in South Africa, Greece (under "the colonels"), Iran, and South Korea. Through the Nixon Doctrine, some traditional American obligations would be set aside and some material advantages secured for the American position of continued primacy:

> A . . . way of reducing costs was a change in the instruments of primacy. There would be fewer overt military interventions, more covert action; less open advice to friends and allies as to preferred behavior (as in the days when European supranational integration was an American objective) and more "conditioning," i.e., moves at placing others in situations in which they would act as one wished; fewer troops and bases, but more transfers of arms and investments; less food aid and military assistance, more food and arms sales, to help America's balance of payments and to make buyers indebted to American banks.[6]

In the words of the new administration, the time had come for "a more balanced alliance with our friends," for "more equal partnerships based on a more balanced contribution of both resources and plans." For the rest of the Third World, a measure of disorder and instability was anticipated, but these would be marginal to major American concerns; the United States would not be at the mercy of crisis, but rather in a position to ignore it, or, where national interests overrode, to control and to manipulate it. Diplomacy would be the primary instrument in the new strategy for the United States in the decade of the seventies.

The shah welcomed much of the new American strategy. It promised a weakening of the appearance (and reality) of Iranian dependence on the United States, the opportunity to launch independent initiatives in the Persian Gulf regions as the British departed, and the establishment of ties with the Soviet Union that would permit the shah to accord lower priority to the security of his northern frontiers. Moreover, he could play a significant role in Third World councils, including OPEC and the "Non-Aligned" movement. The shah, however, had other aspirations and plans, which required continued coupling with the United States if they were to reach fruition. The vital interests of Iran could involve confrontation and hostilities with radical Arab states in the Persian Gulf; certainly, protection of these same interests would produce a collision with radical regimes in Syria, Libya, and Iraq. Finally, the shah was deeply troubled by the growing power of a Soviet-armed India in South Asia, the enfeeblement of Pakistan, and the penetration of Afghanistan by the Soviet Union through economic and military assistance programs. He was fearful of the encirclement of Iran by an "Arab Sea" and the final isolation of his country (a fear that underlay the close working relationship with Israel). So he moved to intensify the American connection and to ensure that not all of the vestiges of "vertical politics" would be interred with the rise of detente.

Iran had a number of advantages in its efforts to secure a reaffirmation of American support. First, despite the Nixon-Kissinger "Grand Design," the Middle East remained an intractable problem area. Second, the new administration was distressed over the growth of radical forces in the Middle East, and the advantages that accrued to the Soviet Union from such growth. Third, the Middle East contains nearly two-thirds of the known reserves of the world's petroleum, and the Persian Gulf region accounted for almost one-half of that total. Fourth, with the overthrow of King Idris of Libya in September 1969 by a young captain of the army and self-proclaimed Arab revolutionary, Muhammar al-Qaddafi, and the avowedly radical posture of Algeria under Colonel Houari Boumedienne, the American stake in maintaining harmonious relations with Iran was growing rapidly. Fifth, the U.S. government was deeply concerned over the possible consequences attending the British withdrawal from the Persian Gulf, including a "domino theory" involving the overthrow of weak sheikhdoms by radical Arab revolutionary forces. Finally, there was the American investment in Iran, including more than $2 billion in economic and military aid over the previous two decades.

During the 1960s, the United States had tended to view its oil interests in the Middle East as basically two-dimensional. The first was oil's strategic importance—western Europe and Japan were heavily dependent on Middle Eastern sources of supply to sustain their industries, and any interdiction by reason of conflict or coup would be cause for alarm. The second American interest arose out of the commercial advantages that accrued from the involvement of American companies in the petroleum exploitation of Middle East fields. Annually, these companies earned and repatriated approximately $2 billion from operations in the North African and Persian Gulf areas. However, in the 1960s the United States itself was not heavily dependent on Middle Eastern oil to meet its domestic consumption or strategic stockpile requirements. Domestic production was satisfactory to meet these needs. But in 1970–71, the advantageous position occupied by the United States began to change drastically. America's consumption of petroleum skyrocketed at a time when its production capacities appeared to have achieved a plateau well below demand. The United States had no choice but to look abroad for additional supplies to satisfy consumer demand. Necessity, however, also meant dependency, and precisely at a point when the oil-producing states in the Middle East were beginning to understand the implications of their bargaining power. Arab producers in particular were becoming more assertive, not only on production matters and on pricing but on political imperatives—above all, the Arab-Israeli question.

The initial reaction in Washington was ambivalent, even when Libya unilaterally increased the price of its oil exports. The belief persisted among high government officials that market forces in the United States would lead inevitably to price increases and a reduction in American consumer demand. This proved too optimistic an assessment. The price of American oil was well below that of other industrialized nations, and an overheating economy was bound to produce yet higher consumer demand in the years ahead, demands which the American production base could not hope to meet. With the Vietnam war still in progress, the Nixon administration had no wish to embark on an emergency program that would require public sacrifices of an heroic nature. Conservation through pricing or rationing would be anathema to an American people troubled by war and bored with the prospect of yet another "crusade."

Mohammed Reza Shah moved boldly and swiftly to take advantage of the opportunity. In January 1971, an OPEC conference was convened in Tehran, during which the shah seized the initiative in proposing a significant rise in the f.o.b. price of petroleum—an initiative welcomed by attending Arab states. Given the obvious desire of the majority of Arab producers to utilize OPEC as an instrument in their campaign against Israel, the message to Washington became increasingly clear. Despite its ties to Israel, Iran would support the Arab cause if Washington were to fail to meet the shah's needs in the area of Iranian security. In May 1972, Nixon and Kissinger agreed for the first time in the long history of postwar American-Iranian relations to sell Iran virtually any conventional weapon it wanted, and so instructed the American foreign affairs bureaucracy in July 1972.

On initial examination, the decision appeared appropriate for the circumstances that were shortly to confront the Nixon administration. The eruption of the fourth round of Arab-Israeli hostilities, the Yom Kippur War of October 1973, generated an Arab embargo on the sale of oil to Western supporters of Israel and a quadrupling in the price of oil to be made available, during and after the embargo. The oil card had now been played, to the shock and chagrin of most European nations and of Japan. The connection with Tehran assumed even greater priority, since Washington now was badly in need of Middle Eastern friends and allies. The shah had cooperated, after all, by abstaining from the embargo, even though he had followed the Saudi lead in raising oil prices.* Iran henceforth became the balance wheel in the region, the leverage state, which would influence attitudes and policies of neighboring governments, even that of the Soviet Union, whose oil depen-

---

*A great deal of foolishness has been written about the increase of oil prices in 1973–74, suggesting that the American government somehow masterminded (or at least actively encouraged) this very serious blow to Western economies. CBS News on its "60 Minutes" broadcast of May 4, 1980, went so far as to suggest that Nixon and Kissinger actually wanted Iran to raise oil prices so that the shah could buy more and more American weapons.

So far as can be reasonably confirmed, the actual facts are roughly as they were perceived and reported at the time: (1) The increase had been discussed for a long time, and had been supported by radical Arab leaders and by the Soviets; (2) the determinant factor was the sudden spurt in the "spot market" price of oil, which reached three to four times the official price shortly after the Saudi production cut; (3) the shah's leadership was therefore based on the demonstrated market situation, and not on any political skulduggery with the Americans.

dency might be expected to grow in the years immediately ahead.

All this meant, of course, that Iran's relationship with Washington had altered drastically by 1972, and even more so in the wake of the Arab-Israeli war of 1973. Iran was no longer in the position of a dependent satellite. It now had "reverse leverage" with Washington, and the shah could magnify his role on the world stage—something the United States would not only be compelled by the erosion of its position in the Mediterranean area to applaud, but to support materially and diplomatically as well. The shah, in the words of David Ronfeldt of the Rand Corporation, could now exploit the "geopolitical interests of the patron superpower"—and the vulnerabilities of that same superpower as well. This he proceeded to do with a subtlety and panache that was relatively painless to the United States. Nixon and Kissinger went to Tehran in 1972, and the shah emerged from the meetings with the President's recognition as the personification of Iran, a natural ally and an individual sharing a "mutuality of interest with the United States." For the shah, the symbol of his successful negotiation with President Nixon and Dr. Kissinger would be a substantially increased program of military sales to Iran, involving the most advanced equipment to be produced by American arms manufacturers. Iran could easily afford the military modernization that the shah contemplated: the United States, western Europe, and Japan were subsidizing the program through their importation of Iranian oil.

The American special relationship with Iran has been much criticized, but in context it must be considered an excellent decision by both parties. With strictly supervised restraints imposed upon the Nixon administration by an increasingly suspicious and hostile Congress, there was a desperate need for strong allies who could replace American power in vital areas of the world. In most crucial areas of foreign policy the shah's interests were virtually identical with America's, and the strengthening of the Iranian military establishment had the attractive side effect of helping the U.S. government's international balance sheet. Furthermore, there were only limited international political risks involved in strengthening Mohammed Reza, for there was little chance that he would turn this military might against the United States in the foreseeable future—a very real possibility in the case of other, more radical Middle Eastern countries.

If the United States wished to maintain a strong military presence in the region, it had only two choices: either project American military power into the area, or find a strong ally capable of playing this role. The first option was almost impossible to execute under prevailing domestic political conditions. The second, by contrast, was readily available, since it met the requirements of Mohammed Reza Shah as well as the United States. These requirements were not only military; the special relationship was based on overlapping economic, strategic, military, and philosophical considerations:

Economics: By 1971 it was becoming apparent that the United States would have to depend upon foreign sources to meet its energy requirements. Iran was pivotal, both because of its leadership role in OPEC and its capacity to meet Western oil needs. Moreover, as the United States' balance-of-payments position deteriorated, Iran was perceived as an excellent customer that could partially offset the worsening American economic position. Iranian imports of American military and other equipment more than quadrupled during the first eight years of the decade beginning in January 1970.

Strategic planning: With the British decision in 1968 to withdraw militarily from their forward position east of Suez, Iran loomed even larger in American military planning. It was conceived as a "free world" bastion in an otherwise turbulent region of the world, one that might conceivably play a stabilizing role not only in the Persian Gulf region but on the seas beyond. The shah was encouraged by American officials to contemplate just such a role for himself and his nation in the period after 1971. This encouragement also meant that the United States could count on continuing access to important stations in northern Iran from which Soviet strategic weapons programs could be monitored.

Military necessity: The growing importance of Iran to American military planning was underscored by events in adjacent countries and regions. For example, the 1974 invasion of Cyprus by Turkish military forces engendered violent reactions in NATO and, as might be expected, in Athens and Washington. The American Congress imposed a partial embargo on the sale of arms and associated military equipment to Turkey, an action that neither appeased the Greek government nor produced any change in policy by the government of Turkey. Both countries subsequently cut back drastically on their participation in NATO, and closed most American military installations in their respective countries. From the perspective of American defense strategists, Iran assumed greater importance as these events unfolded.

The new international order: Under the Nixon and Ford administrations, Kissinger had hammered out a new approach to the international community, one predicated not on a policy of containment of the Soviet Union but on a new "structure of peace," in which the triangular relationship between the United States, the Soviet Union, and the People's Republic of China would assume paramount importance. Within this framework, the Nixon "Doctrine" was enunciated in 1969—one that shifted the burden of responsibility for security to America's friends and allies. America would be prepared to sell the necessary arms and to make essential training available to allies and friends, but the primary responsibility for self-defense would be theirs. The strategy had several advantages. It promised a reduction of American forces abroad and a realignment of responsibilities without terminating U.S. security commitments and obligations to friends and allies; it enhanced the posture and competitive position of American business abroad, particularly corporations involved in aerospace research and arms development; it ensured continued compatibility in weapons, doctrine, and command and control between the United States and its closest friends and allies in the Third World; and it encouraged these same friends and allies to assume leadership responsibilities within their regions that the United States could support, either formally or indirectly.

In the case of Iran, the dividends from the new policy in the 1970s were expected to be substantial. Washington already shared with Tehran a common perspective on security requirements in the region and actions that might be taken to support those requirements, not only in the Middle East but elsewhere. Iran, for example, was the primary source of supply in the energy field for Israel, South Africa, and the regime of Prime Minister Ian Smith in Rhodesia. Since Washington was disposed to "tilt" in favor of white governments in southern Africa, Iran's support in the form of oil supplies was deemed essential. Similarly, the shah and his government were viewed as an effective counterpoise to radical regimes in neighboring Iraq and Afghanistan. Through a discreet form of covert paramilitary assistance to groups opposed to these governments, Washington hoped to keep Baghdad and Kabul—and by extension Moscow—off balance. These programs included clandestine support for Kurdish independence movements, and arms aid to dissident groups in Afghanistan.

The intelligence and covert operations portion of the American connection was of particular significance for the shah. It permitted him to play a complex game in which his personal ambitions could be accommodated, while ensuring a congruence of American and other interests with the goals and objectives of his government. It was not a case of the tail wagging the dog, but rather an instructive exercise in joint ventures for jointly perceived benefits. These ventures included the establishment of escape routes for Soviet defectors wishing to flee to the West, reverse penetration routes for intelligence collection, reconnaissance missions into Soviet territory, the establishment of border listening posts to intercept Soviet communications, the launching of joint exercises to counter the efforts of Arab terrorists to destabilize sensitive geographic areas, and the sharing of intelligence estimates on particular countries of mutual concern to Tehran and Washington. Indeed, collaboration reached the point during the 1970s where SAVAK agents were permitted to enter the United States and to engage not only in information gathering but in programs against Iranian students involved in demonstrations against the shah. The full extent of collaboration is not known, but it is clear from the available evidence that the Nixon, Ford, and Carter administrations all turned a blind eye to these SAVAK activities, which involved steps by the CIA to neutralize the FBI's efforts to intercede in what the latter regarded as blatant Iranian violation of American sovereignty. Throughout, the State Department under the stewardship of Secretaries Kissinger and Vance turned a blind eye to the activities of SAVAK in the United States.

The singular lack of willingness of senior officials in the Nixon, Ford, and Carter administrations to intercede in efforts to terminate SAVAK surveillance and counterterror activities in the United States was predicated on considerations of overriding national interest, and shows how strongly the American government appreciated the Iranian alliance. The Iranian "listening posts" were crucial for

American monitoring of Soviet missile tests, and Washington was loath to antagonize the shah and thus jeopardize these activities. Furthermore, the shah provided assistance to the government of South Vietnam as the Paris peace negotiations were coming to a close in 1973—the assistance being several squadrons of F-5 aircraft to bolster Saigon's defense capabilities. Again, he served as an intermediary with Pakistan's leaders in the wake of the 1971 war with India, in an effort to ensure that Pakistan maintained a position favorable to the West despite Washington's lack of effective support during the hostilities. With respect to Soviet efforts to enlarge its beachhead in the Horn of Africa after the overthrow of Emperor Haile Selassie in 1974, Washington looked to Tehran (and Riyadh) to develop an effective counterstrategy it could support. The strategy called for the creation of a Red Sea Entente of moderate Arab nations, to challenge Soviet influence and eliminate the Soviet military presence in Somalia and the People's Democratic Republic of South Yemen. Egypt and Sudan would provide the strategic and military screen for the venture; Iran and Saudi Arabia would supply arms where necessary and the financial underpinnings. The United States would be expected to provide both material and psychological backing when the "ripe moment" arrived—the "ripe moment" being when the Somali government was prevailed upon to withdraw from its close association with the Soviet Union and to order both the termination of the Soviet military supply mission and access to military installations located at Berbera and Hargeisa. As will be seen, these plans misfired, despite the most energetic political and material support tendered by the shah, when Carter failed to follow through on the agreement. Nevertheless it bespoke the general importance that the United States attached to Iran as an influential "middle power" in the Middle East.

This influence was not confined to the Middle East alone. During the 1970s the shah had bought into the so-called Safari Club, a group of Middle Eastern and African nations implacably opposed to the spread of Soviet influence in both regions, and pledged to the provision of assistance to moderate Arab and African regimes that appeared to be threatened by more radical neighbors. The principal membership included Iran, Saudi Arabia, Morocco, Egypt (after the Sadat rupture with Moscow), the Ivory Coast, and Senegal. France was the sole European partner in what has proved to be one of the most effective consultative systems to be fashioned by moderate leaders in the Third World. The span of interest and the field of maneuver of the Safari Club has included the two Shaba crises in 1977 and 1978, which involved the insertion of Moroccan and French forces *inter alia* to counter the activities of Soviet- and Cuban-backed ex-Katangan gendarmes in the copper-rich province of Zaire. In addition, the Club has been active in supporting the Moroccan effort to retain control over the Western Sahara (formerly a Spanish colonial possession) in the face of Libyan- and Algerian-backed guerrilla attacks by the Polisario movement. Elsewhere the Club moved to counter the efforts of President Qaddafi of Libya to topple Arab and African regimes of which he disapproved.

The American government had not taken official cognizance of the Safari Club, or of Iran's major role in this informal coalition. However, it had viewed with enthusiasm Iran's support for the general goals espoused by the Club. Nor can it be disputed that the membership's interventions in such crisis areas as Zaire in 1977 was entirely welcome in Washington. Additionally, there were some members of the Carter administration who welcomed Saudi Arabia's interventions in support of Morocco. The point here is that Iran was a pivotal member of an association whose activities the United States could reasonably detach from the mainstream of American policy, while occasionally tacitly welcoming involvement in geographic areas where American public opinion or the public posturizing of a particular administration effectively denied Washington a leadership role. Under President Carter, for example, the public posture against armed American involvement in the 1977 Zaire crisis effectively eliminated any real opportunity to defuse the crisis. Having backed itself into a public and ideological corner, the administration was relieved when Moroccan forces were rushed to Zaire to protect that country's threatened Shaba Province.

FROM THE SHAH'S PERSPECTIVE, the intimate relationship with the United States was a mixed blessing. In the words of the famous lament from *The King and I,* if one has allies strong enough to be protective, "may they not protect me out of what I own?" The shah constantly tested the waters, probing his American interlocutors for any sign of discontent in Washington. Mohammed Reza's anxieties were so well known in the State Department that over the years there were numerous "hand-holding missions" to Tehran. For many old Iranian observers, the shah was a professional worrier. This undoubtedly contributed to the extraordinary slowness with which the American government recognized the gravity of the Iranian crisis in 1978—having heard the shah worry so often, there was a tendency to assume he was simply crying "wolf" again.

The shah had other worries about the Americans, for it seemed to him, and many other allies, that the United States was experiencing a precipitous decline. If that were true, then a close working relationship with the Americans would only provoke the Russians and other enemies of the United States, without offering solid security to Iran. Disturbed by the erosion of morale and will in the United States at the time of its defeat in Vietnam and Cambodia, distressed by the implications of the Watergate debacle, and unclear as to the prospects for the successful completion of Kissingerian-style "shuttle diplomacy" after the Yom Kippur War, the shah often worried aloud about the "traumatization" of the Americans and the evaporation of their resolve. He determined nevertheless to increase America's dependency on Iran, through commercial and military channels. Paradoxically, he applied to the Americans the very strategy that Kissinger had elaborated for the unfolding U.S.–Soviet relationship: the fashioning of a network of interdependence predicated on Iran's newly acquired oil wealth, a network that would ensure American fealty to the security ties established with Iran. In this way the shah hoped America would be harnessed to Iranian needs, and any temptation to sever the links would be resisted not only by Mohammed Reza's diplomatic supporters, but also by domestic American constituencies that depended for their well-being on the Tehran connection. The shah would take advantage of the continuing White House desire for primacy in international society and a stable international economic order to achieve his own ends.

His strategy was exquisitely conceived and worked all too well. Within a brief period the American business community, hypnotized by the lure of vast profits, had created a network of dependent relationships that ensured they would serve as a vigorous pro-shah constituency with the American government. Their efforts to lobby in support of Iran were not discouraged by the Treasury and Commerce departments, both worried over the worsening terms of

American trade abroad, or by the White House's own committee created to facilitate and expand the promotion of American exports abroad. Within the military production and export sector an effective promotional lobby also began to materialize. It expended considerable time and effort on reducing congressional restraints on the export not only of advanced American weaponry but of the technology and manufacturing capacity associated with the new weapons systems. These programs were generally supported by key segments of the foreign affairs bureaucracy, which saw in the evolving relationship opportunities for meeting the needs of their services or achieving goals that might prove unattainable without the acquiescence of the government of Iran. Thus senior officers within the Defense Security Assistance Agency in the Pentagon were disposed to implement the White House directive of July 1972 without reservation or restraint. Export goals would be complied with, as would bureaucratic targets established within the Department of Defense that offered the prospect of recognition and career advancement for civilians and military alike. For the chief of naval operations of the day—Admiral Thomas E. Moorer—the new program sales offered different vistas. He contemplated the establishment of a naval base in southern Iran which, when taken together with U.S. training programs and sale of Spruance Class destroyers, would provide the American Navy with access to an important naval facility bordering on the Indian Ocean in time of crisis, and with a faithful ally to maintain the facility. So great was his zeal for the extension of American naval power that Moorer far exceeded his authority, and had to be restrained by Secretary of Defense James Schlesinger.

As commercial, bureaucratic, and foreign policy interests began to converge, the U.S. approach to Iran started to lose focus, and the consequences became troublesome to some segments of the Washington community. The Senate Committee on Foreign Relations commissioned a staff study in 1976 to examine the implications of the explosion in arms transfers to Iran that had taken place. Government-to-government military sales to Iran had increased more than sevenfold, from $524 million in fiscal year (FY) 1972 to $3.91 billion in FY 1974, making Iran the largest single purchaser of American military equipment worldwide. In the five-calendar-year period 1972 through 1976, American contracts to deliver military hardware to Iran would exceed $10 billion. The number of Americans associated with military programs grew from approximately 15,000 in 1972 to roughly 24,000 in 1976, and was expected at existing growth rates to exceed 45,000 by 1980. The findings of the committee staff were both instructive and worrisome:

- Iran had purchased large quantities of advanced equipment and, upon delivery in 1977–81, could be regarded "as a regional superpower."

- However, the government of Iran was attempting to create an extremely modern military establishment in a country that lacked the technical, educational, and industrial base to provide the necessary trained personnel and management capabilities to operate such an establishment effectively.

- The 1972 decision by President Nixon to sell Iran virtually anything it wanted effectively exempted Iran from arms sales review processes in the state and defense departments. This lack of policy review on individual sales requests had created a "bonanza" for U.S. weapons manufacturers, the procurement branches of the three U.S. services, and the Defense Security Assistance Agency.

- The presence of large and growing numbers of Americans in Iran had already given rise to socioeconomic problems. Although many of these had proved to be "manageable," they threatened to worsen if a major change in U.S.–Iranian relations materialized.

In a prescient passage in the staff report, it was noted that "Anti-Americanism could become a serious problem in Iran . . . if there were to be a change of government." In a crisis situation, "United States personnel in Iran could become, in a sense, hostages." On the other hand, the committee staff offered no way out of the maze of dependent relationships that had developed in the military supply and security areas:

> The U.S. cannot abandon, substantially diminish, or even redirect its arms programs without precipitating a major crisis in U.S.–Iranian relations. . . . Since Iran has memories of the abrupt cut-off of U.S. arms to Pakistan in 1965, and to Turkey in 1974, and because of the political symbolism that stems from a close supplier-client arms relationship, it is not clear who really has influence over whom in time of an ambiguous crisis situation. Senior U.S. officials have expressed concern about the U.S. being labeled as an unreliable supplier; this concern undoubtedly inhibits the U.S. will to exercise its capability to terminate its support.[7]

Although the U.S. government lacked either the will or the desire to modify or terminate its military supply relationship with Iran, and although any drastic change in military sales would have serious political resonance, some senior officials were deeply concerned that the relationship was "getting out of hand" and that Iran was becoming a warehouse for unneeded or unusable military supplies. The Senate study team found a singular lack of willingness at the senior reaches of the State Department to tolerate debate over the "possible adverse implications of unrestricted arms sales to Iran." Within the Department of Defense, on the other hand, an air of disquiet had descended on the office of the Secretary. Dr. James Schlesinger, a former Rand Corporation scholar and deputy director of the White House Office of Management and Budget, was disturbed by the inclination of the American private sector to "dump" what he felt was "unnecessary and very sophisticated equipment upon unsuspecting recipients." Schlesinger believed that the military supply relationship with Iran might well be getting out of control. If his assessment were correct, the shah's long-run confidence in the Department of Defense might be eroded, since DOD was serving as the main agent for arms sales to Iran. In addition, if "Iranian defense resources were badly allocated, the operational effectiveness of its forces would be downgraded with adverse effects upon the regional security posture."[8] In late 1973, Schlesinger briefed the shah on the far-reaching implications of purchasing sophisticated weaponry that Iran could not readily absorb. The shah responded by requesting that the Secretary make available a qualified adviser in such matters. Schlesinger dispatched Richard Hallock, a retired army colonel and former member of the Rand Corporation staff at Santa Monica, California, to Iran. Hallock "operated outside the DOD chain of command, in part because he and the Secretary suspected that some DOD components might have been functioning primarily as salesmen rather than advisers."[9]

The Secretary and other senior personnel in the Department of Defense subsequently became disenchanted with Hallock's performance. Moreover, it was felt that a more direct system of supervision and control should be established over regular Department of Defense personnel assigned to Iran. Erich Von Marbod, an experienced professional and former comptroller of the Defense Security Assistance Agency, was selected for this task and sent to Iran late in 1975. The U.S. Embassy staff initially objected to the appointment but finally relented. It had become apparent that the situation was getting increasingly out of control, as official and commercial salesmen flocked to Iran. The Von Marbod mission extended over a period of approximately one and a half years, and brought some order out of the near chaos that prevailed at the time of his arrival. But the principal challenge to Washington was not met: how to see the problems accumulating in Iran as a result of the oil boom not through the prism of American policy and narrow bureaucratic interests alone, but within the context of the troubles that the shah through his grandiose schemes was piling up for Iran and himself.

As the Senate study team observed in 1976, there existed in Washington no apparent disposition to reflect on where the Iranian connection was leading the two countries. This was hardly surprising, although in retrospect it was a serious error. For an embattled Republican administration there were far more pressing matters on the docket in 1975–76, and no dramatic warning signs were emerging from Tehran. Even the most prescient Western governments—the French and the Israeli—were unaware of the explosiveness of the Iranian crisis prior to the spring of 1978.

Yet there were serious problems. Revenues had actually been declining while government expenditures had been increasing almost geometrically; by 1975–76, Iran was a country flirting with widening economic dislocations. It was producing less in manufactured goods than had been anticipated under the shah's five-year plan for the economic modernization of the country. Iran was now also a net importer of food products, indicating a mounting birth rate, a movement of peasants away from farmlands that had been turned over to them a decade earlier, and an inability to increase agricultural productivity adequately. Equally important, Iranian society was out of equilibrium. The rush to the cities in the wake of the oil "boom" had produced demands for services that the government found itself incapable of providing; housing was scarce, employment opportunities even scarcer. Yet a whole generation of young Iranians was emerging from high schools, colleges, and universities in search of employment opportunities suitable to their "skills," and these included highly politicized alumni returning from universities abroad. With the exception of military service, such opportunities were rapidly drying up for the new generation. The civilian bureaucracy was already bloated, service in the provinces as a teacher was to be avoided for reasons of class and status, and the private sector of business and trade already had its full complement of recruits. Corruption was rapidly expanding to frightening proportions.

Equally frustrating to the shah was the performance of his own armed forces midway through the modernization program. The military was swollen with equipment, much of which it could not maintain with any appreciable degree of efficiency. In addition, the Iranian armed forces had not distinguished themselves during service in Oman, nor in periodic border collisions with Iraqi forces. In brief, Iran was spinning toward crisis, and the one-man system created by the shah would need exceedingly good luck and much help from Washington to overcome the immediate obstacles. Yet this was the very moment that the shah's traditional good luck began to run out. It can now be seen that the 1972 agreement with the United States was the apogee of the shah's fortunes. Two years later he learned from his French doctors that he had contracted a relatively slow-moving cancer, and while chances for cure in such cases are fairly good, the discovery represented a psychological blow to Mohammed Reza.

Finally, for the first time since the Mossadeq crisis, the shah had to make major decisions without the assistance of at least a handful of strong-willed associates. Alam was dead, along with Generals Zahedi and Foroughi. The few generals who dared tell the shah the truth were removed from the Palace, some as far away as the United States. Those who remained in command would never challenge a royal decision, nor would they fight strongly for a position that was clearly not the shah's own. Of the top advisers to the throne, perhaps the strongest personality was the son of General Zahedi, Ambassador Ardeshir Zahedi. But he was in Washington, trying to convince the Americans of the gravity of the Iranian crisis and to stave off the growing attacks upon his country's human rights policies from the new Carter administration. And the shah never entirely trusted Ardeshir, for he always harbored a lingering suspicion that the son might attempt to avenge the removal of his father nearly three decades before. Further, while Mohammed Reza respected Zahedi's character and courage, he was never a great admirer of the ambassador's intellect. Even when Zahedi gave the shah excellent advice, as he did throughout the last difficult months, Mohammed Reza was not disposed to accept it.

Thus the shah of Iran found himself ill-prepared for his final crisis, while his American allies were not proving at all what he had hoped.

THREE

Carter and Iran

THE LEADING MEMBERS of the Carter administration who took office on January 20, 1977, were anxious to distinguish themselves from their immediate predecessors in the field of foreign policy. Not only had the basic principles of American international relations been major issues in the presidential campaign, but the actual methods by which policy was conducted had been at the center of the Carter-Ford debates. In particular, many on the Carter team wanted to put considerable distance between themselves and retiring Secretary of State Henry A. Kissinger. Since many of Carter's policymakers had been in office during the most intense moments of the Vietnam war (people like Secretary of State Cyrus Vance himself, along with State Department officials Leslie Gelb and Anthony Lake, and Secretary of Defense Harold Brown), they were eager to show that they were not about to repeat the discredited efforts of the recent past. There was a great deal of emphasis in the early days of the new administration upon "open diplomacy"—by which it was meant that the President would not continue the secret negotiations that had characterized some of the Nixon and Ford years—and upon a more moralistic basis for American foreign policy.

There were mixed motives for the new approach. For some officials, notably Vance and Brown among the cabinet members, there was an intense desire to avoid any repetition of the Vietnam experience. They had lived through a period of the most anguished decisionmaking in the late 1960s and early 1970s, had been subjected to sharp criticism from close friends, family members, and the media, and were determined at all costs to avoid similar humiliation and traumas. This attitude was as much a matter of understandable human psychology as it was the result of political and strategic analysis, and it also produced a reluctance to use American military power and covert intelligence capabilities as arms of foreign policy. These positions were enthusiastically shared by the President himself, who early on demonstrated an almost visceral repugnance for weaponry, particularly of the nuclear variety. Almost unknown at the time—and little discussed afterwards—the President's first action in the foreign policy area was to instruct the joint chiefs of staff to arrange for the immediate withdrawal of American nuclear weapons from South Korea. This order was given within twenty-four hours of the inauguration, without any consultation with congressional leaders, the military experts at the Pentagon, the South Koreans themselves, or other allies likely to be affected by the move. Nor was there any effort to discuss the matter with the North Koreans in order to secure a reduction in tension on the peninsula. In the event, the alarm produced by Carter's instructions was so great that the Pentagon managed to have the withdrawal delayed and eventually reconsidered. But the fact that the new President would take a decision of this magnitude without the broad consultation within the bureaucracy and the international community that generally attends such steps indicated that Carter was quite prepared to take decisive action to set off his administration, symbolically and otherwise, from those of Nixon and Ford.

In addition to the stricture "No more Vietnams," the leading policymakers of the young administration embraced another slogan: "No more Pinochets." This meant that the United States should steer away from close working relationships with dictatorships, whether friendly or hostile. Moreover, it meant that Washington would be extremely reluctant to provide clandestine assistance to right-wing movements in countries challenged by "radical" forces. In practice, the Carter administration strove to develop closer ties with governments claiming to be "progressive," even when they were overtly hostile to the United States. The most visible spokesman for

this policy was Ambassador Andrew Young, whose frequent ideological sorties on behalf of radical Third World regimes were sometimes indistinguishable from the pronouncements of Cuban dictator
Fidel Castro. Young was convinced that the long-term interests of
the United States lay in persuading the leaders of countries like
Angola, Cuba, Vietnam, and Cambodia that Jimmy Carter was a
friend of theirs. Young consequently downplayed the role of Cuban
armed forces in Africa, warned against the results of countervailing
American or European efforts on that continent, and preached patience to American leaders. In time, he said, such countries would
inevitably turn to the United States for assistance and expel the
Soviet proxies. In line with these views, Young and many other
leading Carter administration officials urged closer ties with such
movements as the Palestine Liberation Organization and the Polisario Front that was waging war against King Hassan of Morocco.
These efforts undoubtedly won some friends for the United States
among similar-minded African and other Third World leaders, but
it profoundly worried the more moderate, traditional American
friends and allies.

Finally, virtually every major official in Carter's advisory group
believed that it was time to redefine the relationship between the
United States and the Soviet Union. As early as March 1977, the
President announced that the United States had lost its traditional,
exaggerated fear of communism. The Secretary of State stressed his
conviction that America's approach to the Soviet Union had to be
based upon "positive incentives" rather than upon a policy of containment. Vance rejected the notion that "the United States can
dominate the Soviet Union" or otherwise "order the world just the
way we want it to be." The period of the *Pax Americana* was at an
end; henceforth the United States must accept a more limited role
in world affairs. In such a world, Vance argued, America would have
to abandon the search for military solutions to its problems with the
Soviets. And he was optimistic, for, as he put it on the eve of the
Vienna summit in 1978, President Carter and Chairman Brezhnev
"shared common dreams."

Implicit in the statements of Carter administration officials was
the conviction that the United States had itself been the root cause
of many of the problems of the recent past. And there was more than
a hint that America would—and should—do a sort of penance for

its presumed sins in Vietnam, Chile, and other areas. Carter's foreign policy thus rested upon a drastic reassessment of America's proper role in international affairs, and of the methods by which foreign policy should be conducted.

For other top advisers, the new foreign policy seems to have been the result of a domestic political analysis. Carter's chief pollster, Patrick Caddell, was sensitive to the gradual disintegration of the traditional foreign policy consensus in the country. In the first days of the new administration he wrote a fascinating recommendation stressing the need for a political campaign in which the image of the President as a man of the people, a moral figure, and a genuine leader would be progressively enhanced. Caddell, the President, and the political advisers at the White House (notably Hamilton Jordan and Jody Powell) realized that no administration could conduct an effective foreign policy without a solid domestic political consensus. They consequently set about to construct a political base from which the President could gain support for whatever kind of policy he wished to pursue.

In large measure, this political operation was an undoubted success in the United States, although it was viewed with alarm in many foreign capitals. The keystone of the political campaign was the argument that the United States had betrayed its own principles by supporting too many dictatorships throughout the world, and cutting itself off from "progressive" forces striving for greater democracy and social justice. Examples included Franco's Spain, Salazar's Portugal, Greece under "the colonels," and the various Latin American authoritarian regimes in countries like Brazil and Argentina. However, the human rights policy also appealed to some "hawks": there were suggestions—above all from the National Security Council staff and its head, Zbigniew Brzezinski—that the United States had recently been "too soft" on the Soviet Union, and that the human rights campaign must inevitably call attention to the deplorable repression conducted by Soviet totalitarianism.

In all probability, the architects of the human rights policy had not thought through the international consequences of the presidential rhetoric. From the beginning there were only two real possibilities: either the administration was serious, in which case some form of "linkage" would have to be adopted, which meant in practical terms that the United States would have to punish governments of which it did not approve by withholding trade benefits or aid packages; or there would be no linkage, in which case the human rights campaign would shortly be regarded as mere rhetoric with no concrete payoff. For both ideological and practical reasons, the first was the only acceptable development, and the advocates of the human rights campaign quickly became a major force on policymaking.

The human rights enthusiasts were not numerous, but they were often highly talented, and they had impressive connections with some of the most powerful people in Washington. Within the State Department, the "hub" of the movement was in the Bureau for Human Rights and Refugee Affairs, directed by Patricia Derian. A civil rights advocate in the sixties, deeply suspicious of the Washington bureaucracy and decidedly impatient with the inherent conservatism of the State Department, Derian privately lectured foreign service officers and old-line ambassadors, most of whom she presumed to be in opposition to the new approach. She openly voiced her suspicions of such types, and often remarked that she considered it her task to keep the professionals in line with the President's desires. She also exerted pressure over new ambassadorial appointments.

Derian was hardly an expert on international questions. She had never been a student of foreign affairs, had not traveled abroad extensively prior to her appointment, possessed little familiarity with the background, mores, or traditions of the countries she would be monitoring and little if any knowledge of diplomatic tradition or protocol. Her first direct contact with foreign cultures was sometimes traumatic, as when she read reports of female circumcision in an African country. Even though this was a centuries-old tradition unchallenged in the country in question, Derian instructed the American ambassador to intervene vigorously with its government to eliminate the barbaric custom. The ambassador reacted with commendable prudence, but did report to Washington that he had raised the matter, and that the host government had taken note of the American protest. Incidents of this sort were not rare under Derian.

Along with her human rights responsibilities, Derian was also supposed to monitor the plight of international refugees, whose numbers grew vertiginously in the late seventies in countries like Vietnam, Cambodia, Haiti, and Cuba. Yet Derian was curiously lethargic in this field, preferring to delegate responsibility to her subordinates. The performance of the human rights bureau in regard to the refugee problem was considered so unsatisfactory by the President that Derian was deprived of her authority in 1979, and the subject handed over to a special assistant to the President for refugee affairs.

Derian's human rights efforts had the support of some powerful individuals throughout the executive branch and in Congress. It became apparent within a few months that the traditional centers of policymaking, the regional bureaus and "desks" in the Department of State, were not enthusiastic about the human rights guidelines. The foreign service officers in those positions recognized that active pursuit of Derian's desires would offend other countries, in the case of efforts not only to obtain better treatment for political opponents of host governments (held to be a desirable objective by many career diplomats, as was the parallel goal of working for the liberalization of political institutions in foreign countries), but to change the mores, cultural standards, and even religious practices of other nations. The career professionals believed that such a program could only result in disaster, no matter how laudable its goals might be. They preferred a more diplomatic approach to cultural and political differences. But Derian often managed to override these objections, thanks to her influential allies. Warren Christopher, the Deputy Secretary of State, was prevailed upon (by Vance as well as Derian) to preside over an inter-agency human rights committee. This undertaking was supported by such stars of the new Carter firmament as director of policy planning Anthony Lake; Leslie Gelb, the head of the Office of Political-Military Affairs; Andrew Young, who kept a small staff on the seventh floor of the State Department, and had the lists of State Department officials rewritten so as to place him in the second position, thus underlining his intention to play a major role in the department and his political clout in administration circles; William Maynes, the assistant secretary of state for international organization; Richard Holbrooke, the former editor of *Foreign Policy* magazine and assistant secretary for East Asian and Pacific affairs; and Richard Moose, assistant secretary for African affairs. It also received enthusiastic support from one of Gelb's assistants in the Office of Political-Military Affairs, Henry Precht, who later became Iran country director at the time of the crisis. These officials had the full support of Secretary Vance, the President, and Vice President Walter Mondale.

The group of human rights advocates was not only powerful; it included some of the most intellectually brilliant individuals in the government. Both Lake and Gelb had outstanding journalistic reputations, as did Holbrooke, who had brought *Foreign Policy* to a position of considerable political influence during the Nixon–Ford period. These people were eminently well qualified to develop and promote the human rights campaign, package it for the media, and gain widespread acceptance of its basic principles. Moreover, the central themes of the campaign were extremely popular in the country, and it can be argued that they were entirely in keeping with the principles of the democratic revolution that lie at the heart of American political history. Yet there were immense practical and abstract problems in the way of successful pursuit of human rights. In the first place, a serious advocacy required that the United States engage in systematic meddling in the internal affairs of other countries. To be taken seriously, the human rights principles had to be backed up with American power. Trade restrictions might have to be applied (as they had been in the case of the embargo against Rhodesia in a previous administration), diplomatic sanctions might have to be considered, and enormous tensions would inevitably be produced. Moreover, efforts at linkage would likely be more successful against American allies than against American enemies, for the simple reason that those who treasured American friendship might be willing to take domestic risks when asked to do so, but those who were opposed, or who strove for a genuinely neutral position, would take such moralistic strictures less seriously. Finally, powerful enemies like the Soviet Union, or weaker countries under Soviet protection —like Cuba, Vietnam, or Libya—could ignore calls for liberalization while denouncing American "imperialism" in response to attacks on their repressive practices.

The human rights campaign was immediately denounced by the Soviet Union as a gross interference in its internal affairs. The KGB carried out an emergency investigation to make sure there would be no American-inspired uprising, the flow of Jewish refugees and other dissidents was slowed down, and religious groups in the Soviet empire were subjected to even greater harassment than before. In subsequent months, the Russians challenged Carter directly by arresting Anatoly Shcharansky on trumped-up spying charges, and then sending him to the gulags over the protests of the administration. In the face of this thoroughgoing—and wholly predictable—Soviet reaction, the administration backed off, preferring to stress the more lawyer-like approach of Vance to the East-West conflict.

Similar unfortunate results occurred in Third World dictatorships. Following American criticism, dictators like Field Marshal Idi Amin in Uganda and President Haile Mariam Menghistu in Ethiopia reacted violently, leading to a near-rupture in American-Ethiopian relations and a confrontation with Uganda in which Amin threatened bodily harm to more than two hundred American missionaries in his country. Similar developments took place throughout Latin America, the Middle East, and Asia.

The human rights advocates themselves were convinced that the United States was on the right course. One of their supporters wrote in 1978 that there had been some tangible results. Several leading Soviet dissidents had obtained exit visas, prisoners in other countries had been released, and some governments were beginning to "improve their behavior." Above all, "In many important quarters, the former reputation of the United States as a supporter of freedom . . . [was] being restored, replacing its more recent image as a patron of tyranny."[1]

There had in fact been some benefits from the human rights campaign, but they had been in unexpected areas. Foremost was the considerable embarrassment caused to the West European Communist parties—the so-called Eurocommunists of Italy, France, and Spain. These parties had been claiming for some time to be true Western, democratic parties, ready to assume power within the NATO orbit. Yet their own history and the passions of the rank-and-file made it impossible for them either to embark upon a systematic criticism of the Soviet Union or to break with the Soviets on basic East-West questions. The campaign placed these parties in a highly difficult position. If they condemned Carter, they risked being branded puppets of the Soviet Union, for the theme of human rights was very popular in western Europe. Yet to endorse Carter's campaign would antagonize both the Russians and the rank-and-file that still believed the Soviet Union was a citadel of socialism. The Eurocommunists attempted to maneuver their way through the impasse, hoping that the storm would abate. In time, the human rights passions in Washington cooled, especially so far as the Soviet Union was concerned, and the European Communists were able to resume their

own efforts to gain public sympathy. But Carter's campaign undoubtedly cost them considerable public support at a time when they
were on the verge of entering the cabinet in Italy, and possibly
winning a general election in France.

In the long run, the full force of the human rights advocates came
to bear on authoritarian regimes that were considered reactionary,
and that were tied more or less closely to the United States. These
included South Korea, Argentina, South Africa, Brazil, Taiwan,
Nicaragua, and Iran. Not only were such countries particularly vulnerable to American threats to reduce military sales or assistance;
they were also heavily dependent on continued American political
support. Thus the demands of the human rights spokesmen were
likely to have considerable effect, either in producing substantial
compliance or in provoking diplomatic wrath. In virtually all these
cases, the human rights demands for greater liberalization at home
were linked to military and economic assistance programs that themselves were viewed as part of a general revision in American foreign
policy.

The Carter administration attempted to reduce the level of military assistance provided overseas, while simultaneously increasing
appropriations in the areas of economic and humanitarian assistance.
This effort was in keeping with the general humanistic concerns of
the administration, but it encountered unexpected hostility from
several quarters. Above all, many members of Congress, eager to
climb aboard the human rights bandwagon, demonstrated considerable independence of the administration in foreign policy. Just as the
executive branch developed its own assessments of the human rights
performance of various countries, so congressional staffs produced
their own favorite targets for linkage. The lists often conflicted,
particularly when congressmen demanded that aid be withheld from
countries that "provided assistance to or sanctuary for terrorists or
terrorist groups." The problem was that "one man's terrorist is
another man's freedom fighter," and virtually every country in the
Middle East could be placed in the category of terrorist supporter.
Oddly enough, the Republic of Somalia—led by an African Marxist,
and blatantly preparing to invade the Ogaden Province of Ethiopia
in clear violation of the United Nations Charter and that of the
Organization of African Unity—was never singled out as a human
rights violator. In fact, as will soon be seen, the regime of Siad Barre

became a recipient of American support shortly after Carter took office.

In the end, the combination of efforts to reduce military assistance programs and link American economic aid to the human rights standards of foreign countries produced a net decrease in support to Africa and Latin America. And this occurred despite the very strong conviction of Carter and his top advisers that the United States should strive for better relations with the Third World. Moreover, the scope of American aid programs was severely limited, with the bulk of the appropriations going to Israel and Egypt as part of the Middle East peace process. Hoist by its own ideological petard, the Carter administration had apparently produced the reverse of its proclaimed intentions. For despite all the rhetoric, foreign assistance programs—the stock in trade of efforts to win friends overseas and support governments in favor—were shrinking.

The human rights yardstick ultimately proved too clumsy a measure for the delicate process of international relations. Just as there are times when a nation must swallow political objections and form an alliance of convenience with an odious foreign country, so it will also occasionally wish to bring an ally under great pressure at a crucial moment. Behavior of the first sort does not represent approval, any more than the second implies condemnation of the foreign country; each simply corresponds to national interests at a given moment. By subjecting American foreign policy to the overall standard of human rights, the Carter administration sometimes tied its own hands before the battle ever started. Worse still, since the campaign was largely directed against smaller countries rather than strong ones, it appeared to many nations that the United States was abandoning its traditional policy of containment of Soviet expansion in favor of a new sort of moral isolationism. No longer could small countries hope to gain economic and political support from the United States merely by shifting their policies; it was now necessary to conform to American moral and political standards as well. And even this requirement was viewed as arbitrary, for the administration continued to advance credits—and ship advanced technology—to the Soviet Union, even though that country had one of the worst human rights records in the world.

In short, even though the President had introduced an admirable element of moralism into the rhetoric of American foreign policy, the impression from the outside was of an administration that was withdrawing from world affairs, that imposed arbitrary standards on its allies and would-be allies, and that was capable of sudden dramatic turnabouts in its relations abroad. Above all, many foreign leaders were baffled by the apparent abandonment of traditional concepts of national self-interest. They often were unable to grasp American objectives. This in itself introduced a destabilizing element into international affairs, for American intentions and desires have always been a major factor in the decisions of other countries. To the extent that these intentions and desires are unclear, other nations find it difficult to structure their own policies—a point that was to be particularly important in the case of the shah of Iran.

THE SHAH WAS SLOW to recognize the uncertainties and confusions in Carter's foreign policy. To be sure, there was a wealth of evidence suggesting that many Washington officials were hostile to him and to his ambassador, Ardeshir Zahedi. Brzezinski himself, before assuming his post at the National Security Council, had said publicly that Zahedi was a "disgrace" because of his lavish parties and his habit of bestowing expensive gifts on members of Congress and press representatives. Robert Hunter, formerly Senator Edward Kennedy's foreign policy adviser, had often expressed his ideological opposition to the shah's regime, even though Hunter, along with Kennedy, had been a guest of the shah in Iran, and had worked energetically to obtain an audience with the king of kings. And of course there were the human rights advocates, who strongly disapproved of the activities of SAVAK.

Within the National Security Council (NSC) there were others who had no love for the shah. David Aaron, deputy special assistant to the President for national security affairs—a person with an intimate working relationship with Vice President Walter Mondale—had been vociferous in his opposition to the shah's regime when he served Mondale in the Senate; in early 1977 he stated publicly that "this is a different administration. If the shah thinks that he will get everything he wants in the arms field, he is in for a surprise."[2] His sentiments were shared by such NSC staffers as Jessica Tuchman and Lieutenant Commander Gary Sick of the Navy, and accurately reflected Mondale's own feelings.

These executive branch critics of the shah could count on considerable support in Congress, especially among those who were members of the "Vietnam generation." Senators Alan Cranston of California and Frank Church of Idaho, along with Representative Donald Fraser of Minnesota, argued that it was immoral for the United States to continue to provide an uninterrupted flow of weapons to a ruler held guilty of egregious violations of human rights. It was therefore not inconceivable that an alliance between the shah's critics on Capitol Hill and the executive branch might carry enough weight to subject Iran to the sort of linkage that had been abandoned earlier on vis-à-vis the Soviet Union.

Despite the impressive number of officials hostile to the shah, there was good reason to believe that the special relationship between Iran and the United States would continue as before. Whatever he might say in public about the activities of Ambassador Zahedi, Brzezinski was quick to recognize the geopolitical importance of Iran, and assured the Iranians—both in conversations with Zahedi and in telephone talks with the shah himself—that American political and military support would continue as before. Zahedi received similar guarantees from the Pentagon, the Department of State, and the Central Intelligence Agency. In time, even Aaron came to realize that Iran's importance to America might transcend moralistic considerations, although he arrived at this conclusion very late in the crisis.

Zahedi, for his part, knew that Iran had many supporters, even in the more hostile atmosphere of the Carter administration. The Bureau of Near Eastern Affairs was under the direction of Roy Atherton, a senior foreign service officer with considerable experience in Middle Eastern affairs, and a strong conviction that the close ties with Iran had been enormously beneficial to the United States. Moreover, the Iran country director at the time was Dr. Charles Naas, an old specialist in Iranian affairs who fully understood the importance of the special relationship with the Iranians. And senior officials in both the Pentagon and CIA headquarters believed that the relationship with the shah was a necessity for the projection of American military power in the Persian Gulf region and for the collection of intelligence on Soviet activities. Consequently, the senior officials of the Pentagon's Security Assistance Agency actively campaigned for the maintenance—and strengthening—of close ties with Tehran, as did most of the members of the various armed services involved in the arms transfer programs. Despite the rhetoric suggesting a drastic change in arms transfer policies, the Carter administration continued to export weaponry to Iran.

The internal division over the proper course of American policy toward the shah revolved around one of the classic problems in American diplomacy: To what extent is it proper for the United States to demand compliance with its own moral and civil standards in return for its cooperation in a working alliance? The problem, as has been seen, is not merely one of foreign policy, for the human rights campaign—whose principles seemed to call for American efforts on behalf of Iranian "reform"—was as much a part of domestic politics as it was an ingredient of international policy. Perhaps the ideal outcome would have been a human rights "success" coupled with a continuation of the highly useful special relationship with Tehran: by compelling the shah to conform to the standards of the human rights themes, without destabilizing Iran or jeopardizing the close working ties between the two countries. What were the chances for such an outcome? And if the chances were judged to be good, what were the best methods for achieving it?

Ironically, the human rights advocates gained considerable encouragement from the reports of Richard Helms, the American ambassador in Tehran. Obviously, a campaign of linkage directed against the shah might be judged too risky if the shah were believed to be vulnerable to his domestic or international enemies. But Helms's reports from Iran painted a picture of a monarch in complete control of the domestic situation, and the shah's military strength was clearly sufficient to withstand attack from any of his radical Arab neighbors. Like most American and foreign observers in the mid- and late 1970s, Helms was impressed by the shah's wealth and power, and was caught up in the mystique that surrounded the *shahanshah.*

It is hardly surprising that Helms reached this evaluation, for it was shared by virtually all experts in the field, whether American or foreign, whether within the government, the press, or academe. In early 1977 scarcely any observers were prepared to speak of the possibility of the shah's fall from power, and the great majority were convinced that the only major political problem on the horizon was posed by the death of the shah, at which time many analysts foresaw the possibility of a struggle for power between the Iranian military and Crown Prince Reza.

Both Helms and his successor William Sullivan were long-time professionals in the American foreign policy establishment, and both had acquired well-deserved reputations for independent analysis and political acumen. Yet each man carried heavy political baggage to Tehran. Helms had been removed from his post as director of the CIA during one of the darkest moments in the history of the American intelligence community, and his job in Iran was a sort of luxurious exile. While he was ambassador, he had to return to Washington on several occasions to testify before congressional committees investigating alleged CIA improprieties, thus adding to the conviction in the administration that Helms was a political embarrassment. After a lifetime in government service, Helms knew that nobody wanted to hear bad news in Washington, above all from the likes of himself; any inclination he might have had to file pessimistic reports from Iran was tempered by the realization that he would be blamed for much of it. He was hardly inclined to take a dark view of the situation, preferring to stress what he saw as the outstanding leadership qualities of the shah, and the monarch's absolute centrality to the Iranian universe.

Helms's intention was to discourage the shah's Washington critics by constantly stressing that Mohammed Reza was irreplaceable. But the picture of a monolithic regime that he presented paradoxically encouraged those who wished to put the shah under moral pressure. For, they reasoned, if the shah was as strong as Helms reported, then a more liberal treatment of his opponents would hardly be fatal to the stability of the country. And if the shah was as central to the system as claimed, then such liberalization would be relatively simple: it could be accomplished by a simple decision on the part of the shah himself.

Helms was replaced by William Sullivan in the first year of Carter's presidency, but there was no dramatic change in reporting from Tehran. Sullivan was a tough-minded professional, whose political independence had earned him the suspicion of successive American administrations. Nixon thought he was a "Johnson man"; the Carter people considered him a "Kissingerian." Thus Sullivan was forced to be purer than Caesar's proverbial wife, meticulously following instructions, attempting to change the views of those with whom he disagreed by subtle methods rather than direct challenge, and generally maintaining a low profile.

Although the United States was well represented in Tehran, the two ambassadors were therefore operating under unusual constraints. Both men were suspect in the eyes of the Washington bureaucracy, and both had to be extremely circumspect in their diplomatic behavior. To have suggested that the human rights campaign might actually contribute to the shah's downfall would not only have antagonized leading figures in the new administration; it would have weakened the credibility of the American ambassador. Helms and Sullivan had learned a basic lesson of bureaucratic behavior over the course of their careers: If your boss won't accept certain assessments, it is better not to present them. The prudent course is to await developments, hoping to be able to influence events at a later date rather than spending too much capital too early.

In any event, the first year of the Carter administration must have reminded the shah of the opening days of the Kennedy administration in 1961, when the Iranian leader had been under mounting pressure to liberalize his rule, moderate his demands for weaponry, and conform to American democratic standards. And just as the shah had made several concessions to the Kennedy administration —all the while eliminating possible sources of real power, and actually strengthening his own position in Iran—so he made similar gestures to the Carter leaders throughout 1977. The number of political prisoners incarcerated without trial decreased dramatically; an active opposition was not only permitted but even encouraged by the Palace; many of SAVAK's worst human rights violations were brought under control or eliminated; and the symbol of SAVAK repression—General Nematollah Nassiri—was removed and sent abroad as ambassador to Pakistan. This last was in response to explicit American pressure, for there were many in Washington who felt that Nassiri's removal would send a clear signal that the human rights campaign had produced dramatic results.*

Curiously, while there was great American pressure for modera-

---

*Nassiri paid a terrible price for his past sins and his unpopularity in Washington. Later arrested by the shah during a subsequent anticorruption campaign, he was in jail when Khomeini took power in 1979. The revolution was merciless: Nassiri was tortured, then shown to the people on television, and finally "killed" three times. He was hanged, cut down while still alive, then shot in the heart and head.

tion of SAVAK excesses in Iran—a country where capricious use of police forces, systematic torture, and little if any legal niceties had been long-established traditions, and where these practices were far more restrained than in neighboring countries like Pakistan, Syria, and Iraq—there was little activity to limit dubious SAVAK efforts in the United States. There was no secret about the extent of SAVAK operations in this country; indeed, a court case resulting from SAVAK harassment of Iranian students took place in the first year of the Carter administration. Yet there does not seem to have been any effort on behalf of the American government to demand that these practices cease.

By and large, the shah's efforts at liberalization seemed to satisfy the President. On his trip to Iran at the turn of the new year, 1977–78, President Carter announced in his toast that "Iran, because of the great leadership of the Shah, is an island of stability in one of the more troubled areas of the world." And he remarked that "The cause of human rights is one that also is shared deeply by our people and by the leaders of our two nations." One could hardly imagine more reassuring words to the shah, who was always searching for clues that his American allies and protectors were reconsidering their relationship with him. He may have known that in Washington people like Robert Hunter, Jessica Tuchman, and David Aaron were remarking that "the shah was the problem" in Iran. But he also knew that despite threats of cutting back on arms shipments to Iran, the American government had not taken any decisive action. And the close working relationship between the two countries had continued in the complicated and often secret affairs of the Persian Gulf.

THERE WAS ONE precise litmus test available to the shah by which he could gauge the tone and texture of his relations with the United States. This was the arms transfer program. At the heart of such transactions is the often extreme vulnerability of the recipient nation, which is totally at the mercy of the policies and idiosyncrasies of another. A mutually beneficial bargain had been struck in the mid-1950s. Now, almost twenty-five years later, the validity of the bargain was to be tested.

Jimmy Carter had campaigned in 1976 on a platform that called for significant restraint over arms transfers. The United States could not achieve moral rebirth in international affairs so long as it remained the world's principal supplier of arms, and the President promised efforts to curtail its own transactions, as well as those of other supplier nations.

The position of the new occupant of the White House was a break with American tradition. Ever since the inception of the American arms transfer program in the years following World War II, the U.S. government had treated transfers of military services and equipment as normal foreign policy transactions. These transfers had been used in support of a wide array of objectives: to strengthen and maintain regional military balances (as in transfers to NATO nations, the Republic of South Korea, and to Israel); to acquire and to maintain base and overflight rights, as with Spain and the Philippines; and to strengthen friendly governments against internal subversion, as with Ethiopia and Jordan. During much of this period, the American policy of exporting military hardware for the purpose of collective security was well understood and supported in the United States. By the mid-1960s, however, this support had begun to erode as a result of events in Vietnam and Cambodia. The use of arms sales and grant assistance as adjuncts of policy was being increasingly challenged within the Congress and the American public at large. Now Jimmy Carter, with little experience in foreign affairs, added his voice to the chorus: henceforth the United States would use its power to try to limit the international flow of arms.

Shortly after Inauguration Day, the President commissioned a study on American arms transfer policy with a view to developing new guidelines for the national security bureaucracy. The study team was headed by Jessica Tuchman of the NSC staff and Leslie Gelb of the Department of State. The study was prepared in some haste, but ultimately met the President's requirements. On May 19, 1977, a Presidential Decision Memorandum was issued to the arms transfer bureaucracy, setting forth Carter's mandate. In his own words:

> To implement a policy of arms restraint, I am establishing the following set of controls, applicable to all transfers except those to countries with which we have major defense treaties (NATO, Japan, Australia, and New Zealand). We will remain faithful to our treaty obligations, and will honor our historic responsibilities to assure the security of the state of Israel. These controls will be binding *unless* extraordinary circumstances necessitate a Presidential exception, *or*

where I determine that countries friendly to the United States must depend on advanced weaponry to offset quantitative or other disadvantages in order to maintain regional balance.[2]

The presidential stricture on arms transfers included the following important elements:

• The dollar value of new commitments under the Foreign Military Sales and Military Assistance programs for weapons and weapons-related items would be reduced to an annual level of $8.6 billion.

• The United States guaranteed that it would never be first to introduce into a region newly developed, advanced weapons systems that could create a new or significantly higher combat capability.

• Development or significant modification of *advanced* weapons systems *solely for export* would not be permitted. (Such weapons could not be sold unless or until they were operationally deployed with U.S. forces.)

• Co-production agreements for significant weapons, equipment, and major components would be prohibited.

• Legislation was introduced requiring policy-level authorization by the Department of State for actions by agents of the United States or private manufacturers, promoting the sale of arms abroad. In addition, embassies and military representatives abroad would not promote the sale of arms.

As one of the administration's senior officials put it, the United States would not "approve arms transfers reflexively," "would give adequate consideration to . . . the long-term implications of arms transfers," and would seek the cooperation of others to do the same. Moreover, human rights factors would weigh heavily in U.S. decisions:

> In formulating security assistance programs consistent with these controls, we will continue our efforts to promote and advance respect for human rights in recipient countries. Also we will assess the economic impact of arms transfers to those less-developed countries receiving U.S. economic assistance.[3]

Iran, of course, was a customer, not a recipient of aid. Nonetheless, the new presidential guidelines appeared likely to slow down the shah's plans for the modernization of his country's armed forces. Mohammed Reza had prepared a program that included the addition of the airborne early warning and command system (AWACS, also made available to NATO); he hoped to make an additional purchase of up to 140 F-16 aircraft; he was concerned to bolster the sea defenses of Iran by acquiring some of the newest frigates already being produced for the American Navy. In addition, his shopping list contained advanced radar and ground early-warning equipment, upgraded M-60 tanks, the F-4G (wild weasel), the F-18, which was in the drawing-board stage, and various special facilities for co-production of advanced weaponry already purchased. The guidelines contained a worldwide arms sale ceiling that would likely constrain contractual negotiations. Moreover, to the extent that the ceiling would be reduced each year, Iran could not expect to maintain its high tempo of acquisition. Finally, presidential limitations on co-production also would put a damper on hopes to quickly develop modern industrial capabilities in this area.

The first months of the Carter presidency confirmed these fears. Leading members of Congress registered their distress over the sale of AWACS and the large numbers of fighter aircraft to Iran. Worse still from the shah's standpoint, during the public debate administration witnesses aired their own worries about the capacity of Iran to safeguard highly sensitive advanced equipment. As might be expected, the shah reacted with considerable heat to what he felt were uncalled-for aspersions. After a brief flurry, the question was laid to rest and the sale of AWACS approved. The shah was disappointed in only one significant area: he had been considering the purchase of an additional 140 F-16 aircraft for some time and, given the prospect of increased costs if the purchase were to be delayed, approached Washington for early consideration of the planned acquisition. Within the administration, the arms transfer bureaucracy reviewed the proposal routinely and presidential approval was recommended in a joint memorandum from the Secretary of Defense and the Secretary of State. Only the intervention of several NSC staffers with their chief led to a review of the request within White House precincts. Brzezinski was initially inclined to support the position of Vance and Brown, but after reading a staff memorandum on the subject, he supported a reduction in the number of aircraft to be sold. The President backed Brzezinski, and the shah was duly informed. He also experienced delays in requests to support the development of the F-18 airplane, to secure early delivery of tanks, to purchase tear gas and napalm for air force training, to acquire the F-4G, and to move ahead with plans for co-production facilities to be located in Iran.

It might appear from these events that the administration was indeed adhering to its restrictive arms transfer policies. In reality, the conduct of business with Iran was virtually unchanged. Not only did Iran continue to receive more military orders than any other country, but the Carter administration embarked upon a clever bookkeeping program that enabled the shah to overcome the obstacles set in his path by the American President. Much of this was designed by Admiral Ray Peet, the director of the Department of Defense's agency concerned with military sales, and involved the following methods:

• Iranian orders for specific major items would be placed on a multi-year basis, thus ensuring that Iran would remain within the annual guidelines;

• Iranian orders were placed early in the fiscal year so that the shah would get a larger dollar allocation than any other purchasers;

• Contracts were refined in order to permit cost estimates to vary, a sort of escalator arrangement to take into account rising production and training costs. This achieved two goals: any actual cost increase would be passed on to the Iranians; and Iran would be permitted to buy a certain quantity of equipment regardless of cost increases. The practical effect was to raise the ceiling on Iranian purchases;

• Finally, parts of orders were displaced outside the United States. Western Europe was not included under the Carter ceiling, and thus parts of the Iranian shopping list could easily be subcontracted to European manufacturers, or relayed through European wholesalers. For example, the hulls and power packages for the shah's frigates could be built in West Germany while the weapons and radar systems were produced in the United States. The shah received what he wanted while the Pentagon remained technically within the guidelines. Not surprisingly, this method led to a spectacular increase in arms sales, and, in one of the more bizarre developments in recent American political history, the Carter administration set a new record for sales of military goods and services in its first full fiscal year: more than $12 billion.

The shah, then, had some good reasons to be pleased with the behavior of the new administration. At the same time, however, there existed signs of internal confusion, and even hostility toward his own person. Also, in the area of arms transfers, some specific items were withheld. The most important case—both for its actual significance to the shah and for its impact on American-Iranian relations—was the "wild weasel."

The shah had long asked the American government for permission to purchase a squadron of advanced F-4 aircraft, known as "wild weasels" because of their sophisticated electronic countermeasure capability. These planes had been sold to Israel in 1973–74, but Iran had been unable to obtain them. On his trip to Washington in the fall of 1977, the shah had made it clear that the wild weasel squadron was his top military priority. He had learned during the Yom Kippur War that F-4s without the electronic countermeasure capability were strikingly vulnerable to Soviet-made antiaircraft missiles, and since Iraq and Syria could be expected to have these Soviet weapons, the shah wanted the wild weasels. He made his appeal in the strongest possible language.

The American government was not eager for Iran to be the second foreign nation to fly the wild weasels, and no decision had been made as late as early July 1978. At that time, Department of Defense experts strongly endorsed Iran's request, and Secretary Harold Brown sent a two-page memorandum to the President urging a positive decision. As was usual in such cases, Carter discussed the matter with Secretary of State Vance, who finally managed to get him to reject the proposal. The decision was reached at a moment when Deputy Assistant Secretary of State David Newsom was in Tehran. He was advised of the President's instructions, via a "flash" cable, just an hour or two before meeting with the shah. Newsom thus had the unenviable task of personally informing Mohammed Reza of the American government's negative decision. Worse still, this unpleasant announcement was part of a conversation that greatly disturbed the shah, for it confirmed a growing suspicion that there had been a basic shift in American geopolitical strategy. The shah feared that this change might cause his own political demise as the ruler of Iran.

VERY FEW OBSERVERS fully appreciated the extent of American-Iranian cooperation in international affairs, for most students of the region—even in relatively high levels of government—only saw one or two elements in the set of interlocking relationships that bound the two countries tightly together. To grasp the complexity of these ties, one must look at the American regional commitments, where the special role of Iran becomes evident.

For more than a quarter of a century, the U.S. government and the monarchies of Iran, Saudi Arabia, and Ethiopia had maintained an intimate relationship predicated on certain well-defined policy goals and operational objectives. These included: (1) continued American support for the three "moderate" monarchical regimes (known as the three kings principle); (2) provision of security and other forms of assistance to these regimes to deal effectively with both foreign and domestic threats; (3) active opposition to expansion of Soviet influence in the region; and (4) frequent consultations to secure coordinated policies and approaches to the solution of common problems. Over a period of more than two decades a pattern of consensus, collaboration, and consistency of performance had evolved that led the three areas involved to believe that Washington would fully support stability in the region.

The American performance in meeting regional crises and supporting the ambitions of the "three kings" underscored the value of the American connection. The United States had backed Emperor Haile Selassie even when he terminated Eritrea's status as an autonomous member of the Ethiopian federation (a status upheld by a United Nations mandate), just as Washington had been instrumental in foiling a coup attempt by Ethiopia's imperial bodyguard in 1960. The United States had also accorded a special status to Iran on Persian Gulf matters, and welcomed the intervention of the shah's forces to quash the Dhofar rebellion. And, of course, there was the extremely close bond to Saudi Arabia, where over the years Washington had developed a web of security relationships based on an interlocking network of military assistance and sales agreements.

The three kings worked closely together, in keeping both with the traditional link between the world's few surviving monarchs and with a virtual identity of geopolitical interests. All feared the spread of radical Arab governments—even the Saudis, whose devotion to what would later be termed "radical Islam" was second to none. All were concerned about Soviet penetration of the Middle East, having had considerable experience with Soviet-supported movements during the Nasser period.

In addition, as has been seen, the three monarchs worked closely with two other countries: Morocco and Pakistan. The five countries constantly consulted with each other on foreign policy questions, maintained close working relationships between their respective intelligence services, and often presented a common front to the Americans on serious international problems. On occasion, they were joined by Jordan's King Hussein, and four of them—Morocco, Iran, Ethiopia, and Pakistan—had limited but fruitful relations with Israel.

With the arrival of the Carter administration in January 1977, Saudi Arabia indicated to the new President that it was deeply troubled by events in Yemen and the African Horn, and the shah signaled his own concern at the same time. The half-decade of 1972 through 1976 had been tumultuous; it had been punctuated by political upheaval and civil strife in the Horn, growing prospects of a border war, and increased likelihood of great power confrontation. The period had opened with the violent termination in 1974 of more than fifty years of rule by Emperor Haile Selassie. In 1975, internal conflict had spread throughout Ethiopia as the military leaders who had replaced the emperor sought to suppress their opponents. Equally disturbing, Colonel Menghistu, the emerging leader of the governing military committee *(Dergue),* was embracing Marxist ideology and actively wooing Moscow for arms. Secessionist forces were active in the Ethiopian provinces, threatening to balkanize Ethiopia; at the same time, Menghistu's policies and problems were unsettling the Nimeiri regime in neighboring Sudan.

In response to the expressions of concern emerging from Riyadh and Tehran, the Carter administration communicated to leaders in both capitals its intention to attach a high priority to the shoring up of moderate forces in the region. Senior presidential representatives conducted discussions with the Saudis, seeking to form a strategic alliance with the leading petroleum-exporting country, to vouchsafe American access to energy supplies at a "reasonable price," to secure Saudi support for new administration peace initiatives in the Middle East, and to support Saudi plans to buttress the position of moderate forces in the Red Sea region. The Saudi plan was to thicken security and economic ties with like-minded leaders in a form of regional entente. Taking advantage of the Egyptian and Sudanese rupture with Moscow, as well as the growing Somali disenchantment with Soviet restraints, Saudi strategy emphasized:

• Increased Saudi and Iranian financial subventions to all three nations as they shifted closer to the West;

• U.S. military assistance to Cairo, Khartoum, and Mogadishu, as well as stepped-up aid to Taiz in the face of growing signs of intervention by the radical South Yemeni regime;

• Support for Somali claims to the Ogaden region of Ethiopia, particularly if the Menghistu regime gave continued evidence of wishing to buttress its relationship with the Soviet Union.

An Ethiopian economic delegation that visited Moscow in mid-1976 was hosted by Soviet Foreign Minister Gromyko and received by Premier Kosygin. While proclamations of friendship had emanated from these meetings, the Soviet leaders apparently made no firm offers of a material nature. Moscow was obviously seeking to strike a balance between Ethiopian needs and Somali ambitions. By the end of 1976, however, the Soviet Union decided to enter into an arms transfer agreement with Ethiopia, reportedly to undergird the Menghistu faction, which was under attack by moderate elements in the *Dergue.* The power struggle was finally resolved on February 3, 1977, when gunfire erupted in the midst of a *Dergue* meeting, an exchange that left the leader of the moderate element, General Teferi Banti, and six of his confederates dead.

During this strained period, Washington proceeded to take a series of policy initiatives that heartened the potential members of the Red Sea Entente. In rapid succession, Moscow and the Menghistu regime were denounced for human rights abuses. The Menghistu regime was singled out for excesses committed under the "Red Terror" purges then in progress; the State Department announced that all grant military assistance would be terminated as a sign of disapproval (although arms transfers under sales arrangements were to continue), and that economic assistance funds projected under bilateral and multilateral agreements would be subjected to careful scrutiny, with approval predicated upon improved performance by Addis Ababa in the human rights field. As might have been anticipated, the Menghistu regime, sorely pressed by secessionists and dissidents outside the capital and disputatious factions within, denounced Washington for meddling in Ethiopia's internal affairs, excoriated the U.S. policymakers for their erstwhile support of the "repressive and feudalistic Selassie regime," and promptly terminated all activities of the American Military Assistance Advisory Group (MAAG), USIA, and the military installation at Kagnew (Asmara). The size of the U.S. diplomatic staff was also drawn down drastically. The immediate reaction in the White House was best characterized as one of puzzled irritation; but the entente forces, convinced that the administration was signaling its intention to "push Menghistu to the wall," felt encouraged by this Washington-inspired "lurch towards polarization."

Further heartening to the Red Sea Entente leaders was the White House decision, taken in June, to dispatch a military survey mission to Sudan to review that nation's military equipment requirements in the wake of President Nimeiri's decision to request the withdrawal of Soviet military advisers the previous year. The survey mission recommended, *inter alia,* the sale of a squadron of F-5 aircraft to buttress Sudan's air defense capabilities.* Finally, in one of those paradoxes that characterized Carter's presidency, the White House determined that the United States should make "defensive weapons" available to Somalia, particularly if the Siad Barre government decided to end its military supply relationship with Moscow. This decision was conveyed to Somalia early in July. Barely one month later, regular Somali forces crossed the Ethiopian border.

Washington's decision to provide "defensive weapons" had come at a delicate juncture in Somalia's frayed dialogue with the Soviet Union. Several months earlier the Russians, in tandem with Fidel Castro, had embarked on a vigorous campaign to ameliorate relations between the two "socialist regimes" in the Horn region— Ethiopia and Somalia. Castro visited Africa during March and, after urgent consultations with Moscow, on April 5–6 made clear his support for an "alliance of Ethiopia, Somalia, and South Yemen," as a "common anti-imperialist front." Castro urged the leaders of all three nations to meet in an effort to resolve their differences, and to fashion the basis for a political confederation of socialist countries in the Red Sea area. Castro and the Soviet Union made clear their opposition to any Somali "adventures in the Ogaden" in the midst

---

*Almost five years after the initial Sudanese approach for aid, the squadron was still undelivered, in marked contrast to the Soviet performance in delivering almost $1 billion in military hardware to neighboring Ethiopia within six months after the Somali attempt to seize control of the Ogaden in mid-1977.

of Menghistu's travails with Eritrean secessionists and other opponents of the Ethiopian revolution. The Soviet Union would close its military supply pipeline to Somalia should its president, Siad Barre, not heed its strong "advice."

On May 19, Siad Barre rejected the proposal to form a confederation, due to "irreconcilable differences with Ethiopia over the Ogaden." Menghistu had himself taken a position against "dismemberment" of Ethiopia—a position that indicated the Ogaden was not negotiable even within the framework of confederation. Siad had hedged his bets, however. Early in 1977 he had apprised the Saudis and Iranians of his interest in joining the Red Sea Entente—an action that Moscow greeted with distress, given its dependence on access to military installations at Berbera and Hargeisa. Moscow quite properly perceived that it could be "squeezed" by Siad Barre to support his irredentist ambitions against Russia's new Ethiopian client, caught up in the turmoil of revolutionary change. To mitigate against such pressure, Moscow had produced the alliance strategy, which now threatened to abort.

The United States stumbled into this unfolding situation. Because of Washington's unwitting signals, all of the major actors in the region began to operate on assumptions that proved erroneous and, in the resulting crisis, destabilizing. Washington's assumption seemed to be that it could diminish Soviet influence in Somalia by serving as an alternative arms supplier without provoking a wider conflict between traditional foes. President Siad Barre misread the American position, assuming that the Carter administration implicitly approved the unleashing of his regular forces to invade the Ogaden. The Saudis felt confident of an ultimate Somali victory, especially in view of the safety net that the Carter administration was providing. The Sudanese government intensified its support for the Eritrean secessionists now that the entente appeared to be maturing; and Sadat pledged his support for the entire venture in hopes that the moderate Arab alliance, operating under the benign mantle of Washington, would win its Horn of Africa gamble.

The role of the shah in this effort to shore up moderate regimes in the Red Sea region is frequently overlooked. For the effort to succeed, the architects of the strategy—in Riyadh and Cairo—required the clear support of the new administration in Washington. President Sadat, early in 1977, had canvassed the Carter team on the possibilities of Egyptian forces serving as a "fire brigade" in Africa to provide muscle for a peacekeeping effort, given mounting signs of Soviet penetration below the Sahara. The initial American reaction was circumspect. Therefore, it was imperative that an extra-regional backer enter the lists with the Carter administration to secure at least tacit American support for the Red Sea Entente. This the shah did enthusiastically, for he was alarmed at the overthrow of Haile Selassie and the rise of revolutionary forces in both Ethiopia and the People's Democratic Republic of South Yemen. The shah knew that the stability of the Red Sea and that of the Persian Gulf were irrevocably linked. Barring a major American effort to counter Soviet penetration—something that appeared unlikely, given the Vietnam syndrome prevailing in the United States—moderate nations in the region would have to rely primarily on their own devices, with the United States as a counterpoise only if the Soviet Union decided to intervene directly in the contest for regional supremacy. Tacit Washington backing would be sufficient, and the shah, through Ambassador Ardeshir Zahedi, undertook to enlighten the Carter administration about the threat of radicalism in the region and the counterstrategy that had been formulated. The senior White House staff was fully briefed on the latter score, and signaled to Zahedi their backing for the venture.

The support of the shah placed him squarely at odds with the Soviet Union. The bases at Aden and at Berbera were very important for the operations of Soviet naval forces in the Indian Ocean—both as way stations for support of allies in Vietnam, Cambodia, and Laos, and as power centers for control of the sea-lanes from the Middle East oilfields to the West. The entente clearly threatened Moscow's investments in the Red Sea, laboriously constructed over the previous decade at great expense to the Kremlin. Taken together with the elimination of the Soviet presence in Egypt and Sudan, successful implementation of the Red Sea Entente strategy would mean a debacle for the residual Soviet position in the southern Middle East area. Thus, the activities of Mohammed Reza were undoubtedly viewed in Moscow with a combination of alarm and outrage. The shah was offering mounting financial support for the Siad Barre government, urging that the Soviet Union be required to remove its personnel from Berbera, and promising military aid should the Soviet pipeline "dry up."

The shah had reason to believe that he was not exceeding the American brief in launching his own initiatives with Somalia. He had been approached by Ambassador William Sullivan, at the behest of the U.S. government, to ensure that Iran would make arms available to the Siad Barre regime in the event that Washington experienced delays in meeting its obligations in a timely fashion. As a result, he had ordered his armed forces to establish contingency plans for an airlift to Somalia; should the need arise, Tehran could ship several tons of weapons within a forty-eight-hour period using its 6-130 transport aircraft. Moreover, the signal from Washington was not couched in the usual diplomatic obfuscations. The arms were to be made available if the Somali military experienced unanticipated difficulties with the Soviet Union, or if the Ethiopians were gaining a clear advantage over Somali forces. Apparently, there were no references to purely "defensive weapons." At the same time, Egypt could be expected to compensate for any deficiencies that might arise if the Soviet Union curtailed its supply of replacements or spare parts. The Egyptian military still possessed a considerable supply of Russian equipment, which, *in extremis,* could be cannibalized and placed at the disposal of the Somali armed forces.

The stage for a dramatic denouement was set. With the Somali invasion of the Ogaden in July 1977, the Soviet Union called for withdrawal of the invading forces. The ultimatum did not contain a deadline, but it was clear that the Soviet pipeline would indeed dry up in the event of refusal. In the meantime the Somalis were sweeping the Ethiopians before them, and by September controlled more than 90 percent of the Ogaden. Only two major towns, Harar and Dire Dawa, remained to be taken. Following an Organization of African Unity denunciation of the Somali invasion as a blatant act of aggression in violation of the OAU Charter, the Soviet Union terminated its arms aid to Somalia and closed its military facilities there. At the same time, a massive airlift of arms aid to Ethiopia was launched, in which Soviet transport aircraft violated the airspace of Sudan, Saudi Arabia, and Iran. Approximately 17,000 Cuban troops were rushed to Ethiopia in due course to provide training and conduct combat operations in the Ogaden against Somali forces.

As might be expected, Saudi Arabia, Egypt, and Iran immediately looked to Washington for leadership in countering the Soviet-Cuban involvement in the Horn crisis. But the Carter administration reversed its field, initially urging President Siad Barre to withdraw his forces, and several weeks later condemning the act of Somali aggression. The President refused to honor his pledge to provide defensive weapons, and subsequently turned a deaf ear to entreaties from Riyadh, Tehran, and Cairo that he do so. Indeed, the State Department did everything to convey the impression that it wished to share in the OAU condemnation of Somalia. While expressing public concern over the Soviet-Cuban military involvement in the Horn, it could not bypass the Ethiopian argument that Addis Ababa had a legitimate right to seek emergency assistance, in the face of aggression, from whatever source it found convenient. To outrage the entente nations further, the United States even withdrew its support for emergency airlifts of American-built military equipment by Iran. Since Iran looked overwhelmingly to the United States for military supplies, this was tantamount to reneging on promises for the covert arms transfer program that the shah had prepared for Somalia. In due course the entente crumbled, the Somalis returned to home territory (although not without keeping rebellion in the Ogaden alive through the Western Somalia Liberation Front), and angry recriminations against American duplicity and "hypocrisy" followed from various spokesmen in the region.

DIPLOMACY IS A HIGHLY REFINED art form, but the dialectic of diplomacy has one hallowed commandment: precision in communication. While verb forms are sometimes opaque, purposes must be clear. Bold initiatives, in particular, need to be carefully planned and executed, and precisely timed, with a clear understanding of the goals and objectives of the principal players. The Carter administration launched its 1977 initiative without any such understanding and with a singular lack of judiciousness.

The Red Sea strategy was backed by a White House staff with only limited experience in the area, but which tended to view forces operating in the Red Sea from a *realpolitik* perspective, one that makes superpower rivalry the dominant reality. The pattern of alliances in the region, together with American vulnerability on the energy front, gave the Saudi-Iranian approach a seductive appeal for those of a globalist persuasion. The problem was that the Red Sea did not fit neatly into any traditional "bipolar" equation, for when

Somali troops marched into the Ogaden, all of black Africa united against the Siad Barre regime.

Within the State Department, those experts who might have provided a degree of realism were shunted aside. William Schaufele, the experienced assistant secretary for African affairs, was departing. His successor, Richard Moose, had little concrete appreciation of the African Horn, and was disinclined to contest the views of White House globalists, preferring instead to concentrate his energies on what was to prove an abortive southern Africa human rights strategy. The assistant secretary of state for Near Eastern affairs was also otherwise engaged; the Arab-Israeli question was first on the agenda of issues confronting him. Elsewhere in the department, the period of "breaking in" that is normally associated with the arrival of a new administration had not been completed. Among the new arrivals there were few officials who had any familiarity with Horn of Africa or Persian Gulf affairs.

Ultimately, of course, the decision on how to deal with the Horn crisis rested with President Carter. He had advertised early in his tenure that he intended to be the final arbiter of American foreign policy, and that he would oversee every significant initiative. There is compelling evidence that the President was attentive to the stratagems of Red Sea Entente nations, that he was anxious to support the Saudi and Iranian effort, and that he was most willing to lend his backing to efforts to reduce the Soviet presence in the region. A former naval officer himself, he recognized the utility of acting to eliminate the Russian presence in Berbera. There can be little doubt that he understood the importance of working closely with the Saudis in the region, particularly given the Arab-Israeli strategy that he and his staff had fashioned. If the United States expected to register any success at the conference table, Riyadh, Cairo, and other Arab capitals had to listen with a sympathetic ear to the American policy position.

The President did not anticipate the Somali invasion of July 1977, or the reaction to it. In particular, the unanimity of the Organization of African Unity member states placed the United States in an awkward position. It now had to choose between supporting an aggressor state, Somalia—thus risking the southern Africa strategy that had been devised by Ambassador Andrew Young and his colleagues—and turning away from the Red Sea Entente. The President tempo-rized, possibly hoping that a military stalemate might result, and so permit other parties to mediate the dispute. When this tactic proved ineffective, he had to deal with a second, far greater problem: the Soviet airlift of arms, and the infusion of Cuban combat forces. Carter now had to determine whether the situation in the Horn had changed qualitatively, as argued by Riyadh, Tehran, Cairo, and Mogadishu. All four capitals were calling on Washington to meet its obligations under the original scenario by offsetting the Russian effort with an emergency airlift to Somalia. The President tempo-rized once again. The U.S. government encouraged Riyadh and Cairo to turn to western Europe for emergency arms aid; in the case of Tehran, Carter raised no objection to aiding Siad Barre. However, at the last moment, when Iranian aircraft were being loaded with American equipment, Washington transmitted an urgent communi-cation to its embassy in Tehran insisting that only non-American weapons be supplied. The administration felt compelled to act this way because of the provisions of the Arms Export Control Act of 1976, which stipulated that the U.S. government could not endorse third-country transfers of American military equipment unless the United States was itself prepared to make such equipment available from its own resources.

The upshot of this sequence of events was that the President had severely damaged American credibility and embarrassed, if not humiliated, some of its most important partners in the Middle East. From their own vantage points, the leaders of Iran, Saudi Arabia, Egypt, Morocco, Sudan, and Somalia had seen the Carter adminis-tration make promises it did not keep. Moreover, these same leaders had mobilized themselves on the basis of the American guarantees —or presumed guarantees—and had then been forced to back off, in front of their own people and other leaders in the region who had been informed of the plans.

In any working alliance, the greatest strains come over plans that backfire to the detriment of one or another of the partners, and there is no doubt that the Horn of Africa fiasco in 1977 subjected the American-Iranian alliance to considerable stress. The shah was deeply disturbed by the American about-face, and wondered if it portended a more general shift in Carter's foreign policy. The follow-ing year, his suspicions increased when, following the Soviet-inspired coup in Afghanistan that brought the Taraki government to power, the Americans urged the shah to support the new regime. This request did not come only through the usual diplomatic channels; it was repeated to him by Secretary Newsom in July. It baffled the shah, for he could not understand why the Carter administration would be so eager to sanction the Soviet move into a country bordering his own. Was this simply an American concession of an inability to project power into Afghanistan? Or was it, possibly, another symptom of a growing Soviet-American condominium over the entire Persian Gulf and Middle Eastern regions? The shah's own inclinations were to challenge the Soviet move in Kabul, both by supporting the local opponents of the new regime, and by mounting some sort of propaganda campaign against the newest Soviet interference in the internal affairs of another country. But the Americans were not interested in such actions, preferring to have the shah strive for good relations with Nur Mohammed Taraki.

In dozens of conversations with leading Americans and Europeans throughout the summer of 1978, the shah wondered out loud whether Carter and Brezhnev had prepared a plan for a *de facto* partition of Iran. After all, the extension of Soviet power into Afghanistan—a move that could well lead to the basing of the Red Army on Iran's northeastern frontiers—would obviously increase the Kremlin's leverage on Iranian events. If the Americans not only acquiesced but actually seemed to encourage such a development, it could only mean (in the shah's view of the world) that Carter was prepared to see Iran move closer to the Soviet Union, at least on some questions. Perhaps the Russians would be given greater control over the northern part of the country, while the Americans would retain their interests in the south.

To be sure, the shah was not entirely convinced of the existence of such a plan, but the first year and a half of Carter's presidency had been gravely unsettling to the king of kings. He no longer believed that the United States was a thoroughly reliable ally (having already been disturbed by the nature of the American withdrawal from Vietnam and the refusal of the United States to challenge the Cuban brigades in Angola in 1975). And for the first time in two decades, he was forced to contemplate the possibility that his American protectors might prefer a different kind of Iranian government to his own.

FOUR

The Crisis, I

LIKE MOST SUCCESSFUL REVOLUTIONS, the Iranian uprising that removed Mohammed Reza Shah advanced by fits and starts, not in a smooth progression. And like all such phenomena, much of its success was due to error and inspiration; the crucial ingredients were human decisions rather than vast, impersonal forces. The determining factors were that the shah—and his domestic and foreign supporters—made a series of mistakes, while Khomeini and his allies showed great skill, tenacity, and resourcefulness.

The major actors in the drama were unaware of the first crucial turning point in the long struggle between Mohammed Reza Shah and the Ayatollah Ruhollah Khomeini, for it was tucked away in the text of the Algiers Treaty between Iran and Iraq signed in March 1975. The treaty signaled an end to the limited hostilities between the two countries, and marked the shah's abandonment of the Kurds, who had fought for years against Iraq on Mohammed Reza's behalf. In one of the treaty's clauses there was a proviso that 10,000 Iranian pilgrims could cross the border into Iraq each year for religious trips. This agreement made it possible for Khomeini to maintain a constant flow of couriers and acolytes from his exile in Najaf into the Shi'ite centers of Iran. The effects began to be felt by early 1977, when Iranian universities were the sites of significant protests against the shah's government. It was not immediately clear that there was a religious impetus behind the protests, for there were many local issues, such as the dates of examinations and the cost of food in student cafeterias. By the fall of the year there were ugly signs of religiously inspired violence. There were riots at Tehran University in October, where masked students distributed pamphlets demanding a total separation of male and female activities outside the classroom, and warning women that any violation of this Islamic stricture would result in loss of life. In the same month, roughly one hundred religious zealots at a shrine outside Tehran demonstrated on behalf of Seyyed Mehdi Hashemi, a relatively unknown mullah sentenced to death for his activities in connection with the assassinations of several moderate clerics in Isfahan. Hashemi was a follower of Khomeini, whom he had visited in Iraq in 1976, and the demonstrations followed similar protests and hunger strikes by Iranian students in Paris. The international dimensions of the Khomeini movement could thus be perceived. Finally, October saw the first mild challenges to the shah in the Majlis, where parliamentary interrogations were raised about governmental failures regarding social services, economic development, and overcentralization. Although the questions were fairly meek, the very fact that they were raised marked a breakthrough compared with previous practice.

There was, in short, a substantial protest against the performance of the government, and while nobody believed there was enough opposition strength to threaten either the stability of the country or the continuation of the dynasty, there was enough to concern prudent leaders. For the preceding two years, the shah had been promising greater democratization for the country and a substantially higher degree of participation for the political and intellectual elites. The events of the last months of 1977 suggested that greater democratization might lead to disorder, and that greater participation might entail challenges to the existing leaders. Yet to reverse himself on these matters would have cost the shah heavily, both among his American allies, who were tirelessly reminding him about human rights (a theme strongly reinforced by British Ambassador Anthony Parsons), and in the eyes of the Iranian people, who would have viewed an abrupt about-face as an admission of failure.

The protests came at an awkward time. Although steadily rising oil prices had given Iran unprecedented quantities of money, the mismanagement of the national economy had produced widespread unemployment, urban slums, the worst inflation ever, and visible signs of strain throughout the governmental apparatus. In August, the shah replaced his premier of eleven years, Abbas Hoveida, with a distinguished technocrat, Jamshid Amuzegar. The purpose of the change was to place a competent economic planner in charge of the government, and bring the social problems under control. The move was not a great success, for economic growth actually slowed: there was a drop in most major sectors in 1977–78, as compared with 1976–77. To be sure, this was only to be expected of a deflationary program; but the political crisis demanded short-term amelioration rather than long-term programs, unless the political volcano could somehow be capped.

In any event, the shah's response was extraordinarily and unexpectedly mild. The traditional monarchical reaction to such demonstrations and socioeconomic difficulties would have been increased repression, restrictions on public expressions of hostility to governmental policies, and far sterner action against those who dared attack the government or the shah himself. Criticism from Western governments or journalists would have been dismissed with the usual observation that Iran was not yet ready for democracy. Instead, the shah stuck with his liberalization program, encouraged Amuzegar to take the painful steps required to bring the economy back into line, and permitted the increasingly open criticism to continue.

He also at first attempted to co-opt his more moderate critics by embarking upon a personal campaign for the liberalization of Iran. He traveled the country, promising greater democracy, a reduction of torture by SAVAK, and announcing more humane treatment of prisoners as well as the virtual abolition of press censorship. At the same time, he strongly criticized the religious leaders, attempting thereby to isolate the mullahs and ayatollahs from the more reformist-minded elements in Iran. Finally, SAVAK was unleashed in its full fury against the clandestine guerrilla groups—the *Mujahidin* and the *Feday'i*—to bring an end to a flurry of bombings and assassinations, including some against American government and private officials. The question of the guerrillas will be discussed at greater length shortly, but it is useful to note that a couple of hundred of these individuals were killed or arrested in the last few months of 1977 and early 1978.

The shah's strategy of splitting his opposition failed, and it was a failure of ominous proportions, for his inability to divide the secular reformers from the religious zealots meant that his opponents were willing to set aside their profound differences in order to bring down the Pahlavi dynasty. The shah was no doubt especially sensitive to this possibility, for the history of Iran ever since the late nineteenth century has been characterized by precisely this sort of apparently incongruous antigovernmental alliance between progressive or radical secular forces and intensely fundamentalist religious leaders. Indeed, every major revolt against the central government from the 1890s to the present has had this profile, whether the movement was directed against foreign economic interests (as in the case of tobacco in the 1890s or oil in the 1950s and 1960s), or efforts by one shah or another to introduce Western social standards.

Yet Mohammed Reza's tactics were poorly designed, fanning the very flames he was trying to extinguish. From the summer of 1977 to the early weeks of 1978, his moves against the religious leadership were misconceived, and only strengthened the coalition that eventually doomed him. The opening moves were economic. For many years, the ayatollahs had received money from the Iranian government. Some of it was channeled through "sweetened" government contracts with the bazaar merchants, who then passed on part of the frosting to the clerics. Other funds, by far the most significant quantity, came in the form of direct cash subsidies from government officials to specific ayatollahs and mullahs. The money was part of the secret account in the prime minister's office, which in Iran—as in other countries—went to special friends who would not wish to have any formal accounting made of the transactions. For example, in addition to the subsidies to the ayatollahs, the shah's government also provided a relatively small stipend to some of the surviving monarchs of other countries in exile.

The subsidies to the religious leaders were initiated, according to most accounts, after the first great wave of protests against the White Revolution. The ayatollahs were evidently placated, at least in part, by governmental reassurances that their temporary losses would be compensated by a more regular and secure flow of government money. Thus despite the continued friction between the Pahlavi dynasty and the religious leadership of Iran, there was a fairly consistent economic relationship. Significantly, Khomeini refused an offer of money from the shah's representatives during the disturbances of 1963 that led to Khomeini's long exile. Most other ayatollahs were less scrupulous in their response to offers of governmental largesse, and the payments were estimated at some $80 million by early 1977.

The shah apparently believed that he could bring the clerics under control by turning off the cash spigot in mid-1977, and soon the subsidies had been reduced from $80 to $30 million. But the effect was the reverse of what he had desired: instead of altering their political stance to win back their stipends, the religious leaders only intensified their opposition to the shah. This opposition was increased further when the shah took similar economic measures against the bazaaris, imposing a new tax upon them and requiring that they keep their books in order. The two ill-conceived measures alienated those religious leaders, whether among the clerics or within the bazaar, who had been willing to go along with modernization so long as they received a satisfactory slice of the new Iranian pie. As soon as they were threatened with economic losses along with cultural isolation, they went headlong into opposition.

These economic mistakes were compounded by a political error of great symbolic importance early in 1978. On January 7, the Tehran daily *Ettela'at* was forced to publish an attack against Khomeini entitled "Iran and the Red and Black Imperialism." The article was evidently written by Information Minister Daryush Homayun (a fact revealed by the editorial staff of the newspaper in the next phase of press liberalization later in the year), who told the editors that the shah himself insisted upon its immediate publication. The article was of unprecedented violence, accusing Khomeini of homosexuality, reactionary ideas, opportunism, ignorance of the true principles of Islam, obscure ties to British imperialism, and other dark links to foreign countries (his Indian origins were referred to as an "unknown past"). Furthermore, the article contained suggestions that Iran was in the grips of a new conspiracy representing a union of Communist ("red") and clerical ("black") forces attempting to destroy the country. The latter point was well taken, but the outrageously unrestrained tone of the article offended the entire religious community —who viewed it as an attack against all of Islam—and even those moderates who were uncomfortable with the fundamentalist approach of Khomeini. The newspaper's editors were embarrassed (they had in fact urged that publication be postponed, or that it be printed in an unobtrusive corner of the paper), and they had to deal with the rage of the ayatollahs and mullahs. Even the most moderate of the ayatollahs, Kazem Shariatmadari, condemned the article for "besmirching the faith," and suggested that the publication of the attack had "shocked all Muslims in Iran." Under the circumstances, no one could defend the article in *Ettela'at,* and the alliance of convenience between religious and more secular religious leaders opposed to the shah became even stronger.

The publication came at a time when violence was once again erupting in the streets. New demonstrations took place in the holy city of Qum on January 7 and 9. Religious leaders claimed that the actions were in response to the *Ettela'at* article, while the government maintained that they were timed to coincide with two of the most important dates in the history of the westernization of Iran: January 7, when women had been formally emancipated in 1935; and January 9, when the shah's agrarian program had been formally launched in 1962. Whatever the actual explanation, the demonstrations were serious, with the second leading to violent clashes with police. At least six people were killed in the fighting.

The deaths in Qum marked the beginning of six months of periodic violence throughout the country. Once the mandatory sixty days of mourning had passed, demonstrations were launched anew, producing new clashes with government troops, fresh martyrs, and the beginning of another cycle of forty days. This relentless rhythm continued until June, when the pattern was broken and violence became almost nonstop.

The violence was not limited to religious centers, although it almost always had some religious ingredient. For the first time since 1963, there was an antigovernment protest in the Tehran bazaar, where the shopkeepers staged a strike in the face of official threats to revoke the licenses of all participants. And as always, there were periodic explosions on university campuses.

In June, the crisis took on a new dimension. Both the number of demonstrations and their clear religious content pointed to a guiding hand with single-minded resolve:

The dominant role of the religious leader in the events of 1978 was emphasized by the nature of the targets attacked by rioters, many of

which had religious significance or stood for secular influence or a
Western life-style in the eyes of the demonstrators. Others were chosen
because they were seen as symbols of capitalism and social inequality,
or of the power of the regime. Many targets fell into more than one
of these categories. Recurrent attacks were made on cinemas and
theatres, liquor stores, television sale rooms, shops for luxury goods,
expensive cars, banks, the headquarters of women's organizations,
police stations, and the offices of the *Rastakhiz* party. A different
religious element came to the fore in the attacks on businesses owned
or headed by members of the Bahai sect. . . . Yet another indication
was that riots usually started at centers of religious life. . . . Sermons
and religious lectures were the principal means for spreading opposition propaganda. . . .[1]

In addition to all these targets, the demonstrations increasingly
centered upon the person of the shah himself, and upon his deviation
from Islamic standards of behavior and belief. In particular, there
was a growing demand that the shah abandon the Imperial calendar
(dated from the accession of Cyrus the Great) and reinstate the
Islamic one (starting with the hejira of Mohammed in 622).

In the face of this heightened violence against him, the shah reversed his tactics by attempting to appease his religious enemies.
Military commanders were instructed to show maximum restraint in
dealing with religious-led demonstrations, and it was not until an
outburst of unusually destructive violence swept Isfahan in early
August, shortly after the beginning of the holy month of Ramadan,
that martial law was temporarily declared in that city. The shah had
once again gotten the worst of both worlds: having provoked the
wrath of the mullahs, he then backed away from their challenge. The
impression in the eyes of his enemies was of a man who was losing
his grip on power, unsure of his strategy, and vulnerable to attack
—an impression that had been heightened in June when the shah
announced that the dreaded chief of SAVAK, General Nematollah
Nassiri, had been relieved of his responsibilities. There are many
versions of the reasons for Nassiri's removal, and it is impossible to
select any one of them with confidence. Some experts, including at
least one high-ranking official of the U.S. State Department, believed
that the shah was responding to direct American suggestions that
Nassiri should be removed. The general was the symbol of human
rights violations to many in the American foreign policy establish-

ment, some of whom considered SAVAK one of the most odious organizations in the world. Others simply downplay this explanation of Nassiri's removal, pointing instead to his failure to predict the Soviet-inspired coup in Afghanistan earlier in the year, and his inability to stem the revolutionary tide. Still others who knew Nassiri personally argue that he in fact resigned in protest against the shah's refusal to crack down on his opponents.

In any event, the reasons for Nassiri's departure are less important than the effect of the action, for the shah's opponents could only have been heartened by the event. And they were also encouraged by Mohammed Reza's refusal to use traditional Iranian methods of quelling disturbances. Admitting that torture had been used in the past, the shah told journalists in the autumn of 1978 that he had long since ordered the practice stopped. There was, he said, "no torture, for sure. No holding of prisoners without charge."

Given the traditions of the region, it is unlikely that all physical violence against prisoners had been terminated, but there was unquestionably a striking decrease in the more brutal forms of torture, and claims of massive incarceration of political prisoners were announced by the International Red Cross to be grossly inflated. Only three thousand or so prisoners were reported in 1977. By the time the shah left the country, there were less than one thousand political prisoners in Iran.

In short, the tidal wave of opposition was swelling without encountering any real obstacles. And while there are those who suggest that the shah had authorized some clandestine activities by SAVAK against the Khomeini forces (for example, the murder of such key figures as the son of the Ayatollah Khomeini, and the popularizer of Islamic revolution, Ali Shariati), the bulk of the shah's activities were conciliatory, even when carried out secretly. In 1977, Mohammed Reza asked Jordan's King Hussein to approach the leaders of Khomeini's movement in Syria and Iraq to see whether some compromise could be struck. The Syrian government refused to help, and Khomeini replied from Najaf that he would deal only if he were permitted back into Iran. The shah could not accept this condition. When the next secret approach was made—again through Hussein —to Khomeini in France in December 1978, the ayatollah's conditions were more severe: the termination of the Pahlavi dynasty.

The shah's tactics might have worked with an opposition of limited dimensions and grievances, but his opponents in the late seventies were of a sort never seen before in the Islamic world. Once Khomeini seized power in Iran, academics and journalists the world over hastened to explain that the ayatollah had simply enacted a scenario that was implicit in Shi'ite Islam, and that similar events might well spread throughout the Islamic world. Yet, prior to Khomeini's success, it was considered a contradiction in terms to hypothesize a disciplined, systematic Shi'ite revolutionary movement. Experts could well imagine entire nations caught up in a whirlwind of Shi'ite passion; such tumultuous occurrences are not unknown to the history of the Middle East. But Khomeini did something altogether unprecedented by organizing the chaotic, centrifugal forces of the Iranian Shi'ite community into a fairly disciplined network with a single goal, the overthrow of Mohammed Reza Shah. And he did it thanks to considerable foreign support and the assistance of international terrorists. As the head of another Middle Eastern state put it shortly after the shah's fall:

> When the history of this period is written you will see that Tehran was probably the first street battle fought by international terrorism. The men and women who have been trained and indoctrinated in the guerrilla camps of Lebanon, Libya, Algeria, South Yemen, and Cuba, which includes many Iranians, threw all their effectives into the battle. Iran was their first combined operation. My own intelligence leaves no doubt on this score. It was a very skillful operation which required years of preparation but very few people understood what was going on as they maneuvered behind the smokescreen of Khomeini's forces.[2]

IT IS TOO EARLY to present anything like a definitive picture of Khomeini's movement, but the basic outlines are fairly visible by now. At the center sat the ayatollah himself, with a vision of an entire Islamic world liberated from unbelievers of all sorts, totally under the theocratic control of Shi'ite visionaries. Around him revolved the components of his striking force: Islamic and Marxist guerrillas, recruited for the most part from Iranian youth, but supplemented and trained by radical Palestinians and other members of the terrorist international; the Iranian clerics, who collected funds and spread the doctrine in the mosques and in the streets, by word of mouth; supportive Arab government officials in Damascus, Baghdad, and

Tripoli, providing logistical help, funds, and sanctuary for Iranian exiles and their friends; and a far-flung network of acolytes and supporters throughout the Arab world and the West, organizing similar movements for purposes of propaganda and exerting pressure on local governments to weaken the shah. Once in motion, the movement acquired such tremendous gravity that it attracted the weaker secular political groups that had long been considered the only true alternative to the Pahlavi dynasty by most observers; it also received support from the Soviet Union, although the full extent of this assistance can only be guessed at.

The world view of the Ayatollah Ruhollah Khomeini is contained in two volumes: *Islamic Government,* a collection of his lectures in Najaf published in Arabic in 1970; and *Khomeini and His Movement,* a collection of his speeches and harangues published in Farsi in 1975. The central theme is the same in both volumes—the shah must fall, for he is an enemy of Islam. In the 1975 book, Khomeini put it in unmistakable terms: "The rationale of [the shah's] government and some of its members is the abolition of the laws of Islam." What precisely were the shah's sins? First and foremost was the effort to westernize Iran, thus depriving the country of its moral base and the mullahs of their rightful place in society. Khomeini condemns the hiring of women in boys' high schools, and of men in girls' high schools, "the moral wrongness of which is clear to all." Moreover, it is wrong to have women in high places, which the shah had permitted.

But some of the harshest language is reserved for the practice of appointing lay persons to high positions in the national courts: "In order to accomplish its own designs and to abolish manliness and adherence to Islam as qualities for judges, the government's Ministry of Justice has shown its opposition to the established law of Islam. From this point on, Jews, Christians, and enemies of Islam and of the Muslims must interfere in the affairs of Muslims. . . ." The words "enemies of Islam" are a code-phrase for the Baha'is, who were targeted by the Khomeini movement as early as the demonstrations in 1977–78, and later singled out for violent treatment once the revolution succeeded.

The shah was criticized not only for his attempts at modernization, but also for his leniency toward sinners: "We want," said Khomeini in the earlier volume, "a ruler who would cut off the hand of his own son if he steals, and would flog and stone his near relative if he fornicates." Prior to the revolution, Khomeini's many apologists in the West suggested that one should not take such words literally, but the course of events has shown that a literal interpretation was closer to the truth. The same volume contains a preview of the actions of some of the leaders of the Khomeini period:

> If a just mullah is placed in charge of the enforcement of canonical punishments . . . would he enforce them otherwise than how they were enforced in the days of the Prophet? . . . Would the Prophet have imposed more than a hundred lashes on the fornicator not previously chaste? Can the mullah reduce the amount of this punishment, thereby creating a divergence between his practice and that of the Prophet? Certainly not! The ruler . . . is no more than the executor of God's command and decree.[3]

Furthermore, Khomeini attacked the shah for his close working relationship with two foreign powers: the United States and Israel. The latter is singled out for intense hatred, and the former is linked to Israeli schemes for the destruction of Islam. Israel, "through its evil agents . . . has dealt a blow to us. It strikes at you, the nation; it wishes to seize your economy; it wishes to carry off your commerce and agriculture; it wishes to make itself the owner of wealth . . . the Koran bars its way—it must be removed. . . . The Iranian government [of the shah] in pursuance to the purposes and schemes of Israel has humiliated us and continues to do so." Those not familiar with the relationship between Israel and Iran might well wonder at the intensity of Khomeini's rage in 1975. It is not widely known that every Israeli prime minister from David Ben-Gurion to Menachem Begin visited Tehran during this period, as did other leading Israeli personages. Moshe Dayan and Yitzhak Rabin, for example, went secretly to Iran to discuss matters of joint interest with their Iranian counterparts. And there was considerable cooperation between the two countries. Iran was Israel's most reliable oil supplier; Israel responded by assisting Iran on military preparedness, a certain degree of intelligence sharing, and even technical assistance. There was no Israeli embassy in Tehran, but the head of the Israeli mission during the last days, Uri Lubrani, was as much an ambassador as any diplomat bearing the official title. It is doubtful that Khomeini knew the full extent of bilateral relations, but he was not imagining the existence of close ties between the shah and the leaders of Israel.

Khomeini's rage at this relationship stemmed from his hatred of the Jews. He was infuriated by the regime's efforts to tone down anti-Semitic and anti-Zionist outpourings in Iran: ". . . what is this relationship and association between the shah and Israel that the SAVAK says, 'Do not speak about the shah or about Israel.' Is the shah in the view of the SAVAK an Israeli? Or, in the view of the SAVAK, is the shah a Jew?" Behind this Jewish conspiracy to defraud and emasculate Iran, Khomeini saw the long hand of the United States of America:

> It is America which supports Israel and its well-wishers; it is America which gives Israel the power to turn Muslim Arabs into vagrants; it is America which directly or indirectly imposes its agents on the nation of Iran; it is America which considers Islam and the glorious Koran a source of harm to itself and wishes to remove both from its path.[3]

Opposition to a secular ruler on the part of the Shi'ite leaders was hardly new in Iranian history, but never before had anyone called for the removal of a shah in favor of an Islamic republic. The reason for this lies in Shi'ite doctrine. Shi'ites hold a messianic view of history, according to which there will one day be a return of the twelfth— or "missing"—Imam, who disappeared in the ninth century. Until that day, when he will assume full religious and secular powers, all temporal rulers are usurpers. On the other hand, Shi'ites have generally accepted secular rulers who contented themselves with state affairs, because such rulers made no attempt to present themselves as religious authorities and left matters up to the ayatollahs. Any conflicts between the shahs and the mullahs usually broke out over matters held to be the province of religious law.

Within the Iranian Shi'ite leadership there was a secret hierarchy, details of which remain hazy. But there was a long-standing tradition according to which one ayatollah became a sort of *primus inter pares,* a so-called *marja'e taqlid,* "the source of imitation." This chief ayatollah was not chosen by any formal selection process, but rather emerged through a rough consensus. This meant both that there was great competition between ayatollahs for popular acclaim (with each ayatollah developing his own following) and that ayatollahs were often inclined to take positions on many political, social, and even economic issues in order to gain popularity among the religious population. By the early 1960s, Khomeini felt he had become the *marja'e taqlid,* although this was contested by, among others, Ayatollah Shariatmadari, who was supported by the shah's government.

Khomeini believed that his stature as chief religious leader of the Shi'ite community enabled him to move outside the traditional sphere of delimited religious influence in two directions. First, since Shi'ism admitted no separation of "church" and "state," and since he declared the shah to be in violation of Islamic law, Khomeini wished to restore religious authority to Iran by overthrowing the monarchy and reestablishing the clerics as the sole interpreters of law in the country. Secondly, since the principles of Shi'ism were held to be universally valid for the "Islamic nation," Khomeini foresaw a vast revolutionary movement that would eventually govern all Muslims. Khomeini's revolution was to be an Iranian one only in the first instance; eventually, it would become as broad as Mohammed's empire. This last phase would represent the vindication of Shi'ism over the Sunnis, who had long held the majority within the Islamic world. These were Khomeini's doctrinal innovations.

The method by which the *marja'e taqlid* emerged from the ranks of the ayatollahs indicates the unstructured nature of the Shi'ite community, and here again Khomeini was an innovator. Heretofore it had been impossible to meld the Shi'ite ayatollahs into a coherent organization, since each religious leader insisted on creating his own organization to compete with the others. Khomeini managed to gain the upper hand over most of the other ayatollahs, both by dint of his powerful rhetoric and through more earthly methods of persuasion (as, for example, the assassination of his competitors, carried out by henchmen like Mehdi Hashemi). Moreover, he gradually developed an effective network of international contacts.

Khomeini's high status among Shi'ites made him a personage of considerable importance throughout the Middle East. By the early 1970s there was not a Muslim country in the region where Khomeini was not known and supported by at least some leading mullahs and ayatollahs. His most vital connections, of course, were with allies in nearby countries like Iraq, Syria, Lebanon, and Jordan.

The first base outside Najaf or Iran for the Khomeini movement was in southern Lebanon in the late 1960s, where Khomeini's close ally the Imam Moussa Sadr had established himself as the leader of the country's Shi'ites. Moussa Sadr had close ties with the PLO groups that lived in the same villages and training camps as his own Shi'ite followers, and Sadr was able to offer sanctuary, money, and guerrilla training to anti-shah Iranians who had been forced into exile in the late 1960s and early 1970s.

The Imam Moussa Sadr, acting on behalf of Khomeini, was instrumental in propping up the Syrian regime of President Hafez al-Assad between 1971 and 1973. Assad was an Alawi—a small Shi'ite sect whose roughly 1 million followers live mostly in northern Syria—and had come under considerable pressure from the Sunni majority. As in the case of the Shi'ite attacks against the shah, Assad was accused of abandoning Islam because of his adoption of more strictly secular principles (indeed, the Ba'ath Party oath of office contained no reference to Allah), and his Sunni opponents observed that the constitution drafted by Assad did not even require the Syrian leader to be a Muslim.

Assad looked for an ally, and found it in Khomeini's tiny but prestigious organization. At the ayatollah's suggestion, Moussa Sadr undertook the Shi'ite legitimization of the Alawis, and hence of Assad's regime. For years, Sadr preached sermons on behalf of the Alawis, and had the Shi'ite mufti of Tripoli, Ali Mansur, appointed to tend to both the Shi'ite and Alawite communities. The Alawites were thereby given incontrovertible status by some of the most prestigious Shi'ite ayatollahs. It became extremely difficult for Assad's opponents to challenge him on religious grounds, particularly once he corrected the oversights in the constitution and the oath of office.

Assad thus owed Khomeini a great debt, which he would repay in full over the next half-decade. Members of Khomeini's movement such as Sadeq Ghotbzadeh were given Syrian passports, and money and training were also provided. The details of Assad's collaboration with Khomeini may never be known, but some of the best Middle Eastern sources suspect that much of the infrastructure of Khomeini's movement may have been Syrian. This hypothesis is fully consistent with what is known about the enthusiastic support given to Khomeini by Assad.

Along with support from Syria, Khomeini's most important source of foreign aid was the Palestine Liberation Organization (PLO). It is no accident that PLO leader Yassir Arafat was the first foreign dignitary invited to Iran after the revolution, and the only invited guest on the occasion of the revolution's first anniversary a year later. Without the assistance of the PLO—itself closely linked both to Khomeini's friends in southern Lebanon and to his allies in Damascus—it is unlikely that the revolution could have succeeded. PLO assistance covered a wide spectrum of activities, ranging from supplying couriers to carry money and instructions between the various groups of Khomeini's far-flung organization to providing instructors and sites for guerrilla training in Syria, Lebanon, South Yemen, and Jordan, and helping to spread the message of the ayatollah. There was also a purely practical element that bound Khomeini's followers to the PLO, and especially to the more radical Popular Front for the Liberation of Palestine (George Habash's PFLP): during the Lebanese civil war, Iranian and Palestinian guerrillas fought shoulder to shoulder, thus establishing a "brotherhood of the trenches."

The first discussions between Khomeini and the Palestinians occurred shortly after his arrival in Iraq, when he was contacted by representatives of the PFLP (or, before the formal constitution of that group, of its predecessor, the Qawmyun al Arab). In 1968, Abu Jihad, one of the leaders of the fledgling PLO, got in touch with Khomeini, and joint activities began shortly thereafter. Thanks to the PLO connection, thousands of anti-shah Iranian guerrillas were trained. By the early seventies there was a fairly impressive organization in place outside Iran:

> Together the exiles, the Syrians and the Palestinians prepared cadres for revolutionary activity inside Iran. They organized arms smuggling operations into the country, using food transport trucks leaving Beirut to conceal weapons and explosives. They recruited supporters from the pro-Khomeini Iranian student movement, which they organized throughout the Middle East, Western Europe, and the United States. They prepared and infiltrated propaganda and agitators back into Iran. They were free to move about Lebanon and Syria, visit Libya and Algeria, and organize a revolution. . . .⁴

Lastly, Khomeini worked with the infamous Dr. Wadi Haddad, the head of operations for the PFLP, who was generally believed to have masterminded many of that organization's most violent acts. Haddad was able to arrange for extreme left-wing Iranians to undergo guerrilla training in the camps of the Marxist regime in South

Yemen, where activities were supervised by East German intelligence officers assisted by Cuban terrorist experts. By and large these Iranian recruits were drawn from the Marxist *Feday'i* and from the Tudeh Party, rather than from the more strictly Islamic opposition groups. Khomeini was well aware that in the long run men like Haddad and Habash (both Christians, after all) would prove allies of convenience, whereas some of the other figures in the international terrorist network could be considered more enduring friends on religious grounds. But during the preparation and execution of the revolution, all support was welcomed.

Despite this considerable international activity, there was no major terrorist outbreak in Iran until the very end. Some assassinations and bombings took place, but there was nothing approaching the level of terrorism in the same period in countries like Italy, Spain, and Turkey, let alone the explosions that had occurred in Latin America in an earlier period. Two major terrorist organizations were operating in Iran*: the Marxist-oriented *Feday'i* and the Islamic *Mujahidin*. An Islamic *Feday'i* group had been credited with the assassination of General Haji Ali Razmara in the early fifties, but by the 1970s the major organization bearing that name was a Marxist group along the lines of Che Guevara's guerrilla bands in Latin America. The attack against the gendarmerie post in Siakal in February 1971 is generally considered the genesis of the modern Iranian guerrilla movement, even though the operation was a fiasco. Within a brief period, virtually all of the founders of the Marxist *Feday'i* had been killed or arrested. However, the violence of the assault was such that it soon became possible to recruit new members, almost exclusively from the ranks of educated Iranians. Most of the *Feday'i* came from the northern cities and, unlike the *Mujahidin* guerrillas, they were drawn from lay as well as Shi'ite families.

The *Mujahidin* had also made their first major appearance in 1971, in time for the Persepolis extravaganza. They managed to bomb an electrical works, and failed in an attempt to hijack an Air Iran plane. The response of SAVAK was terribly effective: nine guerrillas were arrested and tortured, one of them betrayed the group, and sixty-six others then fell into the hands of the shah's secret police. Yet even

---

*Albeit with considerable internal fission, leading to a proliferation of splinter groups that rearranged themselves into new organizations from time to time.

after losing, like the *Feday'i,* virtually all of their original leaders, the *Mujahidin* were similarly able to regroup, and to expand their operations. The *Mujahidin* were drawn primarily from the central provinces, almost exclusively from Shi'ite families, and with virtually no lower-class elements.

The relatively low level of activity of these organizations (along with other even smaller ones) can be gauged from the fact that between February 1971 and October 1977, only 341 guerrillas were killed in Iran.[5] But if the actual level of violence was not particularly alarming, there was good reason to be concerned. First, it was ascertained that the guerrillas had international connections with countries hostile to the shah: Syria, South Yemen, Libya, and, behind these enemies, the specter of the Soviet Union. Second, all these hostile organizations, with their small numbers of intense young people, were linked in one way or another with Khomeini, and hence to a large segment of the Iranian Shi'ite community. Third, the guerrillas—and particularly the Islamic *Mujahidin*—became the vehicle for and promoter of the ideas of Ali Shariati, the Iranian counterpart of the Algerian revolutionary Franz Fanon. Through men like Shariati, the ideas of the *Mujahidin* reached a large audience, and their influence was far out of proportion to their relatively modest numbers.

Shariati was perhaps one of the last major figures in the tradition of the itinerant sage. Author of some two hundred books, he lived primarily as a roving lecturer after studying in Meshed and in Paris. His basic message concerned the revolutionary content of Islam, particularly its Shi'ite version. According to his view, a good Shi'ite should strive for self-fulfillment through conflict with the world, thereby achieving *azadegi*—a state of liberation and of oneness with the sublime. Only a person in such a state could hope to achieve correct social reform. Shariati's message thus closely coincided with that of Khomeini, and could be used to justify the most extreme forms of revolutionary activity like those of the *Mujahidin.*

It was understandable that the *Mujahidin* should invite Shariati to speak at their Tehran lecture hall in the late 1960s and early 1970s. Shariati preached the virtues of revolution, and even spoke of the dream of a classless society to thousands of listeners, who sat through five- or six-hour lectures. When he died in 1977, apparently of a heart attack, his funeral in Damascus was attended by lumin-

aries from the Khomeini movement and Yassir Arafat himself.
The guerrillas were smashed repeatedly by SAVAK, which despite
its reputation for fairly mediocre intelligence collection never seemed
to have great trouble infiltrating the terrorist organizations. The last
SAVAK roundup occurred in late 1977, and was a most telling blow.
But from that time on, the security forces stopped striking against the
guerrillas. Whether as part of the shah's campaign to restrict SAVAK
activities in order to curry favor with the Americans, or as a gesture of
conciliation toward the religious leaders, the termination of antiguer-
rilla activities was another of the shah's mistakes. In February 1979,
the dramatic attack against the imperial guards at Doshan Tappeh
would be carried out by the revived guerrilla movement. Some of
them were members of the handful of survivors of the Islamic *Feday'i*
organization, released from the shah's prisons in another of his poorly
conceived concessions in late 1978, whence they journeyed to France
to sit at the feet of Khomeini. They returned to Tehran in February
under the command of the Ayatollah Sadeq Khalkhali—later re-
nowned as "the butcher of Kurdistan," the bloodthirsty chief of the
Islamic tribunals.

BOTH THE SHAH and the Americans had long been concerned about
the Soviet Union's appetite for expansion, and their concerns were
fully justified. The Soviets had played an aggressive role in Iranian
politics, most recently in the vigorous support given to Mossadeq
and his Communist allies in 1953, and although they had been unable
to mount any serious threat to the shah for nearly three decades,
there was every reason to believe that they continued to covet Iran.
In Mossadeq's time, hundreds of army officers had been discovered
in the employ of Soviet intelligence; no such vast nest of foreign
agents had been unmasked since then, but there had been several
spectacular KGB operations to penetrate the Iranian elite. The most
ominous of these was uncovered by SAVAK at the beginning of 1977,
when it was discovered that Major General Ahmed Mogharrabi, the
deputy chief of army planning and logistics, was working for Soviet
intelligence. After months of painstaking surveillance, SAVAK
struck in September. The car carrying Mogharrabi's KGB control
agents was blocked outside his house by SAVAK Land Rovers, and
the Soviet officials were dragged off to the local police station, where

they were declared *personae non gratae.* Mogharrabi was caught dictating classified information into a tape recorder that was capable of making "burst" transmissions to a receiver in the Soviet car. This device made it possible to transmit a half hour of recorded information in half a minute, rendering an intercept next to impossible. Under interrogation Mogharrabi admitted to passing military secrets to the Soviets. He was executed shortly thereafter.

There were other cases as well in the same period. In 1977, SAVAK uncovered a long-time Soviet espionage agent at a high post in the Ministry of Education, and the following year it was learned that a retired general was receiving a KGB "pension" for services rendered during his period of active espionage service the previous twenty-eight years. American intelligence in Iran was aware of the presence of hundreds of Soviet agents in delicate positions throughout the country, ranging from trade union organizations—especially those in the petroleum industry—to government ministries.[6]

None of this activity was unusual for the Soviet Union, and all of it fitted within the rules of the game; but it pointed to an ongoing Soviet campaign to prepare for the period after the passing of the shah. As early as 1942, Foreign Minister V. M. Molotov had declared that everything south of Baku was part of the Soviet sphere of influence, and this conviction had not weakened with the passage of time. Every leader since Stalin has attempted to bring Soviet power to bear on Tehran, with varying degrees of success, and Russian braggadocio about their ability to bring Iran under control has been constant since Khrushchev's remark that Iran was like a rotten apple; the Russians had only to wait for it to fall into their basket. In 1976, Chairman Leonid Brezhnev told Somalia's Siad Barre: "Iran will be a tough nut, but we will crack it a lot faster than the capitalists seem to think." The following year embassy officials in Tehran began to warn Iranian ministers that the Soviet Union would make the shah pay a terrible price for his anti-Soviet activities in the Horn of Africa.

Ever since 1959, the Soviet Union had operated a clandestine radio station in Baku, known as the "National Voice of Iran" (sometimes called "Our Radio"). For many years there was another station, first broadcasting from East Germany, later from Bulgaria, that spoke for the Tudeh Party, but these broadcasts were terminated in 1976. It may well be that they were stopped because Tudeh sought closer relations with the clerics, and feared that such a well-known link to

the Soviet Union might make it more difficult to gain acceptance from Khomeini and his followers. In any event, the termination of the Tudeh radio station left the National Voice as the sole clandestine station beamed into Iran from the Soviet Union, and its content was entirely predictable: unrestrained attacks on the shah and on "American imperialism," calls for revolution and freedom from Western influence, appeals for better relations with the Soviet Union.

Right up until the fall of the shah, the National Voice was at one with the mullahs in its total embrace of fundamentalist Islamic doctrine. Once demonstrations against the shah made his fall seem plausible, the National Voice doubled its broadcasting time. After Khomeini took over, the line shifted somewhat, urging separatism on the Kurds, the Azerbaijanis, and others.

On some occasions the correspondence between the words of the National Voice and actions in the streets of Iran was impressive. On the day of the first seizure of the American Embassy in Tehran in early February 1979, for example, the National Voice announced that the SAVAK archives had been transferred to the American Embassy. This followed days of inflammatory broadcasting about purported American clandestine operations in Iran after the ayatollah's return: no sooner had Khomeini set foot in the country than the National Voice announced a CIA plot to kill him. And when the American hostages were seized in November 1979, the National Voice hailed the action as one of righteous indignation by young Iranians intent on defending their country from foreign subversion.[7]

Were the broadcasts and the actions coordinated in any of these cases? The question cannot be answered with any confidence. But American officials were in any event unwilling to acknowledge the seriousness of Soviet anti-shah and anti-American activity in Iran, even after the fall of the Pahlavi dynasty. When Director of Central Intelligence Stansfield Turner was asked about Soviet activities in Iran on national television on January 4, 1979, he said: "I would suggest that listening to the tone of propaganda coming out of the Soviet Union back in September or October, they were in the same position as we, I believe particularly because they are a police state. ... It wasn't until it became clear that the shah's days were numbered that they came out as stridently as they are today against the shah's government."[8] Turner was evidently speaking about official Soviet

broadcasts, choosing to ignore the clandestine transmissions from Baku.

Finally, as the shah and the Americans knew, the entire PLO network that functioned as a support system for Khomeini's movement was itself a piece in the Soviet Union's international chess game. Many PLO guerrillas were trained in the Soviet Union, and in Soviet-controlled training camps throughout the Middle East: in Lebanon, Syria, Libya, Algeria, and South Yemen. There was also the Cuban connection, demonstrated both by the presence of Cuban instructors in the training camps and by Cuban participation in some of the terrorist acts. It was impossible to pin down the degree of Soviet control over the PLO, or even over individuals like Dr. Wadi Haddad, who were believed to be Soviet agents. Many analysts thought that such persons acted with considerable autonomy, while others were convinced that they were kept on a relatively tight leash. Whatever the truth of the matter, there was a solid consensus that the intimate PLO involvement in the Khomeini movement would not have been possible without at least tacit approval from the Kremlin.

Yet despite Khomeini's international connections and his claim that the removal of the shah was simply the first step in a strategy that would eventually transform the entire Islamic world, the revolution that removed Mohammed Reza Shah from the throne was a national effort, carried out with Iranian forces. No matter how strong Khomeini's foreign support, his triumph rested in the last analysis on the support of the Iranian people, many of whom lost their lives in the struggle against the shah.

The hundreds of thousands who marched in the streets of Iran throughout the revolutionary period were not all acting out of solid conviction, nor was their wrath against the shah's regime necessarily as uncompromising as Khomeini's. The history of Persia is full of mass movements of extraordinary fickleness; during the Mossadeq crisis, for example, the crowds changed from total support for the premier to total support for the shah in a matter of days. Given the demography of Iran in 1978–79, with its strikingly high proportion of young people, passions could be considered highly volatile, and it was here that Khomeini's excellent organization played a determinant role. And that organization could not have functioned as it did without the international support Khomeini received. He created a revolutionary organization from a Shi'ite community that had always been believed to be extremely chaotic; but he achieved that innovative task because he was able to enlist non-Iranian forces in his struggle.

WHAT WAS THE SHAH to make of his intensifying travails in the summer of 1978? To answer the question with any precision, one would have to know the content of his conversations with his intelligence chiefs, and above all those with General Nassiri, the head of SAVAK. Both Mohammed Reza and Nassiri are dead, and no minutes of the conversations were taken. But one can infer the level of information available to the shah by the degree to which the American intelligence community—and especially those on the scene in Tehran—perceived the gravity of the crisis. For there was very little that SAVAK knew that the CIA did not also know; years of close relations had guaranteed that the Americans got very complete briefings from Iranian officials in such matters. In this case the Iranians may have attempted to withhold some information from the Americans: to have admitted the gravity of the challenge to the shah was tantamount to a confession of failure by SAVAK. It is the sort of bad news that no underling wishes to bring to his Caesar, and SAVAK officials were undoubtedly sensitive to the situation. Nonetheless, it is unlikely that there was a great gulf between the shah's information and that available to American officials.

Very few, if any, Americans believed the shah to be in mortal danger in the late spring or early summer of 1978. There were some friendly governments—notably the French and the Israeli—that were profoundly concerned about the shah's prospects for survival as early as the spring of 1978; but not so the Americans. Neither American nor Iranian intelligence appreciated the strength of the shah's enemies. Nor was there a sense of the weakness of the shah's resolve.

In part, this was due to the American failure to understand the shah's personal drama and his progressively intense psychological agony. No one outside a tiny circle around the shah realized that he was dying of cancer, and thus no one was able to assess the psychological effects of the disease, and of the chemotherapy given him by his French doctors. It is not known which medicines were prescribed, but their effect—according to dozens of persons who met with the shah in the last year—was evidently similar to that of tranquilizers. Many visitors in 1978 found Mohammed Reza unexpectedly passive, introspective, and withdrawn, and one such report —from Treasury Secretary Michael Blumenthal in November— alarmed the Carter administration.

Further information about the shah's disease and its treatment may permit a clearer analysis, but one can assume that he was in the grips of a profound depression. Given his long-time anxieties, it is a virtual certainty that the worsening of his physical condition heightened his sense of insecurity, magnified his suspicions of hostile forces around him, and drove him deeper into withdrawal. At the same time, it must have concentrated his concern that the dynasty should remain after his own death, and the parallel wish that his own image in Iranian history should be as glowing as possible. Accordingly, Mohammed Reza became passionately committed to the view that he must not take action that would produce large-scale bloodshed in his last days. He desired to be remembered as a benevolent monarch, not a ruthless dictator. As he told friends repeatedly in the final months of his rule, he wished to leave Iran not only with an advanced industrial base and military organization but with a modern political system as well. And he wanted to pass on to his son a country with genuine affection for the Pahlavi family. Could this be achieved if the revolution were smashed by the application of what he called "the iron fist"? The shah did not think so. Months after the debacle, Mohammed Reza wrote:

> I am told today that I should have applied martial law more forcefully. This would have cost my country less dear than the bloody anarchy now established there. But a sovereign cannot save his throne by spilling blood of his fellow-countrymen. A dictator can do it because he acts in the name of an ideology which he believes he must make triumphant, no matter what the price. A sovereign is not a dictator. There is between him and his people an alliance which he cannot break. A dictator has nothing to pass on: power belongs to him and him alone. A sovereign receives a crown. I could envisage my son mounting the throne in my own lifetime. . . .[9]

The last sentence is the operative one. The shah knew he was dying, and that the way in which the Iranian crisis was resolved would determine the destiny of his heir. And he remembered that his father's application of "the iron fist" had only managed to delay the day of reckoning with his religious enemies. Would it not be wiser to attempt a more durable solution? As the shah himself remarked, to have applied martial law with vigor would have perhaps saved the monarchy, and even spared the country the degree of bloodshed that followed Khomeini's return; but it would not have solved the problems that had produced the crisis.

The future of the dynasty was not the only factor pushing the shah toward appeasing his enemies and restraining those who wished to take strong measures. There were at least two other elements that pointed in the same direction. One was the shah's belief that modernization had already rendered the mullahs largely anachronistic, and that they would become politically irrelevant as new class structures and political institutions came into being. This was not merely an idiosyncrasy of Mohammed Reza's. The "developmental model" was accepted by most academic and governmental experts throughout the West, even those who had no sympathy with him. Like the shah, they saw religious opposition to the dynasty as the last gasp of a caste that was soon to pass into history. This view encouraged the shah to believe that a durable secular-religious coalition was highly unlikely, for the class interests of the secular bourgeois reformers were opposed to those of the mullahs and ayatollahs. He feared that repression might strengthen the coalition, rather than resolve the conflict in favor of his regime.

The other factor had to do with the United States. Throughout the crisis, the shah was convinced that the American government had a grand strategy for Iran, even though its outlines remained obscure to him. He was certain of the existence of an American strategy, for the geopolitical stakes in the Iranian crisis were so great that it was inconceivable to him that the United States had not developed such a plan. His own life demonstrated the constancy of American activity in his country. He had been restored to the throne in 1953 thanks to the Americans and their British allies. Throughout the 1960s he had had to cope with American efforts to force a particular political direction upon his country; the might of the Iranian military, for all its faults a determinant force in the region, stemmed directly from the United States; the new industries and the new cities were inhabited by tens of thousands of American technicians and their families; and the special relationship in the early 1970s combined with the fortuitous increase in oil prices had made Iran one of the United States's most important allies. The shah believed that this continued American interest in Iran had not been the result of personal sympathy for himself or admiration for his methods. American support was based rather on a cold-blooded analysis of American interest. And, he reasoned, what had taken place to change this position? Was the United States not compelled to ensure the existence of a reliable Iran? Had he not been a good ally? What could the Americans hope to gain if he were overthrown?

Of course there was always the possibility that the United States had decided to neutralize Iran, and divide control over the country with the Soviets. And there was another hypothesis: Perhaps the Americans had decided upon a drastic change in strategy in the Middle East. Heretofore they had based their actions on the creation of military alliances to contain the spread of Soviet power and influence, but the system of alliances had not fully succeeded. Political changes in the United States had made it an unpopular policy, and the American public seemed unwilling to bear the costs. Under the circumstances, the Americans might have decided to launch an alliance with radical Islam in order to undertake a frontal attack against communism. There were many experts in the West who believed that the Soviet Union was facing a growing challenge from Muslims living within the Soviet empire, and this was held to be a potentially revolutionary force against the Kremlin. Indeed, by the time the shah had been removed, Brzezinski himself would be speaking optimistically of precisely this possibility. Had the Americans decided to back the Khomeini forces?

For the moment, the shah had no clear indication of U.S. intentions. The one consistent message that arrived from Washington was the human rights sermon, along with expressions of support from Pentagon and State Department representatives for Iran's military purchases. Mohammed Reza's course of action seemed clear: attempt to meet the human rights demands. In that way, he would satisfy the Americans, avoid the open conflict that might jeopardize his son's chances for a peaceful and durable reign, and ensure that he would not be remembered as the man who had unleashed a bloodbath on his country in his dying days. If it later developed that the Americans wished to see the iron fist deployed, there would be time enough for that.

So the shah continued to pursue a moderate course, awaiting clarification of the American grand design. If they wanted him to remain, they were certainly powerful enough to defend him, just as they had done in 1953. If they wished to replace him, he could not expect to prevail.

Baffled by the growing strength and resolute tactics of his enemies, uncertain of the intentions of his powerful allies in Washington, thrown into a depression by his disease and the medications of his doctors, the shah behaved just as anyone might have expected. In retrospect, it would have been amazing had Mohammed Reza mustered the act of will required to sanction force. For him to have done so would have required the strongest possible support and guidance from the government of the United States.

The Americans for their part did not know that the shah was dying, and they were slow to realize that his regime was imperiled. When the shah expressed concern at the way things were going, the old Iranian hands in the American government were inclined to be extremely skeptical. They considered Mohammed Reza a professional worrier, and had long since become accustomed to his forecasts of terrible developments. Furthermore, many Carter administration officials welcomed the shah's difficulties as vindication of their theory that he was too autocratic to merit wholehearted American support. Depending on the intensity of such sentiments, analysts on the National Security Council and in the State Department saw the challenge to the shah as an opportunity either to press for greater liberalization or even to raise the possibility that Iran's problems could not be solved so long as Mohammed Reza remained in power.

Many American analysts and policymakers did not regard the possibility of the shah's fall as a catastrophe for the United States. Ideologically opposed to the shah's methods, desirous of allies of a more explicitly democratic and progressive orientation, a number of people in the foreign policy establishment examined the Iranian crisis with a low level of sensitivity to the possibility of a serious crisis. Furthermore, the Americans had forgotten a great deal of what had been previously learned about Mohammed Reza Shah. For decades it had been realized that, in J.F.K.'s words, "He may not be much of a shah, but he's our shah." Mohammed Reza was not a tyrant, and not a particularly strong personality. Ironically, by 1977—at a time when the shah was beginning to come unstuck—the image in

Washington was of a brutal and authoritarian personality with strong elements of megalomania (even though there was reportedly a CIA profile outlining the shah's inferiority complex). This image, of course, matched the political mood of the new administration, and later played a crucial role in buttressing American inaction in the final months of the crisis. If the shah was indeed a tough guy, he could be expected to crush his opponents ruthlessly with the help of SAVAK or the armed forces. There was no need for the American government to go out of its way to suggest repressive action.

Thus, even though there were numerous reports of the shah's psychological state, the basic misassessment of Mohammed Reza's personality remained until very late in the day. Individuals like Michael Blumenthal, Lady Bird Johnson, David Rockefeller, Henry Kissinger, and Joseph Kraft felt that the shah appeared disoriented and irresolute. Yet their reports were invariably interpreted as showing the shah "losing his nerve" in the face of the crisis, never as basic ingredients of his makeup, compounded by disease and medication.

American appreciation of the gravity of the political crisis was similarly skewed. Nobody in the Tehran embassy realized that the shah might not survive the crisis until September 1978, at the earliest, and the theme was not sounded in earnest until October. This is not to say that there was no appreciation of the pattern of violent opposition to the shah, or of the existence of a very well organized force in Iran dedicated to his overthrow. The latter theme was stressed in a midsummer (1978) cable, while the former had been reported for well over a year. As early as July 25, 1977, the embassy had sent an airgram to Washington entitled "Straws in the wind: Intellectual and religious opposition in Iran" that touched on some of the elements that made up the shah's opposition; there was another, more detailed study of the Iranian opposition in February of the following year.

Yet the possibility that the shah might fall was not taken seriously for a long time, and the intelligence community in Washington was not well placed to predict it. A subsequent study of the "intelligence failure," conducted by the staff of the House Permanent Select Committee on Intelligence, concluded that leading American policymakers did not realize the gravity of the Iranian situation until October 1978. According to the staff report: "No CIA intelligence reporting based on sources within the religious opposition occurred during a two-year period ending in November 1977, and embassy political

reporting based on contacts with the opposition was rare and sometimes contemptuous."[10] Moreover, the staff said that a CIA assessment in August 1978 had contained the embarrassing statement that
"Iran is not in a revolutionary or even a 'prerevolutionary' situation,"
and a Defense Intelligence Agency (DIA) Intelligence Appraisal
dated September 28 announced that "the shah is expected to remain
actively in power over the next 10 years." As for the Department of
State's Bureau of Intelligence and Research (INR), it possessed no
full-time Iran analyst, and consequently produced not a single intelligence report (as distinct from daily situation reports) during all of
1978, although there is reason to believe that an INR analyst was
asked to look at available information on Iran for the State Department in midsummer, and came to the conclusion that the situation
was very bad. However, if there was such a study, it had little, if any,
impact.

As a matter of fact, nonexperts were far more worried about the
Iranian crisis than were officials in the intelligence community
charged with following the course of events. The Senate Foreign
Relations Committee held closed hearings on Iran on September 15,
at which Henry Precht as country director and Jack Miklos as
former embassy deputy chief of mission testified. When asked why
the government had failed to anticipate the Iranian crisis (which
greatly worsened in September), both foreign service officers suggested that the United States had relied too heavily upon SAVAK
for information. They also pointed out that recent "reforms" designed to protect against excesses on the part of the intelligence
community had made it very difficult for CIA or DIA officials
abroad to conduct covert intelligence-gathering operations.

Twelve days later, the head of CIA's National Foreign Assessment
Center, Dr. Robert Bowie, observed before the same committee that
prior to the Carter administration, with its super-sensitivity about
secret operations of any sort, it had been common practice for the
CIA to penetrate dissident groups in countries like Iran. But under
Carter the practice had been cut back, because such penetrations
were additionally opposed by the shah and by the State Department
as well (on the ground that contact between the American government and the opposition might encourage the shah's opponents and,
if revealed to the public, weaken his image at home).

When pressed on the failure to anticipate the severe disturbances,

Bowie noted that there had been no demand in Washington for in-depth assessments on Iran, and he added that while there were many anti-shah demonstrations in that country, he did not think it likely that the situation would fly out of control.

On the other side of Capitol Hill, Under-Secretary of State for Security Assistance Lucy Benson testified on arms sales to Iran on October 5, and expressed no profound concern over the rapidly changing Iranian situation. When Representative Stephen Solarz asked if she thought the United States should exercise more care in selling arms to Iran, she replied: "I do not believe so, because we were adequately careful and cautious before."[11]

By the time the crisis was in full swing in November, President Carter concluded that his intelligence officials had failed, and he openly criticized their performance. A special committee was appointed to determine whether the intelligence failure reflected a single oversight (and thus was simply a personnel problem) or pointed toward a structural problem (requiring an overhaul of the system itself). The House Select Committee on Intelligence staff concluded that the formulation and evaluation of intelligence on Iran had been influenced by the nature of American policy: "not directly, through the conscious suppression of unfavorable news, but indirectly . . . policymakers were not asking whether the shah's autocracy would survive indefinitely; policy was premised on that assumption."

The American performance seems even worse when compared to the assessments of Israel and France. Over the years, Israel had tended to work intimately with the shah's government on internal matters and defense questions, whereas France collaborated on foreign operations, both paramilitary and diplomatic. But both nations well understood the crucial role played by the shah in supporting Western interests, and both realized that the fall of the shah would be a catastrophe for the West. France and Israel were far more sensitive than the United States to any possibility of a shift in the balance of power in the Persian Gulf, and hence were more likely to react to vague warning signs.

In addition, the two governments were blessed with outstanding diplomatic and intelligence personnel in Tehran. The head of the Israeli mission, Uri Lubrani, had served in intelligence for many years, and had then been posted to Ethiopia as ambassador. Lubrani had early sensed the weakening of Haile Selassie's regime, and had argued vigorously with his American counterpart, who had been extremely reluctant to recognize the emperor's danger. The same kind of discussion took place between Lubrani and William Sullivan in Tehran, although to his credit Sullivan came around to a more realistic view of the crisis before most people in Washington.

In any event, Lubrani began to have the feeling that the shah was in grave danger in the spring of 1978, when he expressed his concern for the first time in a communication to Jerusalem. This was followed in early June by a long cable in which Lubrani wrote that in his opinion the shah was doomed. Henceforth, he said, it was no longer a question of "whether the shah could survive," but only "how long he would last." His own guess was that the shah would not remain in power more than two to three years, although he allowed for the possibility that his reign might endure as long as another half-decade. Lubrani's assessment created a mild sensation in Tel Aviv, and was challenged by many in the Foreign Office. But the Israeli government was sufficiently concerned that it took two steps: it alerted the Jewish community in Iran that the situation looked bad (and encouraged Iranian Jews to make plans for their departure); and it transmitted the substance of Lubrani's concerns to Washington. The reply from the American government, reflecting the view of the intelligence community, was that Lubrani's concerns were alarmist.

The French intelligence community did even better. The SDECE had an excellent representative in Tehran, and his reading was so accurate that he wrote a report in the spring of 1978 in which he said the shah would not be on the throne by the spring of 1979. This report was shown to the Americans in Tehran, and received the same response as the Israeli assessment.

The French and the Israelis arrived at their conclusions without the benefit of a crucial piece of information: the parlous state of the shah's health. But neither intelligence director—and neither government head—had an inflated opinion of the shah's decisiveness and courage to begin with. Thus, while the chiefs of both intelligence communities are extremely critical of their own failure to learn about the shah's cancer, they were at least able to make an accurate assessment of his character. In addition, they gave considerable weight to the information available on Khomeini.

The French had followed the activities of Khomeini in Iraq with concern for some time, and the director general of the SDECE,

Count Alexandre de Maranches, was in a particularly good position to learn about Khomeini because de Maranches had devoted considerable energy to getting to know Iraqi leader Sadaam Hussein. De Maranches and President Giscard d'Estaing both felt that Hussein was far more independent of Soviet influence than was believed by the Americans, and relations between Iraq and France were steadily improving in the 1970s. When the French learned of Khomeini's close ties with the Iranian and Palestinian guerrillas, along with those with Libya and various other Soviet-linked countries and individuals, they were deeply concerned. On at least one occasion French and Iraqi officials talked about Khomeini, exploring the possibility that Iraqi short-term gains from extending warm hospitality to the ayatollah might be offset by long-term costs to the stability of the region. There was therefore no great love in the Elysée Palace for Khomeini long before he sought refuge in France in 1978. The French knew his intentions, and knew he was no friend of the West. In addition, they had a rough sense of his organization's international dimensions.

The Israelis, too, were concerned about Khomeini as the result of their monitoring of PLO activities throughout the Middle East. Like the French, they realized that Khomeini was dangerous; they had an enhanced appreciation of his particular hatred of Jews, and of course of the very existence of Israel.

The Americans did not share these assessments of Khomeini, and it is fair to say that their key policymakers never truly understood the ayatollah. Most observers, from CIA analysts to university professors, from journalists to officials in the State Department and the National Security Council, believed that the opposition to the shah was led by intellectuals and students, with additional technocratic and religious elements, along with the bazaaris and the usual fringe groups. They were convinced that the opposition was of a traditional Western sort, and that their goals were akin to those of a democratic (or even social democratic) westernizing middle class. This was consistent both with the bulk of American contacts in Iran —which tended to be with English-speakers and those educated in the West—and with the developmental models so dear to modern sociology that suggested the rising middle class was the source of opposition to the monarchy and the focus of the emerging elite. Throughout 1977, no one seemed to believe that the opposition was fundamentally religious, or to appreciate the power of the mullahs and ayatollahs. And even when the occasional academic suggested that the clerical component was central to the opposition movement, the mullahs were portrayed either as "moderates" or as people who might play a role in strengthening the opposition, but who would eventually recede if the movement was successful.

The bulk of the available information on the opposition movement came from the leaders of the old Mossadeqist group that was taken to be the largest opposition body, the National Front. In addition, there was input from academics and Iranian exiles close to the Front, who generally reinforced the same message. The leader of the Front was Karim Sanjabi, who had spent many years in the shah's prisons, but emerged to lead a comfortable life in Tehran in his villa with a swimming pool. Sanjabi was convinced that it was possible to work with Khomeini and the mullahs; that the religious leaders, despite their archaic language, had modern ideas; and that—as he put it to the American journalist Joseph Kraft—"Ayatollah Khomeini doesn't want chaos."[12] It was therefore necessary to work with the religious leaders to achieve a democratic republic.

Sanjabi was typical of many of the National Front leaders. Amidst the general confusion, the reformist-minded individuals who composed most of that group's leadership convinced themselves that Khomeini was like them, or, alternatively, that they would be able to control him once the shah had been either brought under control (through a British-style constitutional monarchy) or driven out. This proved to be pathetic wishful thinking, but it was the almost universal testimony of the National Fronters throughout the crisis.

Insofar as there were American contacts with the opposition in Iran, they were with people like Sanjabi, and this pattern of contacts was duplicated in Washington, Paris, London, and Rome. Wherever there were Iranian exiles, there were meetings with Americans, and the majority of the Iranians were able to speak the soothing language of Western-style reformism and social democracy. Hence, both among the senior staff at the Tehran embassy and among the members of the Washington bureaucracy, two convictions were developed and reinforced: the "moderation" of Khomeini, and the "supremacy" of the moderate National Front figures in the opposition movement.

In reality, the National Front had very little mass following, but these impressions were supported by the testimony of the academic experts, based on sources among the Front representatives and in the religious camp. The most influential of the academics was Professor Richard Cottam, of the University of Pittsburgh, a scholar who had once been a foreign service officer in Iran, and who was apparently the first American in years to have a conversation with Khomeini in Najaf in August 1978. Cottam granted that Khomeini was not an entirely attractive character (although just after the revolution he wrote of the ayatollah's "Islamic humanist ideology"), but argued that he was a religious figure who had no interest in government *per se,* and would consequently retire to the holy city of Qum to continue his religious activities, if the shah were to be overthrown. So good were Cottam's contacts among the National Front group and the followers of Mehdi Bazargan (later named as Khomeini's first prime minister) and other allies of the ayatollah that his name surfaced as a possible ambassador to Iran after the revolution.

Thus, even those experts who realized that there was a vital religious component to the opposition forces suggested that it was something the United States could live with, and if need be, work with. The movement was taken to be moderate, and the extremists were held to be religious figures who would take no active role in the post-shah regime.

Above all, there was little understanding of the clerical fascism embodied in the works of Khomeini. This failure of perception and analysis was crucial to the subsequent American response throughout the debacle, as it was to the failure of the Iranian reformers who genuinely wanted a more liberal and Western country. No one in the Carter administration or in the foreign policy bureaucracy seemed aware of the violent ideas and unrestrained passions of the ayatollah. If anything, there was a determined effort to portray Khomeini as a somewhat eccentric but basically admirable religious figure, or even, in the unfortunate words of Ambassador Andrew Young after the revolution, as "some kind of saint." So strong was the desire to cast Khomeini as an acceptable, nay democratic leader, that there was considerable consternation and disgruntlement in the State Department and the CIA when three American newspapers published extensive accounts of Khomeini's writings. The articles showed that Khomeini's books revealed him as a violently anti-Western, anti-American, anti-Zionist, and anti-Semitic individual, who offered an unattractive alternative to the shah. Yet as late as the first week in

February 1979, when Khomeini was returning in triumph to Tehran, Henry Precht told an audience of some two hundred persons at a State Department "open forum" meeting that the newspaper accounts were severely misleading, and he went so far as to accuse Washington *Post* editorial columnist Stephen Rosenfeld of wittingly disseminating excerpts from a book that Precht considered at best a collection of notes taken by students, and at worst a forgery. Precht was hardly an isolated case, for the conviction was widespread that Khomeini's books were either false, exaggerated, or misunderstood. This conviction was strongly reinforced by Khomeini's supporters in the United States, some of whom were regularly consulted by the American government as sources of information on the anti-shah movement.

Astonishingly, there were no copies of Khomeini's works available to the American analysts. The American Embassy staff in Tehran asked the State Department for detailed excerpts from the books in early autumn, 1978 (already quite late in the day), and never received the information. And the *Post*'s Rosenfeld received a telephone call from the CIA asking if it was possible to borrow a copy of one of the books, for there was none available at CIA headquarters.

As in the case of the misperception of the nature of the opposition, American wishful thinking about Khomeini was reinforced by academic experts. Some of these were conveniently located at Georgetown University's Center for Contemporary Arab Studies, which was funded in part by a large contribution from the Libyan government of Qaddafi. There were at least two Islamic experts on the Georgetown faculty in close touch with Khomeini: Professor Mehdi Haeri, whose father had been Khomeini's teacher in Qum; and Professor Thomas Ricks, who was in regular contact with Ghotbzadeh. Haeri had briefed William Miller at the Senate Select Committee on Intelligence, while Ricks worked directly with State Department experts. His views can be readily gathered from his remarks—in an interview—about the press treatment of Khomeini's books, published in the Washington *Post* on January 28:

> . . . those excerpts were incredible. I can't even find one of them. They were published out of context. The original lectures were not in Arabic, he spoke to a Persian audience. Why would he speak in Arabic?
> . . . I have read the Persian lectures and I find no basis to support the

alleged anti-Semitic quotes. There is this passage in the *Post* version that says Khomeini sees the Jews as trying to take over the planet. But there is nothing saying this in his lectures. I have them. I have the book.

The American government had the book translated into English and released later in the winter. But Ricks's words certainly reassured those people who would have thought twice about seeing Iran fall to the Khomeini whose ideas were actually to be found in his works.

It was consequently possible for those who felt, for one reason or another, that the fall of the shah would not be a disaster, to argue that the success of the opposition led at least in part by Khomeini might turn out to be "something we could live with." Yet the question remains: Why did American experts not listen to French and Israeli observers? And why was the CIA and the rest of the intelligence community so poorly informed about the eventual rulers of Iran?

IT MAY SEEM SURPRISING that the small French and Israeli intelligence organizations outperformed the American intelligence community, which had at least ten times the number of the other two groups. The answer is that the American intelligence community under the Carter administration was still in full retreat following the scandals of the mid-seventies. After the appointment of Admiral Stansfield Turner as director of Central Intelligence, morale dropped further when hundreds of officials from the clandestine services were phased out or summarily dismissed by a computerized personnel system transplanted from the armed services. While Turner constantly spoke of the importance of morale at CIA, he rarely behaved in a way to inspire and defend that esprit de corps which is the absolutely essential requirement for an effective intelligence service. Moreover, he continued and amplified some of the misguided procedures of the past, particularly a strange indifference to cultural and linguistic skills in foreign posts. Within two years of assuming his position, Turner had approved the transfer of virtually every CIA station chief in major western European capitals, and these experienced veterans were often replaced with people who had no knowledge of the language, history, or culture of the country to

which they were posted. This is a grave handicap for even the most
talented individual, and inevitably led to a drop in the quality of
reporting.

Furthermore, the CIA has always been particularly sensitive to
the political winds in Washington, and Turner was careful to stay on
the good side of such influential people as Vice President Mondale
and David Aaron, both of whom had expressed a strong dislike for
covert action of any sort. The CIA under Turner was thus more than
usually reticent to undertake the sort of clandestine intelligence-
gathering operation that might have provided first-class information
about the Khomeini movement.

So far as Iran was concerned, there was a surprising paucity of
experts at CIA. Throughout most of the crisis period there were at
most two analysts working full time on Iran, and for much of that
period there was only one individual following and analyzing events
at the agency. For the most part, the CIA analysts who dealt with
Iranian material were not Persian specialists at all, but rather Ara-
bists, a bias that would be demonstrated in mid-December 1978,
when the CIA organized a special task force to follow the course of
the revolution. The head of the task force was from the Arab States
Branch.

For those one or two individuals working on Iran in 1977–78, there
was little time for serious research, since they were forced to cope
with a mounting pile of paper coming in from all directions, and with
the necessity of contacting the few experts in the United States with
knowledge of Iran. And here again, some of the oversights were
surprising. To take only the most impressive example of individuals
ignored by the policymakers during the crisis, on only one occasion
was Richard Helms, former DCI and former ambassador to Tehran,
asked for his assessment and recommendation. The conversation
took place at the White House (without the President) and lasted just
over an hour. Kermit Roosevelt also received summary treatment
during the period.

As the House Select Committee staff report noted, there was indeed a draft of a National Intelligence Estimate produced in midsummer 1978, but it did not represent the latest research. It had
actually been completed nearly three months earlier but had been
delayed for technical reasons, and its preparation had lasted well
over a year. Like all NIEs, this one—entitled "Iran After the Shah"

—embodied the contributions of the various agencies and branches of the intelligence community, and was not a particularly rigorous document. It is in the nature of such collective efforts that the analysts who contribute an estimate state their assumptions explicitly, and this one rested upon the premise that in the event of an Iranian crisis, the military would act to support the dynasty, or at least fight to defend itself against any mass opposition. On this hypothesis, it was hardly surprising that the analysts should have concluded that Iran was not in a revolutionary or even prerevolutionary situation. In fairness to the intelligence community, to have spoken of a revolutionary situation in April one needed the oracle of Delphi—or their modern equivalents in Paris and Jerusalem.

The problem with American intelligence—which itself was just a special case of the American policymaking community—was not that it failed to foresee the coming of the crisis, but that it did not understand the crisis when it came. And the warnings of the French and the Israelis were disregarded because of a mixture of arrogance and suspicion. CIA officials had long felt that the French were inferior intelligence gatherers; without independent confirmation of the French prediction of the fall of the shah, the American officials in question were unlikely to take the matter seriously. There was a different objection to Lubrani's material—one that had to do with international politics. The Carter administration had no great fondness for the Begin government in Jerusalem, and the intelligence community had learned that the White House was always suspicious of any Israeli information suggesting that the sentiments of the President and his top advisers rested on an unsubstantial empirical base. The most obvious case in point was the PLO, which the Israelis treated as a terrorist organization dedicated to their destruction. The Carter team was uncomfortable with this characterization of a group that it wished to involve in the Middle East peace negotiations, and officials from Vance to Turner took pains to avoid calling the PLO a "terrorist" organization. Evidence of PLO terrorist activities was unpleasant to such officials. One reaction to the flood of Israeli information about the PLO was to suggest that it was unreliable, prepared in order to manipulate American foreign policy.

This problem grew worse with time, for the Carter administration's relations with the Israelis deteriorated steadily. Despite the intimate relationship between the two countries (one which closely resembled that between the United States and Iran before the fall of the shah), Washington did not hesitate to exert extreme pressure on the Israeli government when it felt that Tel Aviv was being insufficiently responsive to American desires. In the fall of 1977, for example, Ambassador Sullivan discussed with an Iranian official the possibility of interrupting oil shipments to Israel as a method of bringing pressure to bear on Tel Aviv. There was never any response from the Iranians, but the very fact that an American administration would consider the use of such a weapon against an ally testifies to the tensions between the two countries. Under the circumstances, American officials were always on guard for Israeli "disinformation." When the Israelis forwarded Lubrani's assessment to Washington, many Americans saw it as an attempt to goad the United States into taking a more pro-Israel position in the Middle East. His prescient words were ignored.

Having failed to heed the warnings in the spring and summer, the Americans were poorly placed to catch up in the fall. For by the time the crisis was upon them, the President and his associates were deeply involved in other pressing matters: Camp David and its follow up; normalization of relations with the People's Republic of China; and SALT II. Even at the height of the crisis, Carter never recognized the stakes in Iran. Despite the most impassioned warnings from friendly countries throughout western Europe and the Persian Gulf, suggesting that the fall of the shah would open the way for a Soviet advance toward the oilfields and the sea-lanes of the Middle East, the President never attempted to design a policy to safeguard American interests. In all probability, Carter did not believe that there was any danger of Soviet expansionism in the area, for he told Bill Moyers on national television on the evening of November 13: "We don't have any evidence that the Soviets . . . are trying to disrupt the existing government structure in Iran nor that they are a source of violence in Iran. I think they recognize—they have a very long mutual border with Iran, and a stable government there no matter who its leaders might be is valuable to them."[13]

The U.S. government was always at least one long step behind the realities of the Iranian revolution. At first there was no anticipation of a crisis that might bring down the shah. There were many who never felt that the shah's downfall would be a bad thing for the United States, and thus when the gravity of the crisis was confirmed, it was not viewed with great alarm. Furthermore, the dangers represented by the Khomeini movement were insufficiently understood, and there was no sense of urgency in designing a policy to block his advance. Finally, the ideologically skewed perception of the shah as a nasty tyrant, combined with total ignorance of his physical and mental health, led the President and his advisers to move more slowly in the constant expectation that, come what may, the shah would eventually lower the iron fist on his enemies.

All these failures contributed to the paralysis of the President throughout the revolution. Khomeini's triumph was certainly not inevitable—it could have been prevented by different means at various moments throughout the late 1970s—but the combination of an American President who never designed a policy to defend American interests, and a shah who was immobilized by his own personality and the advance of his fatal illness, made Khomeini's victory possible. Would things have been different if we had foreseen the crisis? The director of Central Intelligence is of two minds on the subject. In March 1979, Admiral Turner said: "If we had been more sensitive [to the cumulative effect of the rate of change in Iran] . . . American policy might have been different."[14] Two months later he told an interviewer: "Even if I'd told the policymakers on October 5 that there was going to be a major upheaval on November 5 in Iran, there was nothing they could do."[15]

It is indeed doubtful that the Carter administration would have done things very differently, even with the finest intelligence.

FIVE

The Crisis, II

THE VIOLENCE REACHED new levels of intensity in August, at the beginning of Ramadan. On the 10th and 11th there were major clashes in Isfahan between demonstrators and police at the home of one of Khomeini's clerical supporters who had issued a call for the overthrow of the Pahlavi dynasty and the creation of an Islamic state. The government responded by moving tanks into the city and declaring martial law, but this only acted as a goad to the revolutionary forces, and riots broke out all over the country. Typically, the implementation of martial law in Isfahan (and a day later in three other small towns nearby) was halfhearted. On the 16th the military governor ordered the tanks removed from Isfahan.

Then, on August 18, occurred the major event of the summer: arsonists set ablaze the Rex Cinema in Abadan, and some four hundred persons died in the panic. In the rage of the moment SAVAK was blamed for the disaster, and although subsequent investigations left the question of responsibility unresolved,[1] it was another step toward the end of the dynasty. The country was in turmoil, and not only because of the mounting tempo of violence. The economic situation was worsening daily in ways calculated to convert the urban poor into a revolutionary mass. Housing prices were out of control, most acutely in Tehran but also in the other major cities. Moreover, the vagaries of the international oil market were hurting Iranian consumers. First of all, the increase in oil prices had driven up production costs in the West, and these costs were passed on to Iranian consumers of foreign goods in the form of higher prices. But simultaneously international demand for oil was dropping, so that Iran's oil revenues were both shrinking and losing purchasing power. There had been bad weather—another sign of the shah's poor luck—and agricultural production was down while food prices were up. Finally, the continued drop in the growth rate contributed to the mood of anger and despair.

The discontent with the worsening economic conditions was centered, as always, in the bazaar. And the worse the bazaaris' balance sheets, the greater the anger against the shah. "Following years of prosperity and rising expectations, the mood in the bazaar was now one of disenchantment. This made it easier for religious leaders to call for business strikes to which the bazaar . . . responded impressively."[2]

The shah played his last conciliatory card by dismissing Jamshid Amuzegar and appointing Ja'far Sharif-Emami prime minister on August 26. Sharif-Emami, a man with a reputation as a moderate, was asked to form a government of "national reconciliation," a theme that had been stressed a week earlier when the shah publicly reiterated his commitment to the principles of Islam. There was a rash of measures designed to placate the critics of the regime, whether secular or religious. The Imperial calendar was withdrawn and the old Islamic one restored; press censorship was lifted—and would stay lifted even after martial law was declared in September —to the extent that photographs of Khomeini were printed in the newspapers for the first time since 1964; the debates in the Majlis were broadcast live throughout the country, giving the shah's opponents in parliament a national platform they never had before; and the shah now began consulting with his opponents on policy matters. Both Karim Sanjabi, the leader of the National Front, and the Ayatollah Shariatmadari, the chief religious figure in Iran, were invited to participate in discussions about the future of the country.

The grievances of the religious leaders got special attention, whether complaints were merely symbolic or questions of substance. Gambling casinos were closed, along with motion picture theaters, and although the new press legislation permitted almost anything to be written about the government, there were strict rules about publication of material considered "harmful to Islam."

As for the working (or unemployed) masses, new programs were initiated to redistribute government wealth. Money was diverted from weapons to social services: salaries were raised at the same time utility rates were frozen, stern warnings were issued about waste and corruption, housing costs and land prices were reduced, and the poor were promised help in housing and medical care.

Finally, the Sharif-Emami government moved against some of the human symbols of the protests. Investigations were opened into corruption in high places; officials and former officials were brought to trial (including former SAVAK chief Nassiri, who had served briefly as ambassador to Pakistan), and thirty-four top SAVAK officials were purged at a single stroke. The shah also adopted a stringent code of behavior for the royal family that made it impossible for them to engage in influence-peddling or any business activity.

The result of the government change and these numerous efforts at reform, which were spread out over a three-month period, was to convince the revolutionaries that the shah had stopped fighting back. Instead of pacifying the country, Mohammed Reza stimulated his enemies. On September 4 there were large demonstrations in Tehran to mark the end of the Ramadan celebration. Thousands of people marched, further alarming military leaders who were already concerned about the liberalization program of the new government. Two days later "unauthorized gatherings" were banned, but on the following day there was another anti-shah demonstration in Tehran. Under pressure from the military leadership, the shah approved the imposition of martial law late in the night of September 7–8. Many people in the city were unaware of this development, and the following day saw yet another demonstration in Jaleh Square in the center of Tehran. Accounts of the tragedy differ, but there were evidently scuffles between the demonstrators and the shah's security forces, a refusal by the demonstrators to leave, and then the orders to open fire by the soldiers. Over one hundred persons were killed, and many times that number injured. The day became known as "Black Friday."

For a moment, it looked as if both sides had understood that the country needed at least a brief respite from the turmoil, and the military issued several strong statements. The military governor of

Tehran, General Gholam Ali Oveissi (commander of the ground forces), announced that any violation of martial law, including evening curfews and a ban on gatherings or demonstrations, would be dealt with severely. Tanks were moved into the major cities. For their part, the religious leaders—including Khomeini—encouraged their followers to avoid confrontations, even after the arrests of some ayatollahs and leaders of the lay opposition like Sanjabi and Dariush Forouhar, another leader of the National Front.

But while the shah wanted order, he dreaded bloodshed, and let it be known to his military commanders that restraint had to be exercised. As a result, the conditions were the worst possible from the standpoint of authority, a situation Joseph Kraft described very well as "martial law without there exactly being martial law." A crackdown was formally in effect, but opponents of the shah learned that they could challenge his authority with impunity:

> That fuzzy condition put an obvious strain on the military leaders. Top commanders were unsure of their responsibilities. At one point, in October, the commander of the ground forces, General Gholam Ali Oveissi, sent an officer to warn the staff of the English-language daily *Kayhan* against articles he considered inaccurate and inflammatory. The reporters thereupon threatened to go on strike, and the Prime Minister backed them up. Unit commanders never knew exactly when to intervene. At least some of the rank and file, and perhaps some of the junior officers, sided with demonstrators. On two occasions, provincial police officers were shot by enlisted men in the Army.[3]

The shah was now beginning to pay the price of his autocracy. The revolution could have been avoided altogether if Mohammed Reza had managed to create the political structures required by the White Revolution. The more ambitious and talented members of the new middle classes would have acquired a real stake in the stability of the country, and it would never have been possible for the highly diverse sentiments of discontent to have become focused narrowly on the shah. But he feared such a political evolution, preferring to render impotent any and all alternative centers of real power. When the crisis came, all the hatred in the country was concentrated against him. Worse still, by preempting efforts to create other centers of power, and by manipulating his appointments to eliminate any semblance of autonomous decisionmaking outside the court, the shah guaranteed that he would arrive at his moment of truth without advisers and assistants capable of independent judgment, or even of telling him the whole truth.

In the past, there had always been a certain number of key individuals willing to assume the burden of responsibility, to make the difficult decision, and then present the shah with a *fait accompli.* Now Alam was dead, and Oveissi in 1978 was not the commander of the fifties and sixties. He had lost touch with his younger officers, and had become comfortable after years of high status and prestige. There was only the shah, and the shah was rapidly losing his powers: " . . . the fundamental fact remains that the decisive person to withdraw his commitment to the state was the shah himself. Once the shah had lost the will to fight, the state crumbled from within and out of its own momentum. . . ."[4]

By the fall of 1978, it was no longer possible to co-opt the opposition; if the shah were to survive, it would be because he used his forces to reestablish order in the country. But this he was unable and unwilling to do on his own. Sometime during the summer or fall of 1978 Mohammed Reza disengaged from the conflict—resolved that he would not permit mass bloodshed; that, whatever happened, he would not go down in history as the perpetrator of a conflict that might well become a civil war—and awaited the inevitable outcome. When *Newsweek* foreign correspondent Arnaud de Borchgrave saw him in early November, and told him that some of his foreign supporters would back the use of military force in Iran, the shah wept. There had already been too much violence, he said; he would not be the cause of more bloodshed.

This was not the first time the shah had encountered a revolutionary movement that menaced the end of the Pahlavi dynasty, nor was it the first time that he had remained immobile in the face of such a challenge. In the 1950s, Mossadeq had driven Mohammed Reza into exile, just as Khomeini would in December. But then the United States had restored the shah to the Peacock Throne, aware of the dangers involved should Iran pass into hostile hands. Mohammed Reza Shah wondered whether Jimmy Carter would do the same.

THE IRANIAN CRISIS that led to the downfall of the shah and his replacement by a man hostile to the United States and the non-

Islamic world was the first major foreign policy test for the Carter administration. Until then the foreign policy difficulties faced by the new President had been largely of his own making, stemming from American initiatives: the quest for a "comprehensive" Middle East settlement, the friction with the Soviet Union because of the submission of drastically new SALT II proposals by Secretary of State Vance in March 1977, the often critical reaction to the human rights program, the mixed responses to the abrupt acceptance of Chinese conditions for normalization of relations with the People's Republic of China, and the embarrassments in the Horn of Africa. All of these problems had been produced at least in part by Carter's attempts to remake the world in accordance with his image of proper international behavior.

The Iranian crisis was quite different. Here, for the first time, a vital American interest was directly challenged by hostile forces, and the United States was intimately involved in the crisis from first to last, in the eyes alike of the major participants in Iran and of all foreign observers. The goal of the Khomeini forces was evidently the removal of the shah and his American allies. Indeed, one of the central themes of the anti-shah movement was the effort to strike a mortal blow at "American imperialism." The shah himself believed that American policy would determine the outcome of his struggle with Khomeini, and that in the end it would be American desires and American will—rather than his own wishes—that would dictate his fate. Other pro-Western governments in the Middle East also viewed the Iranian crisis as a clear test of American will and reliability. It was inconceivable to countries from Israel and Oman to Saudi Arabia and Morocco that Carter would not take an active and direct role in the events in Iran. They were certain that the United States would mount some sort of action, and were anxious to see the nature of its response. Morocco and Saudi Arabia, for example, could conceivably face similar challenges, and could use the American behavior in the Iranian crisis as an indication of what they might expect for themselves. The same held true for American allies, albeit to somewhat lower degree. The leaders of countries like the Federal Republic of Germany had long dreaded an American "disengagement" that would leave them exposed to Soviet power. A forceful and successful U.S. response to the Iranian crisis would encourage its allies, heighten their sense of security, and increase the internal cohesion of alliances.

Finally, the Soviet Union also watched the crisis very closely, both because the leaders in the Kremlin had no love for the shah, and because they too were curious about the Carter administration's behavior during its first major test. The Soviets wanted to gauge the limits of American inaction, the better to prepare their own plans for the near future.

The Carter administration does not seem to have appreciated the potentially catastrophic dimensions of the Iranian crisis, in part because so many leading members of the foreign policy team believed that the United States was condemned to play a reduced role in the world—thus permitting them to argue that there was nothing it *could* have done—in part because many of them wished to see American power more strictly limited—thus arguing that there was nothing the United States *should* have done—and lastly because there was no accurate perception of the nature of the challenge to the shah. At each stage of the crisis the officials in Washington misunderstood the forces at work, underestimated the strength of the opposition, overestimated the resolve of the shah and his domestic supporters, and convinced themselves that the Ayatollah Khomeini was other than what he was. For many in the administration, these were honest mistakes, the result of poor information and simple misunderstandings. For others, it was rather the result of preconceived ideological positions, systematic distortions of reality. But whatever the sources of the mistakes, the Americans were profoundly confused over final goals: the President and his top advisers did not know what they wanted. The confusion did not pass, even after the shah had fallen and the ayatollah had seized power in Iran.

Throughout the long crisis, the Americans were hobbled by their own doctrines. To support the shah was viewed in many quarters as a betrayal of the human rights campaign, especially if the shah used American support as an excuse to use military force against his enemies. But to permit the shah to be toppled was a geopolitical risk of vast dimensions. Moreover, any American action in Iran might be viewed by domestic critics as "meddling," and Carter had sworn to avoid this sort of activity. The balance of political considerations thus tilted toward inaction, especially because until the very end there was no consensus among the analysts that the shah's situation was grave.

In avoiding any clear commitment of American support to the shah, Carter and his advisers undoubtedly believed they were keeping their hands off Iran. As the President repeatedly declared at press conferences in the fall and winter, the question of the survival of the Pahlavi dynasty was one for "the Iranian people," not the government of the United States. This was a self-deception, for the Iranian people, like those in every small country dependent on the policies of the superpowers, were particularly sensitive to anything that looked like a change in policy on the part of the American government. And the behavior of the President encouraged Iranians to believe that there was indeed a new policy—a belief that was widespread, even among self-proclaimed enemies of the United States:

> Richard Falk reports that the proclamation of Carter's human rights policy did embolden the religious opposition. "It was quite a surprise to me," admits Falk. "I had thought that this was right-wing propaganda, used for domestic politics in this country." But Bazargan—Khomeini's senior political adviser—confirmed it. They took appearance for reality.[5]

Both sides in the Iranian conflict thus came to believe that the Carter administration would not tolerate any Iranian "solution" that was incompatible with the human rights policy as defined by Patt Derian and the human rights bureau in the State Department. At best, there was a perception of confusion and indecisiveness that itself contrasted sharply with the policies of past American governments. As will be seen, the shah could never get the same story from the White House and the State Department; the one kept assuring him that the United States was solidly behind him, while the other kept reminding him that force was not acceptable. The confusion had been evident for some time, prompting Ambassador Zahedi to go to New York City in late May 1978 to discuss the problem with his old friend, the former Vice President, Nelson Rockefeller. Zahedi knew that the shah had been frustrated in his efforts to get a clear reading of American desires and intentions, and asked Rockefeller if he could help clarify the situation. Rockefeller did at least two things: he called the shah to reassure him that American support was unequivocal; and he called Brzezinski, who did the same. Brzezinski spoke with the shah after discussing the matter with the President, who was on a speaking tour in Illinois, and Brzezinski's words of encouragement were described to the shah as coming directly from Carter. The shah asked for a confirming cable, but the State Department instead sent a message for Ambassador Sullivan's information. The Palace only got the message when the chief of protocol went over to the embassy to ask for it. On this occasion, as throughout the period, the shah found it difficult if not impossible to get confirmation from Sullivan of Brzezinski's supportive words.

The reason for the difference in tone between the statements coming out of the State Department and those from the National Security Council was that there was a substantive disagreement between the two. The disagreement over Iran was a case study of what eventually came to be known as the Vance-Brzezinski conflict, and while the extent of the two men's differences has been exaggerated, there is little question that they failed to agree about their overall approach to the world. By and large, Brzezinski believed that the nature of the shah's regime was a distinctly secondary question, and that Iran was of such preeminent importance to American Middle East policy that the shah should be encouraged to do whatever was necessary to preserve control of the country. Vance, on the other hand, was eager to demonstrate that the old Kissingerian geopolitical view of the world had been abandoned in favor of a more moralistic approach. Thus the Secretary argued that the United States could not give its support to repression in Iran. This view was heartily endorsed by Ambassador Andrew Young, and received the backing of Under-Secretary of State for Political Affairs David Newsom, along with Henry Precht, Patricia Derian, and their many allies and supporters throughout the bureaucracy. One of the most important of these was William Miller, the chief of staff for the Senate Select Committee on Intelligence. Miller had served in the American Embassy in Tehran in the mid-sixties, where he was known for his emotional and intellectual sympathies with the shah's opponents. He spoke Farsi, and established close ties with the *Dorehs,* or intellectual salons that characterized Iranian social life in that period. Later on, Miller became Peace Corps director for Iran, and was recalled by Corps Director Sargent Shriver because he was using his role in order to maintain contacts with the opposition. Miller had direct access to Vance throughout the crisis, once telling a friend that "all I have to do is call him and tell him who I am, and he answers the phone." Miller maintained that the United States should support Khomeini, because he believed that the ayatollah had no interest in foreign affairs, and was simply a religious figure.

Other potentially important actors carried little weight in the formulation of Iran policy once the crisis got under way. Defense Secretary Harold Brown, who was directly responsible for administering the military sales program to the shah, never took a strong position during the crisis, preferring to let the President and those with firmer views prevail. DCI Turner had a difficult role to play. Publicly chastised by the President for failing to warn the American government of the impending crisis, Turner generally took cautious positions, rarely if ever disagreed with the encouraging views delivered by various American representatives in Iran and Washington, and never voiced the opinion that the situation was desperate. Even when the shah had left the country, Turner—and Vance as well— persisted in the belief that the United States "could live with" the outcome.

When the crisis reached its peak in the late fall and early winter, Brzezinski received considerable support and guidance from Energy Secretary James Schlesinger, one of the best-informed Americans on Iranian affairs thanks to his previous service as Director of Central Intelligence and Secretary of Defense. Schlesinger shared Brzezinski's view of the importance of Iran to the West, and he was able to reinforce his own opinions with the warnings of the leaders of the People's Republic of China. The Chinese had raised the question of Iran with Schlesinger during his trip to Peking in late October and early November, and he relayed their concern over the shah's plight to Brzezinski upon his return to Washington.

The message from China was only the latest in a continuous expression of concern from American allies throughout the world. The most dramatic of these came from Egyptian President Anwar Sadat at Camp David in early September. During the three-way negotiations, Sadat took time out to speak to Carter in very grave tones, warning him about the seriousness of the Iranian situation. And the day after "Black Friday," Sadat called the shah from Camp David and spoke to him for about four minutes, expressing his complete backing and his willingness to come to the monarch's aid if it were necessary. Sadat urged Carter to follow suit. The American

President phoned the shah later in the night, telling him of his support.

The Israelis had long since indicated their concern, in both Tehran and Washington, and Foreign Minister Moshe Dayan stressed the point during the Camp David talks in a conversation with ABC correspondent Barbara Walters in New York. Dayan said that he considered the shah's crisis far more serious than the one being discussed at Camp David. Similar warnings came from Morocco, Oman, and several western European countries.

Finally, there was excellent reporting in early September by Ambassador Sullivan, recently returned to Iran from summer vacation. Sullivan was deeply alarmed by what he found upon his return, and his cables accurately described the gravity of the situation. Sullivan's reporting was all the more significant against the background of his relatively upbeat remarks in Washington the month before, when he had urged approval of the sale of 140 additional F-14s for the shah, and gave no indication that he felt there should be any slowdown in the American military assistance program.

Despite all these warnings, there was no action from Washington aside from some verbal reassurances—and these had been generously distributed for some time. When the crisis had intensified in August, Ambassador Zahedi went to the White House for a conversation with Vance, Mondale, Brzezinski, Turner, and the President. It was a long discussion, and after expressing his hope that the Americans would soften their human rights refrain, Zahedi observed that while he was about to return to Tehran for an extended period, he expected that he would frequently travel to Washington to fulfill his diplomatic obligations. The President urged Zahedi simply to do what was necessary in Tehran, then added: "Don't worry about Washington. I will be your ambassador to the United States."

The shah received several indications that the United States was loath to support any vigorous action against his enemies. Not only did Sullivan—often reinforced by the British ambassador, Anthony Parsons—scrupulously transmit the human rights themes to the Palace, but the shah found it impossible to obtain modern riot-control technology from his American allies. Iranian requests for tear gas canisters were blocked for nearly a year by Derian; it was not until Brzezinski and Sullivan had fought for over two months that the tear gas shipments were finally authorized—by Vance himself—in early November. The requests for rubber-tipped bullets were never granted by the American government; the bullets were finally acquired from the British in December.

Ultimately, not even the verbal assurances from Brzezinski and the President himself convinced the shah that the Americans were firmly behind him. Carter had told the shah during their telephone conversation from Camp David that he hoped there would be no further lives lost in the streets of Tehran and that the regime would be increasingly liberal in its treatment of its opponents. He also promised the shah that he would issue a strong statement of support, but the actual document—prepared by Precht and others in the State Department—was a mild one. Once again there was a divergence between private assurances and public statements.

From Carter's standpoint, there was no convincing reason for American action. The intelligence community did not think the situation in Iran was cause for great alarm, and while Sullivan had issued impassioned warnings in early September, the tone of his cables grew less alarmed with the passage of time, the settling in of the Sharif-Emami government, and the temporary lull in the violence. Furthermore, American analysts had long believed that the road to power in Iran lay through the military, and there were only slight indications in the early autumn of 1978 that the military had lost its internal coherence or loyalty to the shah. If the situation got out of hand, the Americans believed they could always turn to the generals as a last resort. Finally, the bad ratings given Iran by the human rights bureau strengthened the fatal misperception of the shah as a willful tyrant, a man who would invariably crush his opponents rather than open the floodgates to the revolution. Thus, even if the President were convinced of the real nature of the Iranian crisis, there seemed to be no pressing reason for American action.

But American attention was not even focused on Iran, for the President's agenda was filled with more pressing matters. First and foremost was Camp David, and its frenetic follow-up. American diplomats, including Vance, Brzezinski, and Brown, were fully occupied trying to convince other Middle Eastern leaders to support the agreements hammered out between Carter, Sadat, and Begin, leaving them little time to devote to Iran. As if this were not enough to distract them, the foreign policy advisers and the President were also very busy indeed with the SALT II agreement with the Soviet Union, and with the imminent breakthrough on the normalization of relations with the People's Republic of China. It is difficult for a government to work effectively on several fronts even under the best of circumstances, and the American government was overloaded. September and October—the two crucial months in the drama—passed without a single major American initiative in Iran.

THE HALFHEARTED APPLICATION of martial law by Sharif-Emami not only failed to quell the spreading hemorrhage in Iran, but actually encouraged the opposition to take more drastic action. Over the course of the two months of the new government, the opposition forces coalesced into a coherent force for the first time, and by mid-October the shah recognized that his own autocratic rule had come to an end. Henceforth, it was merely a question of whether he could salvage some part of his power.

The clearest sign of a basic change in the nature of the opposition was the siege of strikes, which reached dangerous levels by mid-October, when for the first time in recent history there was a serious possibility that Iranian oil production could no longer be maintained. By the end of October the oilfields were virtually paralyzed. This new, devastating tactic showed the markedly increased strength of the anti-shah forces, now firmly in league with Khomeini.

The ayatollah's enhanced control over events in Iran stemmed from the shah's continued vacillation, and also from a fortuitous development. Early in October Khomeini left Najaf, for reasons that have never been explained, and went to Kuwait. In all probability, Sadaam Hussein had been convinced of the necessity to remove Khomeini from Iraq lest the Iranian situation get out of hand, but it is also possible that Hussein was reacting to the ayatollah's own wish to find a more effective base of operations. In any event, Khomeini was not permitted to stay in Kuwait—a country that had often been well served by the shah—and he reportedly considered going to Algiers before finally settling on France as his destination. The French government learned of Khomeini's decision in time to block his arrival if they had so desired, but after consultations with Tehran, they ascertained that the shah had no objection to having his arch-rival in western Europe, and Khomeini was permitted to come to Paris, through Orly Airport, on October 6.

Of all the shah's mistakes, this was perhaps the most serious, for it transformed the command and control of the revolutionary movement. Even following the Algiers Treaty, communications between Tehran and Najaf were uncertain and slow. To be sure, Khomeini managed to get most of his messages into Iran on the ubiquitous cassettes that were paid for by funds from the bazaar and distributed by the mullah network, headed by the Ayatollah Muhammad Beheshti in Tehran. But as the conflict moved into the decisive phase, such a rudimentary system of communications was insufficient. The move to France solved the problem, for the small villa in the Paris suburb of Neauphle-le-Château to which Khomeini moved was located conveniently in a country with advanced communications systems and, above all, with an attentive media that was in itself a direct line to the Iranian masses. Henceforth the sermons and instructions of the Ayatollah Khomeini would arrive almost instantly in Iran by telephone, radio, television, and the printed press. Significantly, even when the rash of strikes was most effective, there was never any action against the telephone system. Calls from Paris to Tehran went straight through. In addition, Khomeini discovered one of the secrets of the late twentieth century: the mass media of the bourgeois countries can easily become the tool of a revolutionary movement. In the case of Iran, this willing tool was called the British Broadcasting Company. From his arrival in France to his return to Tehran, Khomeini was the object of saturation reportage by BBC correspondents. And although the shah's supporters—particularly the generals—were convinced that the several daily BBC broadcasts to the Middle East containing the latest thoughts and wishes of the ayatollah were evidence of collusion between the British government and the revolutionaries, there was a far simpler explanation: Khomeini was good copy.

Thanks to such attention, Khomeini suddenly became a real person to the Iranians. It must be recalled that, prior to the autumn of 1978, Iranian newspapers were not permitted to print his photograph, and while his cassettes were played in the mosques on Fridays, Khomeini remained a remote figure. Not only was he a disembodied voice, but his message—couched as it was in dense theological prose—was not of the sort readily packaged as a guide to daily tactics. All this changed in October. Now he was seen to be not only a grand ayatollah but a commander, a highly picturesque individual with charismatic qualities that astonished even his most devoted followers.

Ever since Khomeini's success, the question of French assistance has been raised. Andrew Young, who at first hailed the Iranian revolution, later attributed the success of the revolutionary movement to the French government and its media. How could the French have given Khomeini such a superb platform from which to launch his appeals? Why was he not muzzled or expelled from the country? And what was the degree of cooperation between the government of President Giscard d'Estaing and the Khomeini movement?

The last cannot be fully answered yet, for the Elysée is understandably reticent about the matter, especially with foreign researchers. But enough is known to be able to state with some confidence that French complicity was far less than generally suspected, even though it was undoubtedly far more than the shah's supporters would have wished. Giscard's original reaction to the arrival of the ayatollah in France was concern and irritation. The situation was one he would have preferred not to face, for to block Khomeini's request for entry would have antagonized his own Left, by then solidly behind the shah's opponents. On the other hand, to permit Khomeini to set up his revolutionary headquarters in France risked antagonizing the shah, with whose government the French had not only close working relations but many lucrative contracts. The problem at first seemed to be solved in Tehran, when the shah encouraged Giscard to let Khomeini enter. But the shah evidently expected Khomeini to vanish in the welter of political activity in France, not to become an international celebrity. Mohammed Reza overestimated the ability and desire of the French government to keep the ayatollah under wraps.

Once Khomeini began to issue his relentless calls for the mobilization of the Iranian masses against the shah, the French bureaucracy was divided on the proper method of handling the situation. Those who were most sympathetic to the shah pressed for the expulsion of the ayatollah and his entourage, while the professional foreign policy establishment at the Quai d'Orsay suggested that a more prudent course was in order. If Khomeini won his struggle, there might be advantages to having granted him asylum and friendship; whereas if the shah eventually used force, Giscard could always say he had only followed the lead of the shah himself. And there was the possibility that under a Khomeini-inspired regime, France might replace the United States as Iran's key Western friend. This would give the French the immense satisfaction of having both guessed right and outwitted the Americans. Last of all, the presence of Khomeini in France made it possible for the first time to gain invaluable information about the ayatollah and his associates. For all these reasons, Giscard—like every other actor in the drama with the exception of Khomeini—sat and watched.

Rarely has a residence been so closely surveilled as the ayatollah's temporary home in the Paris suburbs. In the nearly three months of his French sojourn, Khomeini's guests were carefully noted, the movements of his associates were watched, and communications of all sorts were probably intercepted. At least two governments were involved in this surveillance: the French and the American. The CIA rented a house not far from Khomeini's, the better to obtain first-hand information; the French were able to use the full range of intelligence collection techniques on home territory.

The results of these inquiries were not reassuring to the French authorities, for they suggested that Khomeini's entourage was well connected to foreign organizations that were not considered close friends of the West. The most distasteful of Khomeini's assistants was Sadeq Ghotbzadeh, later to become foreign minister of Iran. Ghotbzadeh came from a good family—his father was a well-to-do lumber merchant—and had become a world traveler at age twenty-four. Like his comrade-in-arms Abol Hassan Bani Sadr, Ghotbzadeh had spent time as a professional student, when he organized anti-shah activities at Georgetown University in Washington in the 1960s. Early in the seventies he was granted a Syrian passport and passed into the network of Middle East activism. While ostensibly involved in journalism (first selling newspapers in Beirut, later reporting for a Syrian magazine in Paris), he was one of Khomeini's couriers, carrying money from Libya and the PLO to Najaf, and from there to Tehran. Well known to Qaddafi in Libya, trained by the PLO in revolutionary organization and techniques, Ghotbzadeh went to Najaf in 1977, and accompanied Khomeini to Paris.

The French collected an enormous dossier on Ghotbzadeh, whom they considered particularly susceptible to blackmail because of his notorious participation in the debauched nightlife of Paris. He was in regular contact with the KGB *residentura* in Paris, and also with very high-ranking members of both the French and Italian Communist parties. The latter connection was particularly significant to French authorities, for the Italian Communists had always been given considerable responsibility for diplomatic missions in the Middle East on behalf of the Soviet Union, and Ghotbzadeh's contacts with the Italian PCI reinforced the suspicion that he might be working with an international Communist network. In time, most French analysts concluded that Ghotbzadeh was simply an opportunist, seizing whatever chance seemed most attractive at the moment. At the very point when he was in constant touch with the KGB, Ghotbzadeh twice attempted to arrange to talk to a leading CIA official. The request for permission for the American to make contact with Ghotbzadeh went all the way up to Stansfield Turner in Washington. It was ultimately denied, presumably because the policy at the time was to avoid contacts with the shah's enemies.

The combination of the observed behavior of people like Ghotbzadeh and the highly visible actions of Khomeini (despite a verbal agreement with French authorities that he would avoid blatant political activity) led some top French officials to urge Giscard to expel the Khomeini group. Giscard reportedly concurred in mid-November, when a formal document was prepared for his signature. But the expulsion was never carried out. Just as the decision was about to be formalized, word reached the French foreign ministry that the Iranian ambassador to Paris had stated that his government did not wish to see the ayatollah expelled. This message caused considerable consternation in some quarters in Paris, and a leading government official contacted the shah directly in order to be certain that the monarch had not been betrayed by one of his own people. The word from Tehran was the same as before: the Iranian ambassador had carried out the instructions of Mohammed Reza. Under the circumstances, Khomeini was permitted to stay, even though he was certain he would eventually be driven out of Paris. (In December, he asked for, and received, permission to go to India, his birthplace.) The French concluded that the shah would not move against Khomeini.

The shah was in fact now attempting to share power with his ancient foes in the National Front. In mid-October he had announced: "If it could be useful, I would play a less active role." Enlisting former Prime Minister Ali Amini and Ambassador Zahedi as his emissaries to the opposition, he tried to put together a coalition government, and there was even some talk of a constitutional monarchy. But the moment had passed for such a compromise solution; not a single opposition leader endorsed the mid-October proposals. Instead, one by one, they passed into Khomeini's hands. Bazargan went to Paris on October 22, and announced full support for the ayatollah; a week later, National Front leader Sanjabi did the same. At month's end the Ayatollah Shariatmadari, previously considered to be "the shah's ayatollah" and the most influential Shi'ite leader in Iran, endorsed Khomeini: "Our demands are the same."

In the first week of November there were student riots at the University of Tehran, and they quickly spread into the city. Banks, theaters, and the British Embassy were set on fire, and soldiers opened fire on student rioters, killing several of them. Patently unable to guarantee a minimum of order, and having lost credibility, Sharif-Emami resigned under pressure from the military, who now demanded that the shah meet the challenge with the only resource that remained: the armed forces. The shah approved the creation of a military regime.

This decision was taken only after careful soundings in Washington. Having tried unsuccessfully to get through to Carter, the shah arranged for a conversation with Brzezinski, who called Tehran on November 3 through the switchboard of the Iranian Embassy in Washington. Brzezinski's message was encouraging: The shah could take whatever measures he deemed necessary with the full assurance that the American government would "back him to the hilt." Brzezinski later told friends that the shah should never have had any doubts about American support, and that American approval for a military government—and all that that implied—was unreserved.

It was not so. There were grave reservations in Washington about a military government, especially if it used the armed forces to smash the opposition. But even if there had been total support for such a solution, matters had been permitted to reach a point where considerable force would have to be used if the revolution were to be thwarted. This was the consequence of the events of September–October, for if the military had been deployed in September or early October, in all probability it would have restored order without the feared bloodbath. Before the unification of the revolutionary forces in October, and the devastating effects of the strikes in the same period, military force could have been directed against limited targets with fair prospects of splitting the opposition. It is unlikely that the variegated elements would have maintained their coherence and determination under such pressure, especially if the domestic actions were combined with a strong appeal to Giscard either to mute Khomeini's voice or have him removed from France. The opposition leaders themselves expected such a move, for it had always come in the past. It was not until they became thoroughly convinced that the shah would not use violence that the opposition leaders joined irrevocably with Khomeini to demand the full price of Mohammed Reza and the Americans: the termination of the dynasty and the creation of an Islamic state.

Mohammed Reza was not in fact capable of such actions in the autumn of 1978, if indeed he had ever been. He would have deployed force only at American insistence, and throughout the year Jimmy Carter shrank from such a solution. It is hard to imagine Carter approving American calls for military action in September or October, when the government in Washington had not even taken full cognizance of the Iranian crisis. This meant that Carter and his advisers had to design policy options under the worst possible conditions in November.

THE MILITARY GOVERNMENT was appointed on November 5, under the premiership of General Gholam Reza Azhari, the chief of staff. Like most of the other generals, Azhari had little personal following, either among the troops or in the general public. And like almost all of the shah's top officers, he was not suited to a position of true leadership, having learned from a lifetime of first-hand observation that success in Iran was achieved by telling the shah what he wanted to hear and scrupulously carrying out the monarch's every whim. The shah's policy of refusing to take decisive action was carried out to the letter, thus demonstrating that not even a military government was capable of establishing order in the country.

The Azhari government was military only in the most technical sense, a point the prime minister was at pains to stress from the outset. While he wanted it known that his government could effectively establish order with its considerable might, "we do not want to use it." In Azhari's own words, his was "not a military government as known elsewhere in the world."[6]

Rather than take a last stand, the shah continued his backing and filling. In his public announcement of the new government on national television, he spoke of his own role in greatly diminished terms. Instead of calling himself *Shahanshah*—the king of kings—he referred to himself only as *Padeshah*—the king. He spoke of the need to cleanse the government of corruption, and to expand the liberties of the citizenry. He admitted that the strikes and demonstrations of the previous months were "quite justified," and promised to avoid a repetition of past errors. Investigations into charges of official wrongdoing—reaching even to the royal family—were extended, and it was conceivable that the shah himself could be the object of investigation. The hapless Nassiri was arrested, along with several other military figures and former Prime Minister Hoveida. All this encouraged the revolutionary forces, who saw that the military was incapable of meeting their challenge. There was little in the way of military action to quell the anti-shah demonstrations, or a new wave of strikes that virtually shut down the oilfields again within weeks of the installation of the Azhari government.

To make matters worse still, Azhari and his fellow generals proved administratively incompetent in the extreme. Unused to making decisions of such magnitude and complexity, and ill-prepared to oversee the operation of a vast economic infrastructure, the military men placed in office by Azhari were overwhelmed by their tasks.

Meanwhile, the revolution swept up the citizens of the country:

> A friend told me how a group of professors at the University of Tehran decided to form a society for freedom of speech in November 1978. Within two weeks they realized they were so overtaken by events that they changed the formal purpose of their society to the abolition of the monarchy and the establishment of a republic! But such an ex post facto adjustment did not enable Tehran's professors, any more than the liberal or socialist intellectuals in general, to establish a grip on the popular avalanche that had gathered momentum under the direction of the religious party.[7]

There was no longer a moderate force in Iran capable of establishing a government that was not acceptable to the Ayatollah Khomeini. Indeed, the strength of the moderates was generally overrated, by themselves and by most foreign observers. But even if there had ever been a chance for men like Sanjabi and Ali Amini to placate the popular discontent and stop the revolutionary force short of its most extreme objectives, that possibility was not realistic by early to mid-November. The only way that men like Sanjabi and Amini were going to head an effective Iranian government was to be installed by a military organization that had established order in the country. And that action, in turn, awaited a decision in Washington.

The American government turned its full attention to Iran upon the formation of the Azhari government in early November, by which time the foreign service officers in both Washington and Tehran were in a state of considerable alarm. Sullivan resumed his highly pessimistic reporting in late September. In the following month, at the same time that the shah was exploring the possibilities of forming a coalition government involving leading opposition figures, the ambassador recommended that the American government get directly involved in the process. He argued that the shah's one-man rule was doomed, and that American interests were best served by a compromise between unreconstructed shah supporters and the radical religious figures. Embassy officials were in contact with some of the mullahs and ayatollahs, and were given to believe that there were some influential religious leaders who were not enthusiastic about Khomeini's extreme Shi'ite ideas. There were also powerful bazaaris who were concerned about Khomeini on more strictly economic grounds, fearing that the implementation of rigid Islamic moral codes would cost them money, both because some traditional but questionable methods might be punished and because an extremist Islamic state threatened to frighten off Western business. The heads of the bazaar guilds tended to favor Shariatmadari, as they said to contacts who relayed the information to the embassy. Curiously, the bazaaris had trouble making direct contact with top embassy officials.

Although Sullivan did not know of the shah's disease, he was well aware that Mohammed Reza, on his own account, would never call for the use of the iron fist. Sullivan therefore concluded that the only way out, short of the triumph of Khomeini or the unlikely use of the military, was to launch an American effort to mediate the conflict. Sullivan argued, first in cables, then—after it became evident that everything in cable form would find its way into the press—via secure telephone and telecom links with Cyrus Vance, David Newsom, and Deputy Secretary of State Warren Christopher, that the

Americans had to attempt to build a barricade against the ayatollah. Sullivan believed it might be possible to rally the military behind a government involving National Front leaders, other moderates like Bazargan and Bakhtiar, and some of the more reasonable mullahs. But if such a plan were to be enacted, it would be necessary to coordinate with everyone concerned: the shah, who would have to step aside at the crucial moment; the moderates, who would have to form the government and then hold firm against the whirlwind; the military leaders, who would have to transfer their loyalty from the dynasty to something new; and finally, the mullahs and the ayatollah himself.

Sullivan sent off variations on this theme throughout October. On November 11 he fired off a "Cherokee" cable—a secret State Department channel for very limited distribution—suggesting that the Americans make contact with Khomeini in Paris for substantive talks. There was no reply from Washington. Increasingly desperate, Sullivan then sent another communication that unless he was advised to the contrary, he would initiate such discussions with the various forces in Iran. Again receiving no instructions, he established contacts with some of the leading religious figures (including the Ayatollahs Beheshti and Shariatmadari) and some generals (above all, General Abbas Gharabaghi, who would later play a crucial and highly controversial role). But the ambassador's initiatives were never part of an overall policy; with the exception of one proposed secret mission that was canceled at the last moment in January, the Americans never followed through on Sullivan's proposals.

Why was there no action from the President? The major philosophical objection to Sullivan's proposals, like those to American initiatives to unleash the armed forces, was that they required a massive American intervention in Iranian internal affairs. The Sullivan plan required the American government actually to facilitate the fall from power of a loyal ally. And while this well suited those who had long resented the American relationship with the shah, it offered very limited prospects for success. Moreover, it was argued by Brzezinski and his supporters, if the plan required the support of the Iranian military, why not use it for a proven friend?

Whatever the merits of Sullivan's position—and he had many backers in the State Department—the Carter administration was in no condition to formulate and implement policy on Iran. The basic problem throughout the crisis was that the President was notable for his absence. Carter never took an active role in the discussion, never gave any clear indication of the kind of solution he favored, and never put the question of Iran into the general context that would have aided the policymakers at lower levels in formulating options. Thus the American foreign policy establishment spun its wheels, each individual considering the problems according to his own passions and interests, not knowing which way the President was leaning.

There were also problems of organization. The number of persons involved in decisionmaking oscillated wildly between a small select group organized in early November by Brzezinski (the so-called Special Coordinating Committee—SCC—composed of Brzezinski, Vance, Brown, and Turner, with Schlesinger joining for four or five meetings in November and December) and large groups—notably one under Newsom's chairmanship—that ultimately included over forty people in what one foreign service official called the largest discussion of specific policy he had witnessed in three decades of government service. This larger group met only twice, once the futility of attempting to make policy in such a cumbersome committee became evident, and the SCC became the true focus of discussion and planning. Individuals such as Walter Mondale, David Aaron, and Gary Sick were brought in from time to time, and there was also a so-called mini-SCC, which was enlarged to include such people as Newsom and Precht. But in the end—as always when tough decisions have to be made—the crucial group was small, and the final instructions awaited the President.

No consensus emerged from the SCC discussions. Having consulted Precht and Newsom, Vance reflected the State Department's conviction that "the shah was the problem." By this they meant two things: the shah was weak, and thus incapable of recapturing the obedience of the Iranian people; and the shah was hated, thus making him politically unacceptable. The faster he left the scene, the better, so that the Iranians could decide upon a successor regime. Newsom later told an admiring interviewer from *The New Yorker* magazine that "no one realized the dedication of his opponents, how much the man was hated, and how much he had lost touch with the situation in Iran." After the debacle, Newsom's assessment of the American intelligence failure was not that it had misguided the government about Khomeini, nor that it had failed to diagnose the shah's fatal illness, but rather that it had failed to identify the shah's "limitations . . . particularly his failure to realize that he had lost the support of important segments of his society—the middle class, the people in the bazaars, and others."[8]

The fact of the matter was that, aside from Brzezinski and Schlesinger, the President's top advisers had no great fear of the shah's opponents, for they were convinced that the National Fronters were stamped out of a Western social democratic mold. And since the National Front and other similar groups were believed to represent the guiding force of the opposition movement, many policymakers in Washington viewed the removal of the shah with equanimity. Indeed, early in November when the shah was asking for American support of the switch to a military government, a draft of a cable to Sullivan was prepared by the State Department, calling for the ambassador to tell the shah he should consider transferring substantial power to a broad-based civilian coalition. In the event, Brzezinski had the cable killed, and substituted his own personal message to the shah, supporting the Azhari government. But within weeks, Patt Derian had dispatched her deputy, Steven Cohen, to Tehran to ensure that Sullivan would continue to remind the shah of America's commitment to human rights, and that the Iranians would not be subjected to a savage repression.

The department's analysis was accurate up to a certain point: the shah's presence was certainly inflammatory, and he was surely the core of the problem. One had only to listen to the BBC's coverage of Khomeini to confirm the accuracy of the diagnosis. But the remedy proposed by Vance was hardly realistic, for the old men and salon intellectuals who composed the bulk of the National Front were not in a position to challenge Khomeini's mass movement for control of Iran. To be sure, this objection would not have impressed the State Department experts, for they were unaware of the significance of Khomeini and his movement. Given the information at hand, it seemed to many in Washington that the Khomeini forces would nicely round out a grand coalition of anti-shah elements. In keeping with Vance's lawyerly approach to foreign affairs, the Secretary of State and his associates strove for a negotiated settlement in which the American role would consist in removing the major obstacle to the creation of a new, more progressive (and therefore popular) government—the shah and his family. The United States would then exert its influence to bring the Iranian armed forces into a supporting role, thus guaranteeing order and stability.

Unfortunately for this theory, it was unlikely in the extreme that the military would face a *jihad* (holy war) on behalf of some individuals who had neither the legitimacy of the shah nor the messianic appeal of the ayatollah, and with each passing week the notion had ever slighter chances for success. But a variation of the theory had its day in court in the form of a special report prepared for the President by George Ball. A former Under-Secretary of State, former ambassador to the United Nations, distinguished New York businessman, and well-known author of works on international affairs, Ball was recommended to the President by Treasury Secretary Michael Blumenthal and was asked to study the Iranian situation and make recommendations as soon as possible. He arrived in Washington at the beginning of December and prepared his report in the record time of less than two weeks.

Ball had already reached some basic conclusions. He had decided that the shah's decline was irreversible and that the American government had to arrange for a transfer of power posthaste. He recommended the creation of a "Council of Notables," based on the historically ineffective constitution of 1906. Ball believed this to be the best chance: no reformist government headed by the shah could survive, and the only persons in the country with enough political experience and sufficiently solid reputations were those elder statesmen from the Mossadeq period who were still around. They were in their seventies and eighties for the most part, but in Ball's opinion they were the best gamble.

Ball's proposal was not accepted, and may have been killed before it had a chance by being leaked to the press almost as soon as it reached the White House. The reaction from Tehran was immediate and alarmed. Was Ball's opinion that of the President? Sullivan had no informed answer, because he had not been consulted on Ball's project, either to voice an opinion or to provide input into Ball's analysis. The embassy was "cut out of the loop."

The failure of the administration to adopt these recommendations was later explained by Ball himself on the grounds that "the shah was a devil one knew, and one did not know what devil would follow him",[9] but there were other reasons. It was unlikely that Ball convinced the senior policymakers that the fall of the shah was inevitable. The costs of jettisoning the shah were high, and one would have to be confident indeed in one's predictions to take such a drastic step. Was Carter prepared for the domestic and international outcry that would follow such a move? Moreover, there was no agreement that the Council of Notables would work, and no guarantee that the old men who were to compose the body would serve if asked. The ayatollah was claiming veto power over any government in Iran, present and future; would he tolerate such a regime?

The real significance of Ball's exercise was to demonstrate in the most graphic manner that the Carter administration did not have an Iran policy three months after Black Friday. Ball's proposal having been rejected, it still remained to formulate American policy.

Not all Carter's advisers were convinced that the Iranian crisis could only be solved by the shah's departure or his transformation into a constitutional monarch. Both Brzezinski and Schlesinger believed that the fall of the shah would have potentially catastrophic international effects, above and beyond the specific outcome in Iran itself. Although they differed slightly on the proper American response to the crisis, they were agreed on the geopolitical importance of Iran to the United States. Both recognized that with a hostile or even neutral Iran, the American position throughout the zone—and especially in the politically volatile Persian Gulf—would be considerably more precarious. With the removal of Iran as the stabilizing nation in the region, Iraq would automatically become the most powerful military force in the Gulf, and Iraq's relations with Washington were not ones of close friendship and shared interests. But quite aside from the purely military aspects of the situation, both Brzezinski and Schlesinger also believed that the fall of the shah would send a shock wave through the other Middle Eastern monarchies. Given American dependence on the Saudi royal family and the various princes and emirs of the Persian Gulf, a supposed weakening in the reliability of the United States might have grave consequences indeed.

Brzezinski stressed the diplomatic factors, arguing that the United States must not do anything that would suggest a weakening of American support for the shah. His main informant was Ardeshir Zahedi, who spent most of the autumn and winter in Tehran, and who kept assuring the national security adviser that while the situation was grim, the military remained loyal to the shah and could be depended upon to defend him in the event matters became desperate. Brzezinski relied heavily upon Zahedi's assessment of the strength and loyalty of the armed forces, even after the shah left Iran in January. In meeting after meeting, Brzezinski would counter the suggestions of Vance and others that the shah could no longer govern Iran by saying that a force of 400,000 soldiers could certainly prevail over Khomeini's movement. And when the State Department–National Security Council disagreement became increasingly heated, Brzezinski vented his spleen on those, like Henry Precht, who believed that each day the shah remained on the throne only exacerbated the crisis and made the eventual outcome more difficult and more violent.

Schlesinger's emphasis was somewhat different. He stressed that it was not only the shah who was under attack in Iran; there was also a direct challenge to the United States. He accordingly urged the President to demonstrate graphically the American commitment to the shah and thereby discourage other countries—notably the Soviet Union and Libya—from meddling in the Iranian crisis. He also believed that a convincing show of American military power would help bring order back to Iran, since it would indicate to the shah's enemies that there were indeed limits to what they could hope to achieve, and that demands that the shah be removed were not viewed with favor in Washington.

The Energy Secretary was not talking about a purely symbolic act, but arguing that the United States undertake to project considerable military force into the Persian Gulf, in the form of strengthening American forces in places like Diego Garcia, moving aircraft carriers into the area, and stationing significant numbers of Marines within striking range of Iran. Schlesinger knew it would be difficult to convince Vance, Brown, and the President of the need for such an operation, and he first attempted an end run by explaining his position to the leading friends and associates of Carter: Jody Powell, Hamilton Jordan, Charles Kirbo, and Attorney General Griffin Bell. When this failed to produce results, he took his case to the Special Coordinating Committee, and finally managed to get one small gesture approved by the President. At the end of the year Carter agreed with Schlesinger (and Brzezinski) that, at a minimum, the carrier *Constellation* should be dispatched from Subic Bay in the Philippines toward the Indian Ocean. Its first destination was evidently an area near Singapore, where it could continue on toward the Gulf if the President wanted to pursue the gesture. In preparation for this move, a draft cable that would have authorized the voyage to the Gulf was prepared and circulated. But, according to a highly reliable Pentagon source, opponents of the move were so upset that they leaked the contents of the cable. Faced with public knowledge of the plan, the White House denied that it was planning to carry it out, and the President ordered the *Constellation* back to the Philippines. Whether the President made this final decision by himself, or whether he consulted with others, such as Vance, who would probably have approved, is not known. Neither Brzezinski nor Brown challenged the President's decision, and the effect of the short voyage of the U.S.S. *Constellation* was to underline the indecisiveness in the White House.

The *Constellation* affair may well stand as a symbol of the President's unwillingness to consider the Iranian crisis in its full international dimensions, but his attitude was already manifest more than a month earlier, when the Soviet Union felt sufficiently encouraged by events to issue a warning. On November 19, Brezhnev admonished Carter about any thought of intervening to save the shah:

> It must be clear that any interference, especially military interference in the affairs of Iran—a state which directly borders on the Soviet Union—would be regarded as a matter affecting security interests. . . . The events taking place in that country constitute purely internal affairs, and the questions involved in them should be decided by the Iranians themselves . . . the shah has ruled with an iron will.[10]

The import of the Soviet message was ominous: Brezhnev was serving notice on the Americans that there must be no attempt to save the shah from his enemies. In the highly formalized political drama of the Middle East, a direct challenge to American resolve had been issued, offering Carter another opportunity to indicate the depth of American concern and the intensity of American resolve. Instead, Secretary Vance responded the following day with a feeble declaration:

> . . . The United States will continue to support the shah in his efforts to restore domestic tranquility . . . the United States does not intend to interfere in the affairs of any other country. Reports to the contrary

are totally without foundation. We note the Soviet Union has said it will not interfere in the affairs of Iran and will respect its territorial integrity, sovereignty, and independence.[11]

The emphasis of the Secretary of State was on America's policy of nonintervention, and there was not even a response in kind to the possibility of Soviet action. Foreign observers were entitled to conclude that the United States had left the shah to his fate—an impression that was heightened on December 7 when a questioner at the President's press conference asked Carter if the shah was expected to prevail. The reply was: "I don't know, I hope so. This is something in the hands of the people of Iran." And he went on:

> We have never had any intention and don't have any intention of trying to intercede in the internal political affairs of Iran.
> We primarily want an absence of violence and bloodshed, and stability. We personally prefer that the shah maintain a major role in the government, but that's a decision for the Iranian people to make.[12]

By this time, as one of the most acute analysts of the period has written, "everyone who mattered in Iran knew the Americans were dumping the shah."[13] American policy was easier to understand in Tehran than in Washington, where an intense debate was under way. But, as usual, the shah was getting the worst of the bargain. Not only was there no effective demonstration of American power to ward off his attackers, but the litany of American rhetorical support served only to inflame the revolutionaries even further, and the human rights leitmotif raised their spirits.

SIX

The Revolution

THE SHAH'S RULE effectively came to an end during the *Moharram* celebrations in early December, even though the details of his departure and the formal dismantling of his state required more time. *Moharram* reaches a climax on the *Ashurah,* the day that marks the death of the Imam Hussein and other early Shi'ite leaders, and is characterized by mass outbursts of intense religious passion, generally in the form of bloody self-flagellation—"The processions, with blood drenching the garments of frenzied believers, are a revolutionary's dream."[1] It was only fitting that the *Ashurah* should have marked Khomeini's triumph, for it was an anticipation of what was to come.

Throughout November and early December the shah searched for ways to create a broad-based government that would satisfy both his political opponents and his Washington critics. But quite naturally, the greater his willingness to compromise and appease, the more intransigent the ayatollah's demands became. Every time an opposition leader hinted at his willingness to join a coalition, Khomeini thundered his disapproval. There could be no compromise with the "criminal shah." Nothing could be discussed before the shah had been removed from the throne. And the final outcome of the crisis must be the creation of an "Islamic republic." Any refusal to comply with Khomeini's demands would result in a call for *jihad*—holy war —by the ayatollah.

The shah had been negotiating with the opposition through Ali Amini and Ardeshir Zahedi, but to no avail, and in truth there was no longer anything worth negotiating without the assent of Khomeini. On one occasion later in December, Amini proposed the creation of a Regency Council of four persons, including himself and Shariatmadari, a concept the shah accepted in principle. But when Amini raised the question of control over the military, the shah backed off, for he knew that if control over the armed forces passed into the hands of the Regency Council, his power would be merely formal, while Amini knew that if the shah retained control over the military, the Regency Council would be little more than a fig leaf to cover the continuation of the absolutist monarchy against which the revolution was raging. Thus even when the shah had been defeated, he clung to the trappings of power, perhaps hoping his son might yet rule. But the discussions highlighted the central problem of the final weeks: What would the generals do?

The armed forces were being kept on a tight leash. As the *Ashurah* drew near, Zahedi was approached by the leaders of the bazaar, who promised that the mass demonstrations for which Khomeini had called would remain peaceful so long as the military did not attempt to stop them. The bazaaris further guaranteed that the demonstrations would be policed by the *Mujahidin,* and that there would be no destruction of the cities. After consulting with the shah, Zahedi agreed, and the soldiers did not intervene. Two precautionary measures were taken, however: the troops were placed on alert in north Tehran—in case of an attack on the Palace—and the airport was closed to prevent the arrival of Khomeini.

The *Ashurah* marches were the largest in Iranian history, with millions taking to the streets. There was no longer any possibility of saving the monarchy by any but the most extreme means. Henceforth, if there were to be an iron fist, it would have to be brought down on tens of thousands of Iranian heads. And, for the first time, there were some serious questions about the reliability of the armed forces. For months Khomeini had called upon the soldiers to revolt against their officers, and the street demonstrators had taken to placing carnations in the barrels of the soldiers' guns. The young men who composed the military rank-and-file could not remain indifferent to the popular frenzy, and many of them were won over by the opposition. On the *Ashurah,* for example, twelve officers of the imperial guard—generally considered to be the most loyal to the shah— were killed by their own men, and a week later troops in Tabriz refused to shoot demonstrators, joining their ranks instead. While the armed forces were still considered solidly behind the shah, there was now a distinct crack in the military edifice.

There was also some erosion of military support at the top, for while the rank-and-file had been exposed to the revolutionary appeals in the streets, the officers had seen the disintegration of the shah and the absence of any supporting moves from the Americans. Military leaders inevitably began to consider their own options, and the confused American policy probably encouraged some generals to make their peace with the mullahs, or depart. It will be recalled that Ambassador Sullivan had undertaken to place religious and military leaders in touch with one another, in an attempt to produce some sort of military-supported coalition. He himself discussed ways in which the two groups might cooperate, and as early as November had proposed to the State Department that American representatives begin to talk with Khomeini in Paris. While no coalition was created in Iran, Sullivan's initiatives had a certain effect. First, military chieftains like General Abbas Gharabaghi, the commander of the gendarmerie, were encouraged to meet with religious leaders to see what kind of compromise, if any, would be acceptable to both sides. Sullivan's suggestion was hardly necessary in a traditional society like Iran's, for the country's religious and military elites quite naturally had innumerable social and familial ties (Gharabaghi, for example, appears to be Shariatmadari's wife's nephew), so that conversations were going on throughout the crisis. But the fact that the American ambassador actively encouraged substantive talks was highly significant to the Iranians, for it provided an insight into the much-discussed American master plan for Iran. If Sullivan wanted the generals to talk to the ayatollahs, it was reasoned, then the Americans must want a compromise rather than the iron fist. From the standpoint of the generals, this hypothesis was most convincing, for not only did they have no indication from any American official that a military solution was being contemplated in Washington, but there were numerous indications that the U.S. government viewed the possible use of force by the military with antipathy.

There was also positive evidence of American interest in a negotiated settlement with Khomeini. In Paris, a leading member of the
political section of the American Embassy—Warren Zimmerman—
was in touch with Ibrahim Yazdi (Khomeini's long-time "official"
representative in the United States) at Neauphle-le-Château, and
while little was known of the content of their discussions, the fact
that talks were in progress demonstrated that the United States was
willing to deal with the ayatollah.

Where did this leave the generals? They feared only one thing: the
total victory of Khomeini, which would leave them unprotected
against the vengeful wrath of the mullahs. So long as the shah
remained, they knew they were an indispensable part of the state; but
if the shah were to leave, and a new form of government to replace
the monarchy, their position would become more delicate. Furthermore, there was a psychological element of great importance: Every
military officer had sworn an oath of loyalty to the shah, and command of the armed forces had always depended directly upon Mohammed Reza's decisions. The shah was therefore far more than the
chief government official. He was the true center of gravity for the
armed forces, the keystone of the military structure. To remove him
would threaten its stability, and the weaker the shah grew, the faster
the discipline and coherence of the armed forces disintegrated. As
this process gathered momentum in November and December, individual military leaders began to make their peace with the religious
movement, both to safeguard their personal safety and to accommodate to what they saw as the American design.

The military could not remain intact when everything around
them was being drawn into the whirlwind, and by the end of December, Khomeini's forces were beginning to conquer territory. Control
of a few cities passed to the revolution, and with little challenge from
the shah's forces, revolutionary courts were established (ordering the
execution of SAVAK officials and military officers) and revolutionary guards created to impose the ayatollah's rule.

The chaos in Iran was matched by the confusion in Washington.
Having been caught unawares by the Iranian crisis, Carter followed
a time-worn but futile principle, turning to old-timers and special
envoys for better information and advice than he had received from
his own bureaucracy. The Ball project was only one of many such
experiences. Another, to take a typical example, was to send former

CIA station chief Arthur Callahan to Iran to obtain a first-hand report in late November–early December. Callahan had served under Richard Helms, and knew Iran very well, better perhaps than the current station chief, who had been transferred to Tehran from a post in the Far East just a few months earlier. DCI Turner was predictably irritated by what was manifestly an expression of dissatisfaction with the performance of his man on the scene; but the Callahan mission provided little in the way of startling new information, though he did add another voice to the chorus of those who had seen the shah in a state of virtual collapse.

There was also an emissary from the President in the same period. Senate Majority Leader Robert Byrd went to Tehran in November. Byrd's son-in-law was Iranian, and he had many excellent contacts in the country. He was able to discuss the crisis with members of his own family before speaking with the shah, and came away convinced that the situation was far more serious than he had been led to believe in Washington, and that there was at best a slim possibility that the shah could prevail. Byrd was also convinced that the shah was not inclined to take strong action, and reported so upon his return to Washington.

The special representatives, like all the professional analysts, agreed on the essentials of the Iranian situation and were strikingly unanimous about the centrality of the armed forces to any resolution of the conflict. The discussion in Tehran between the shah and Ali Amini over control of the military was repeated in Washington, where there was a debate between those who wanted military support for the shah and those who wanted the armed forces lined up behind a different government. In the Vance-Brzezinski struggle of the moment, Brzezinski appeared to gain the upper hand in late November and early December, although his was a purely bureaucratic triumph, with virtually nothing to show for it on the level of real policy.

Brzezinski entered the debate rather late, by which time a good deal of work had been done by lower-ranking officials in the NSC and the State Department. As has been seen, most of these younger officials felt that the opposition forces were progressive in nature, and hence that even if the shah were to be replaced, it would not be a disaster for the United States. A good deal of official American rhetoric through the late summer and early fall was produced at a relatively low level in the bureaucracy. As Country Director Precht told a State Department audience the following year, it was one of those happy occasions on which a desk officer can have a major impact on policy.

Brzezinski, on the other hand, was concerned about the effects of the shah's decline, and insisted that the American government maintain a solid front behind its Iranian ally. He took steps in November to ensure that American statements followed that line, even though he was unable to get any meaningful action (aside from prying loose the tear gas canisters from the grasp of the bureau of human rights; a task made easier when Vance supported him).

The chief result of Brzezinski's internal success was to provoke a torrent of leaks to the press, mostly from angry State Department officials. These began early in December, and reached a peak by the turn of the year. Some of them were deliberate leaks, while others were the product of a more traditional kind of journalism: a journalist would get a hint from a low-level official, then confront a high-level official with the same material. The results were often spectacular, especially in the case of *The New York Times*'s Bernard Gwertzman, who frequently ended up with quotations that came word for word from secret cables, or, more often, from closed discussions.

On December 7, 1978, the *Times* reported deep divisions within the Carter administration over the threat of Soviet action in Iran. Some administration officials were described as perceiving a Soviet "test" of Western determination around the world, and particularly in Afghanistan, Iran, and the Persian Gulf; others were said to doubt that the Russians were "ten feet tall." Insiders knew that the first "group" was actually Brzezinski, and the second was Vance.

On December 27, with the shah about to schedule his departure from Iran, the administration publicly stated its hope that he would continue to "play an important role" in leading Iran to a new government of "national reconciliation." Gwertzman reported that administration officials privately expressed the fear that "his abdication would raise problems for Iran's military forces," but did not contest the ultimate desirability of the shah's departure from the political scene. This was, in fact, the State Department position. It was certainly not Brzezinski's.

On December 29, the voyage of the *Constellation* was announced. At the same time the *Times* reported the view of American officials that "the future of the shah is unclear." The key question, according to the unnamed officials, was "whether his opponents would agree to a new civilian government, with the shah remaining in power." Gwertzman reported, moreover, that "there is no air of crisis in the administration. President Carter remained at Camp David, where he has been mixing pleasure with work all week, and Secretary of Defense Harold Brown flew to California for a holiday. Zbigniew Brzezinski . . . was also not at work today."

For the shah, who closely followed the American press, the message was clear: The Iranian crisis was not judged significant enough to keep the top foreign policy team of the cabinet at work in Washington. And all the stories reinforced his suspicions that the Americans were plotting something that they were not sharing with him. At the end, when the time had come for him to leave his country, the shah could have learned from *The New York Times* that Sullivan believed he had "emerged as something of a Hamlet figure with only a limited following in Iran." True enough; but Sullivan had yet to tell Mohammed Reza that the American government thought his time was up. And Brzezinski, in constant telephone contact with Zahedi, was still urging the shah to hold firm.

Moreover, there was another major participant in the story: Rosalynn Carter, the President's wife, who carried on a fairly extensive correspondence with Empress Farah Diba, constantly telling her of America's support for Mohammed Reza. These letters undoubtedly encouraged the royal family to believe the President would eventually come to the support of the shah.

The State Department officials, frustrated at Brzezinski's conduct of Iran policy, and suspicious that the national security adviser was involved in some clandestine collaboration with Zahedi and his allies in Tehran, conducted their own efforts in the press. Little if anything seems to have been done by the White House to stop this practice, for there was still a strong feeling that a demand for discipline in the foreign policy community recalled the two previous administrations.

In the midst of this unseemly competition, Energy Secretary Schlesinger entered the debate in a serious way in late November and early December, when he attended several meetings of the Special Coordinating Committee. Schlesinger had previously expressed his conviction that American military power should be projected into the area, and he now added his thoughts about the proper handling of the Iranian domestic crisis. His reasoning was that since it was necessary to reestablish order in Iran, it would be easier to do so (and more desirable, for all the reasons advanced by Brzezinski) with the shah in place than with some successor regime. If that were the case, then the U.S. government needed to tell the shah so in clear language. To date, the shah had received two conflicting versions of American desires, and this had to stop. But who could convince the shah at this late hour that the Americans wanted action?

Schlesinger proposed that a special representative of the President be sent to Tehran—a person with such prestige and authority, and such close ties to the President, that the shah could not possibly doubt the authenticity of what he was told. The special representative would assure the shah that he could indeed believe the Americans would back him up, whatever course of action he chose. Schlesinger felt that if the shah were given proper encouragement, he would eventually choose to defend himself against his enemies, and that he would use force.

Schlesinger realized that the strategy might fail; even if the shah elected to fight, there were no guarantees that the military would prevail at that late date. But sending a special representative would at least make the situation clear to the shah (and those others who looked to Washington) and give him a choice in the matter, whereas a continuation of the previous methods would only reinforce his paralysis. Furthermore, a special representative would be able to explain that the United States could maintain considerable offshore military strength in order to deter any foreign intervention in the event an open struggle broke out in Iran. These were not popular subjects in the White House, but Schlesinger argued that the stakes were very high. Not only America's interests, but those of the entire industrialized West might be at stake in the outcome of the Iranian crisis. When the stakes were that high, the government should be willing to take some risks. If the gamble paid off, there would be substantial rewards.

The proposal was couched in terms that might conceivably appeal to a President who was unlikely to approve any explicit American support for military action in Iran. Such a step would have come close to violating the stricture "no more Pinochets"; Carter did not want Iran to fall under military rule if he could avoid it. While this was undoubtedly what Schlesinger had in mind, he did not propose it, but presumably he—and Brzezinski, who supported the proposal —rather hoped that the special representative would find it possible to whisper in the shah's ear.

Brzezinski agreed with the broad lines of Schlesinger's analysis, and he too knew that any attempt to sell the President on an aggressive course of action would fail. Brzezinski was also sensitive to his reputation as the administration "hawk," and did not want to go on record as advocating force. In addition, he had convinced himself that it would somehow be sufficient to *imply* to the shah that any solution he desired would be backed up in Washington. If anything more explicit were attempted, it would be blocked by State Department officials, just as Brzezinski had blocked the state cable calling for the end of the shah's rule in November. By sending a special emissary, Brzezinski and Schlesinger hoped that the shah would decide to act. For political purposes, dispatching an envoy to Tehran was greatly preferable to having a decision emanate from the White House. If the iron fist was parried, it could always be said to have been the shah's decision (even though the world would view it as an American defeat).

Schlesinger told the President that Brzezinski should go to Tehran as the special presidential emissary. Brzezinski had spoken several times by telephone with the shah, and had been one of his most active supporters in Washington. There could be no question about his authority. A lesser personage would not be granted the hearing Brzezinski would receive, and Brzezinski had the enthusiasm and conviction required to fulfill the mission. Finally, he was in constant touch with Ardeshir Zahedi in Tehran, and was presumably very well informed about the state of affairs in Iran.

Brzezinski did not want the mission, although he approved the concept. In a neat turnabout, he urged Carter to send Schlesinger to Tehran. But the President, after a few days, told Brzezinski that he had decided to second General Robert Huyser from his NATO post in Stuttgart.

THE INTENDED IMPLICATION of Schlesinger's and Brzezinski's proposal for a high-level mission to Iran was that the United States wanted the shah to fight for his throne with all the weapons at his disposal. But Jimmy Carter was viscerally opposed to such actions,

especially in a country where his own administration had criticized
far milder forms of the use of force. The President's methods were
well known to his top advisers: he would listen attentively to all
points of view, closet himself privately with one or two intimates, and
then announce his decision. It is not known with whom the President
conferred before transforming the Brzezinski-Schlesinger proposal
into the fateful trip of Air Force General Robert Huyser, but Vance
was almost certainly consulted, along with Defense Secretary Brown,
and the chairman of the joint chiefs of staff, General David Jones.
In all likelihood, Huyser was selected from a short list prepared by
Jones.

As has been seen, by mid-December, if not earlier, both factions
in the administration were agreed that the Iranian military was the
key to the situation and had to be kept intact if things were to develop
acceptably. If one wished the iron fist, the military would have to
deliver the blow; if one wished a purely political solution—the presumed social-democratic option of Ball and the State Department
optimists—the military would have to defend and support it. The
question now facing the President was therefore which government
did he want the Iranian military to fight for? Or did he prefer to stand
back and watch the tidal wave break, with all the incalculable dam-
age that might produce?

Carter did not desire drastic action taken in Iran, and certainly
would not authorize explicit U.S. support for a military move. On
the other hand, it was imperative that something be done to retain
the Iranian military as a piece on the board. The President found a
seemingly neat solution: he approved a mission by a military man.
But Huyser was not close to the President, and his mission was quite
different from the one Schlesinger and Brzezinski had in mind. The
rationale behind the choice of Huyser was deceptively simple: it was
necessary to keep the Iranian military intact, in the event it had to
be used. To be sure, there was no intention to use it unless there were
signs of an imminent catastrophe—but it had to be ready to strike.
So Huyser's primary mission was to talk to the generals, assure
them of American support, and keep the armed forces coherent and
disciplined.

This, of course, begged the question of the mission of the armed
forces. Whom were they supposed to fight for? The question was
quickly mooted, for the shah announced he was leaving the country,

and was appointing Shahpour Bakhtiar as prime minister, replacing Azhari. Huyser was instructed to encourage the Iranian generals to transfer their loyalty from the shah's regime to the Bakhtiar government, and to hold firm. The indecision in Washington had rendered Schlesinger's plan inoperative; Huyser's mission was in essence what Vance preferred. In early January 1979 Schlesinger decided it was all over. He would play no further major role in the Iranian crisis.

The shah had determined to leave for several reasons, not least of which was his exhaustion and depression. He felt that he deserved a better fate, both from his own people and from his American allies. But even in his parlous condition, he knew the game was up. There were no longer any positive responses to his proposals for a coalition government; no one would serve so long as he remained in the country; the streets were full of mobs demanding his death; and there was no sign of an American initiative to save him. He concluded the Americans wanted him to leave, and Sullivan did nothing to dissuade him.

The shah still hoped he might yet survive the challenge by leaving Iran. In 1953 he had gone briefly into exile, and watched while his friends destroyed Mossadeq. Might history not repeat itself? There was at least one person in Tehran who believed it to be possible: Ardeshir Zahedi. In the final days this oft-criticized jet-setter, playboy, and diplomat demonstrated qualities of courage and loyalty that few expected of him. Zahedi's ostentatious parties at the Iranian Embassy in Washington had become a symbol of the shah's corrupt lifestyle, and gave rise to all manner of rumor. But when the "moment of truth" came, Zahedi left no avenue unexplored to resolve the crisis in a way favorable to his sovereign and to his country. He spoke with the mullahs and the generals, urging moderation on the one, discipline and loyalty on the other. Once he perceived that no political solution was available, Zahedi determined that the military must act, but he was in no position to order a military move; only the shah could do that. And the shah did not greatly admire Zahedi nor completely trust his advice. Mohammed Reza had removed Zahedi's father from the premiership, and feared that Ardeshir might try to vindicate his father by striking at the shah. Thus the shah discounted much of what Zahedi told him.

Without the shah's instructions, the generals would not move. But what if the shah were absent? The generals saw the ayatollah's growing power; what would become of them under the Islamic state? Was it not better to try to gain control of the situation? Zahedi knew of these sentiments, as did every other high-level figure in Iran, Washington, and Paris. Almost everyone expected that the military would inevitably attempt to "do something," rather than permit Iran to fall into Khomeini's hands. Zahedi therefore believed it might be possible to organize a *coup d'état* on behalf of the Pahlavi dynasty, but only if the shah left Iran, enabling his friends to fight for him. And so he implored the shah to leave, to trust that his supporters would take matters into their own hands and make the hard decisions that the king of kings could not face. Accounts differ on whether Zahedi intended that the coup be carried out in the shah's name, or in that of his family (thus permitting power to pass to the crown prince, either right away or after a brief interregnum), but there is little question that he saw the shah's departure as the best chance to save the day.

Brzezinski knew all this in detail from his frequent conversations with Zahedi, but there was always a substantial gap between Brzezinski's grasp of a situation and his ability to make effective policy. The national security adviser well understood that with each passing day the Iranian military became weaker, and he had long maintained that there would eventually have to be a military solution in Iran, at least temporarily. But he forgot that the coherence of the armed forces depended upon orders from the shah. He does not seem to have realized that the Huyser mission was virtually certain to produce the disintegration of the armed forces as an effective striking force. If the American government was going to support military action, it could not wait for the politically acceptable moment; that time would never come. The decision therefore rested on an analysis of the Iranian situation, and that dictated quick action. Nobody can say with certainty whether the armed forces could have won against the Khomeini movement in January 1979. Many soldiers would have defected to Khomeini, and there would probably have been considerable loss of life. But the policy of waiting, while making reassuring statements to the shah and concerned Americans, turned out to be the worst of all. It kept tensions at a peak, exposed the armed forces to the increasingly effective propaganda of the opposition, and pointed up the inaction of the shah and the American President in the most damaging way.

Sometime in late December or very early January the shah told the Americans privately that he had decided to leave the country for a vacation, and arrangements were made for him to fly to California, where Henry Kissinger had arranged guest quarters at the Palm Springs mansion of publisher Walter Annenberg. But by the time he left on January 16 he had changed his itinerary, flying instead to Egypt to stay with his friend Anwar Sadat. Some well-informed Americans believed that the change in the shah's plans showed that he expected a coup to take place as soon as he left Iran, and he wanted to be close at hand. The hypothesis is reasonable, but probably incorrect. For from January 16 until the seizure of power by Khomeini in mid-February, leading Iranian military men tried to contact the shah to obtain permission for a coup attempt, but Mohammed Reza refused either to speak to them on the telephone or to give his blessing to such an operation via third parties. Friends and advisers begged him to give his approval, or at least to step aside and tell the military to do whatever they thought best. But he insisted: no bloodshed, no coup.

Meanwhile, a minor drama was being played out across three continents as Sullivan stressed the mounting urgency of talks with Khomeini. While Schlesinger called for a special emissary to the shah, Sullivan demanded a mission to the ayatollah. The American ambassador agreed that it was necessary to keep the military intact, but he told Vance by secure telephone and telecom that the generals had to have some guarantees if they were not to come unstuck. These guarantees necessarily had to involve the eventual outcome of the crisis, and Sullivan argued that this meant the Americans must reach an agreement with Khomeini. If it turned out that there could be no such agreement, it was important to know that as quickly as possible. Vance concurred, and said that this would have to be cleared with the shah. Sullivan went to the monarch, who endorsed the plan.

In another of the turnabouts that characterized the period, the Americans selected Theodore Eliot—the inspector general of the foreign service and a man with considerable experience in Iran—as the emissary. The arrangements were made for a trip to Paris in early January, but at the last minute the mission was canceled, reportedly because Brzezinski talked the President out of the project in the hours following the Guadeloupe summit, arguing that the mission would further undermine the shah. Of course, no special mission was

required to learn the ayatollah's intentions; these were broadcast to
the four winds around the clock. But in retrospect it is remarkable
that no effort seems to have been made to arrive at a working understanding with Khomeini in January. And while there are a few
knowledgeable people who argue that there must have been such
negotiations between early January and Khomeini's return on February 1, there is no available evidence to support the claim. Ironically, there were secret contacts between the shah and Khomeini,
carried out in Paris by SAVAK's number two, General Kaveh.
Nothing is known of their content.

Brzezinski opposed talks with Khomeini because he was convinced that Bakhtiar's government would succeed. If the armed
forces were the key to the situation, why could they not be brought
around to support Bakhtiar, especially since he was a prime minister
working under the aegis of a Regency Council? The Bakhtiar "solution" was a highly seductive one, combining the element of constitutional legality (the 1906 Constitution had provided for the possibility
of a Regency Council) with that of the iron fist. But it was a mirage.
The constitutional subterfuge would not deceive the generals, and
Brzezinski was told as much by a CIA analyst who flatly predicted
the armed forces would collapse shortly after the shah's departure.
But Brzezinski became enthusiastic about Bakhtiar, and it was in
truth the only solution that the President would endorse.

Huyser therefore had to go to Tehran to ask the generals to
transfer their loyalty to Bakhtiar, but without any guarantees for
their future. The mission was one of extraordinary difficulty, requiring considerable diplomatic skill, knowledge of the country and the
crisis, and insight into the Iranian mentality. Huyser was not well
suited to the task. He was deputy commander of U.S. military forces
in Europe, directly below General Alexander Haig, and had previously made several trips to Iran, usually to discuss military contin-
gencies and to study the ways in which Iranian and NATO forces
would cooperate in the event of international crises. He had no
profound knowledge of Iranian society, did not speak Farsi, was not
on intimate terms with the leading Iranian generals (although he
certainly knew several of them), and was not familiar with the details
of the Iranian crisis. Moreover, while Huyser had a fine reputation
as a military man and administrator, he had not demonstrated outstanding political and diplomatic skills, and—a superficially minor

matter, but one of substantial importance in military circles—he was an air force man who would have to deal mostly with army officers.

Huyser was not enthusiastic about the mission himself, but could not fail to obey an order. His instructions were somewhat vague (the letter to him had been drafted by committee, with Brzezinski, Precht, Sick, Duncan, Jones, and Brown all contributing to it at one time or another), but the general direction was clear enough. His instructions arrived in Stuttgart by cable, courier, and telephone. Once his mission had been defined, he left immediately for Tehran, where he arrived on January 3, 1979, for what was officially called a "three-day mission."

The Huyser mission was opposed by his direct superior, NATO Commander Alexander Haig, who angrily complained to General David Jones, David Duncan, Harold Brown, and Brzezinski that his deputy had been taken from him for an operation that could not succeed (and without Haig's input). He warned that Huyser was the wrong man for the job, since a person of considerable political acumen was required at such a delicate moment, and he also predicted that any attempt to hold the Iranian military together through a succession of different governments (or even around a man like Bakhtiar) would only demoralize the generals and produce the disintegration of the armed forces. Echoing Schlesinger's earlier assessment, Haig expressed the view that when confronted by hostile, revolutionary forces, the first obligation was to establish order. In Haig's understanding—without being privy to discussions of the Huyser mission or seeing his deputy's instructions—there was no intention in Washington of asking Huyser to stress the need for order. Despite Haig's strong request that the Huyser mission should be canceled, this suggestion was rejected. He was, however, fully briefed on Huyser's task, which turned out to be rather more complex than had originally appeared.

If the Huyser mission was primarily in keeping with the State Department view that an opposition government with the military solidly behind it was required to defuse the situation, Brzezinski's conviction that revolutions succeeded only when the forces of order did not fight was also represented. Huyser was accordingly told that he must prevent any attempt at a military coup so long as Bakhtiar seemed to have a chance of success, but also that he must prepare a coup, so that there would be a "military safety net" if the situation deteriorated. He was to report every evening to Washington, via a secure telephone link to the Pentagon, where General Jones would receive the call along with either Secretary Brown or Deputy Secretary Duncan listening in. Two note-takers recorded the conversations, and their transcriptions were passed directly to Brzezinski and thence to Carter. Huyser occasionally spoke directly to Brzezinski, but despite his repeated statements to Iranian generals that he was talking every day with the President, he does not seem to have done so.

Huyser was a victim of the Vance-Brzezinski fight, for he was asked to satisfy both American factions as well as to deal effectively with a complex and explosive crisis in Iran. Expected at once to organize and prevent a *coup d'état,* encourage and restrain the Iranian generals, support Bakhtiar and a military organization that had pledged its loyalty to the shah, and master the subtleties of the Iranian whirlwind, Huyser was out of his element. It is unlikely that anyone could have performed this mission effectively, and Huyser was forced to grope through a thicket of operational and political problems from the beginning.

The shah left on January 16, and the generals formally lined up behind the new prime minister. But what kind of support could they provide? With the shah gone, there was no longer any figure in Iran who could command the military, even though a Regency Council had been jerry-built for the occasion. Bakhtiar was always concerned about the possibility of a military coup, and even though he was told by third parties that Huyser had undertaken to prevent any such action from taking place, he retained an ingrained suspicion of the generals. He did not meet with Huyser, for Bakhtiar's contact was with Sullivan. And once again the leaky American bureaucracy in Washington brought bad news to Tehran. *The New York Times* reported that State Department officials had expressed reservations about the new prime minister, given his "limited following in Iran." These same officials, according to the *Times,* indicated that Bakhtiar was well known to the embassy in Tehran, but that the embassy "did not regard Mr. Bakhtiar as a major political figure." These were, in fact, Sullivan's words, and their appearance in the press compromised his ability to deal with the new prime minister, and of course, weakened Bakhtiar's prestige and authority as well.

Bakhtiar's relations with the military were strained from the outset, when he insisted that two of the strongest generals be removed and replaced with more moderate types. Thus Azhari and Oveissi were fired, to be substituted by Najimi Na'ini, Mehdi Rahimi Larejani, and Abbas Gharabaghi as commander of the ground forces, military governor of Tehran, and chief of staff, respectively (Azhari had held the two first posts). Two other strongmen, Manu-chehr Khosrodad and Amir Hussein Rabi'i—of the paratroopers and the air force, respectively—came under tight restrictions. These moves were carried out within twenty-four hours of Huyser's arrival, indicating to the generals that they were likely to be caught between a government that did not trust them and a mass movement that sought to destroy them.

There may have been some talk about a possible coup in the first half of January, between Bakhtiar's selection to head a new govern-ment and the departure of Mohammed Reza on the 16th, but there was no indication of any serious planning. In part this was because one of the major advocates of a coup—Zahedi—lacked the authority to give a go-ahead, and the shah, as has been seen, was strongly opposed. Second, the shah's system of vertical compartmentalization of the military made it difficult for the generals to do joint planning, for they were unused to the coordination necessary for such opera-tions. Third, there was already considerable contact between military officers and the religious leaders, and it must have appeared to many military chiefs that their chances of survival were better by going over to the revolution than by fighting for a leader with a broken will. Fourth, it was a near certainty that by early January some of the generals had made firm agreements with the revolutionaries. Two leading military men were widely rumored to have passed into the opposition camp: Gharabaghi and the sinister Hossein Fardoust. The shah himself accused the two of betraying him, observing that all the other military leaders had either died or fled Iran by early 1980, while Gharabaghi lived on in uncertain circumstances and Fardoust had become the chief of the new secret police, SAVAMA, which had taken over from SAVAK.

Fardoust may well have been a traitor to the shah, and if so his remains one of the most fascinating stories of the period. Selected by the young Mohammed Reza to accompany him to school in Switzer-land, Fardoust rose to the powerful position of court inspector, thus attaining considerable influence over and information about SAVAK and the armed forces. He attended many of the crucial military planning sessions, and was often consulted by the generals when a major decision had to be made. Whenever the subject of a *coup d'état* was raised in January or February, Fardoust was always informed and his opinion solicited. Today many of the survivors from the upper echelons of the Iranian military establishment are convinced that Fardoust betrayed them, and they see his present position as confirmation of his treachery.

The case of Gharabaghi is quite different. After the failure of his mission, General Huyser let it be known privately and publicly that he felt he had been betrayed by Gharabaghi, and hinted darkly that the chief of staff had been in league with the Khomeini forces all along. So far as can be determined, Gharabaghi did nothing of the sort. He was certainly in close touch with the mullahs, but he had done so with the encouragement of Ambassador Sullivan, and hardly for malevolent reasons. Huyser may not have known of Sullivan's actions (he generally disagreed with Sullivan about the state of affairs in Iran), and he certainly did not understand the complex motivations of a man like Gharabaghi. Finally, on several occasions Gharabaghi offered his resignation to Bakhtiar, and once insisted so strongly that Sullivan had to be called in to prevail upon him to remain at his post. This was not the behavior of the ayatollah's "mole" inside the military establishment; it was that of an officer deprived of his commander-in-chief, tossed adrift without any grounds for optimism. There were few people in Iran who believed Bakhtiar could stop Khomeini, and Gharabaghi was not one of them. When the end came, he was saved, probably because of his family ties to Shariatmadari. A year and a half after the revolution, he reached the West.

The fifth reason for the inaction of the military was Huyser himself. It was necessary to support Bakhtiar, and on at least two occasions Huyser warned the generals that any attempted coup would result in the United States "cutting them off at the knees." On both occasions Huyser had been tipped off about plans for military actions. But on the other hand, Huyser had to give the generals some assurance that the United States would not abandon them to the mob, and he promised that at the first sign of violent attacks against the Bakhtiar regime or against military installations, the government of the United States would back decisive action. But the Iranian generals could hardly take this message seriously, inasmuch as the cities of Meshed and Isfahan were already in the hands of the revolutionary guards, and Huyser was not suggesting that they be retaken by the armed forces. Instead of serious military planning, Huyser gave them vague discussions of the possibility that it might be necessary to create a "military safety net" to prevent the country from falling into total chaos. This was never discussed in any detail, nor was anything remotely resembling a plan for concerted military action ever discussed between Huyser and the generals at their frequent meetings.

Some of those Americans who favored the military solution in Iran later pointed out that the possibility of a Washington-approved coup was serious enough for an American oil tanker to have been sent to Band-ar Meshar in January, in the event the armed forces needed emergency supplies. Both Brzezinski and Huyser later said that the tanker contained gasoline for military purposes. That is quite true, but it could not have been used for a coup for the important reason that the revolutionaries—who were in full control of the port—would not permit it to unload. In fact, the tanker remained floating uneasily at anchor in the harbor for several weeks. The cargo was never delivered to its military destination.

The Iranian generals were frankly baffled by Huyser. Like the shah, they assumed that the U.S. government had some sort of plan, but Huyser could not tell them what it was. Relations between Huyser and the generals were not good, since he was forced to work through interpreters and did not have the kind of intimate personal tie to any of the men that is a prerequisite for trust in most parts of the world. Huyser met with the generals—usually about seven in all —virtually every day between January 4 and February 3. The meetings were normally brief, and were almost always at Huyser's request. He worked out of two offices, one in the embassy compound, the other in the Military Assistance Advisory Group (MAAG) headquarters, located in the Iranian supreme commander's staff headquarters. On no occasion did Huyser meet with Bakhtiar—he used Gharabaghi as an intermediary—although he may have had some contact with the opposition.

Present with Huyser was the American MAAG chief, General Phillip Gast of the U.S. Air Force, who stayed on to complete the task after Huyser's hurried departure in early February. Both Gast

and Huyser used Admiral Hassan Habibollahi as their prime inter-
preter, with General Rabi'i of the air force backing up as necessary.
The other Iranian generals with whom Huyser and Gast had regular
contacts included the chief of military procurement and vice-minis-
ter of war Hassan Toufanian, SAVAK head Iraj Moghadam, paratroop chief Manuchehr Khosrodad, and Na'ini of the ground forces.
In addition, General Hashemi Nezhad of the imperial guards and
other officers sat in from time to time. Several of these military
leaders spoke to Huyser and Gast of their concerns, and they insisted
that a policy of simply standing by and hoping the situation would
work out was not likely to succeed. In particular, they pressured
Huyser on three points: Would Khomeini be blocked? Could the
BBC broadcasts be stopped or toned down? And could the Americans help to block the flow of Khomeini's printed and recorded
propaganda into Iran? Huyser conveyed the messages to the White
House via his Pentagon link, but never gave the generals any replies.
The Iranians consequently believed they were not being taken
seriously.

The generals came to the reluctant conclusion that Huyser was not
going to save them. If he could do so, they reasoned, he would have
given them some concrete indication of the plans of his government.
Instead, they got questions about conditions in the country, brave
words about defending Bakhtiar, and occasional hints about the
"safety net." Huyser may have spoken about a possible coup in more
detail with Gharabaghi, but at no time was there any of the systematic planning, organizing, and rehearsing that are required for a
serious *coup d'état*. Yet Huyser repeatedly told his superiors in
Washington that preparations had been made, and that the safety net
could be operational within a day or two of a go-ahead from the
President.

Men like Gharabaghi had spent their lives in a military bureaucracy in which it was necessary to cultivate a certain kind of special-
ized political skill. The Iranian generals had learned to fill their
superiors with confidence by constantly reassuring them that all was
well, and they applied this technique to Huyser. When he asked them
for their opinion of the political situation, they told him what they
believed he wished to hear: All was well, they were solidly behind
Bakhtiar, the armed forces were intact. When he asked if a military
action could be quickly staged in the event of emergency, they as-

sured him they could move in a matter of hours. It was the easiest way to deal with Huyser, for it kept conversation to a minimum, maintained friendly relations, and left the American general in good humor. As time passed, Huyser found it more difficult to gain admittance to the generals' meetings, but the replies to his questions were always the same, even when the armed forces were visibly disintegrating, and when brave men like air force chief Rabi'i feared that his own subordinates might kill him. But the generals eventually concluded that the Americans were not going to block Khomeini; the last hope was that the Americans would at least save the generals.

So it was that Huyser gave the White House highly encouraging information, but the information he transmitted across the secure telephone connection with the Pentagon was not accurate. Operating in a near-vacuum, moving from the embassy to military headquarters and back again at top speed through the streets of Tehran, Huyser had very little contact with the turbulent reality of Iran. Relying almost totally on his conversations with the generals for his information, Huyser inevitably reported that the situation was good and that there was no need to panic. In so doing, he disregarded some of the officers at the military advisory staff, and also Ambassador Sullivan. Huyser was informed by various American officers that the morale of the Iranian armed forces had declined markedly in the previous six months and that discipline might not hold if the military were forced to operate under such high tension without being permitted to strike back. Huyser and Gast were told by several senior officers in the mission that large-scale desertions and mutinies were not unlikely, even among such crack units as the paratroopers (under General Khosrodad) and the imperial guard (General Nezhad). This was Sullivan's view as well.

Huyser elected to believe the Iranian generals rather than the Americans. It is a time-honored tradition within the American military establishment to consider assignment to overseas military assistance advisory groups as a form of penance, often signifying the end of career advancement. Senior officers at such missions are therefore frequently not taken seriously by their peers, and Huyser may have fallen into the trap of viewing the Tehran military advisory staff as a group of "washouts" who were bound to be negative about the Iranian situation. In addition, if Huyser had reinforced Sullivan's gloomy reporting, he risked finding himself on the same road toward private life that Sullivan would travel within a very few months. But the basic reason for Huyser's unabated optimism was the steady flow of encouraging remarks from the Iranians.

From all indications (by which were meant his conversations with the generals), Washington could expect Bakhtiar to succeed. From his first report to the last, Huyser's assessments were upbeat. Indeed, at the very end, when Khomeini had returned in triumph to Tehran and the streets were mobbed with his followers, Huyser flew to Washington and reported directly to the President that everything was going well, that Bakhtiar had every chance of prevailing, that the military was holding together, and that there was no need for drastic action. He did confirm that there was disorder in the streets; but everyone, he said, understood that the first step taken against either the government or the military would lead to instant reaction by the troops. Brzezinski asked Huyser if the coup was still ready to go, as he had repeatedly reported. Huyser said it was ready to go in twenty-four hours; it required only an order from Carter to General Gast.

Huyser's reports were almost completely misleading. The real picture was that painted by the unfortunate Sullivan, who knew that the mullahs were relentlessly gathering strength, that defections among the soldiers were spreading, and that Bakhtiar had failed to obtain even the barest minimum of popular support required to survive. The masses were with the ayatollah; and with each passing day their respect for, and fear of, the military diminished.

Sullivan's messages came through channels similar to those that carried Huyser's reports, and the two men would frequently use the same telephone in Sullivan's residence to call Washington. In one of the more bizarre scenes in recent American diplomatic history, the two men would dine together and discuss the day's developments. After dinner and brandy first one, then the other would call Washington, with almost diametrically different assessments.

That Huyser's reports were taken as gospel, while Sullivan's were rejected out of hand, is tribute to the faith of the President and his top advisers in their newly developed cult of the special emissary and in the Bakhtiar "solution." Sullivan was by then one of the best-informed people in Tehran, but the information he transmitted was bad news, and not acceptable. Huyser, a man with very few sources aside from the frightened generals, was considered to be the ultimate insider, and his information was eagerly awaited and gratefully received. There were many visitors to the White House in the last weeks who told the President and Brzezinski that the news out of Iran seemed grim indeed, and they asked Carter and the national security adviser what the United States intended to do. The President would smile and tell the visitors that if they only had access to the intelligence he was receiving from Tehran, they would not worry. Everything was under control. Bakhtiar was doing well, and the President expected the situation to continue to improve. Brzezinski was rather more colorful in his language, but the message was the same: Don't worry, we have it by the throat. Either things will work out of their own accord, Brzezinski told several people in January and early February (including top congressional leaders), or the military will bring them under control. Those who spoke to him during that period say that Brzezinski was thoroughly confident, certain that Bakhtiar—and the American government—was in an excellent position.

THERE WAS A STRANGE EUPHORIA on each side of the great American debate in the winter of 1978–79, as policymakers from both the State Department and the National Security Council acted as if things were going nicely. The most interesting example of this well-known psychological phenomenon came from those involved in the military assistance program, and was later to be repeated in even more grotesque form in the summer and fall of 1979. In late 1978, American policymakers in the NSC and the Pentagon acted as if there were no reason to worry about the huge military sales program with a country quite clearly on the brink of economic ruin (if the oil could not be pumped, Iran could not pay its bills), and there was a similarly cavalier attitude about the safety of American personnel and property. As early as October 10, 1978, Sullivan had sent a front-channel cable to Washington suggesting that the military program be "cooled down," pending developments; his suggestion was not adopted. Indeed, Gast, as MAAG chief, argued throughout the crisis that the United States should keep its traditionally high profile in Iran.

In many ways the sorry spectacle of American military personnel in Tehran in the winter of 1978–79 recalls a previous retreat from

Saigon. There was no melodramatic rescue of an American ambassador from the roof—in Tehran, Sullivan was taken captive by the mob —but the needlessly large numbers of American troops exposed to hostile Iranians, their deplorable living conditions, and their confusion about the policies of their own government, all recall the last hours of the Vietnam war.

With the virtual paralysis of Iran, some eight hundred American soldiers became superfluous by late November. They had been sent to Iran for tasks ranging from flight instruction to the maintenance of sophisticated equipment. But there was insufficient gasoline for flight practice, most programs were either suspended or closed down, and security could no longer be provided for the Americans, so they left their comfortable barracks and moved into apartments scattered throughout Tehran. Many of them lived through the winter with no heat, and survived almost exclusively on cold C-rations. When it was suggested that some might be sent back to the United States or to another military post outside Iran, Gast invariably insisted the United States maintain its full military presence. As late as January, new servicemen were still arriving in Tehran to face hardships for which they generally were quite unprepared.

A female officer at the American military hospital in Tehran recalled that Sullivan and Gast had insisted that the hospital continue to operate even though there were very few patients, and no obvious reason for existence. The officer later filed an official report in which she observed that "Those of us in the lower echelon . . . felt we were used as political pawns in establishing the U.S. role. . . . Eleven (medical) personnel were kept behind and isolated in the hospital, where they had 2 Khomeini guards for protection." These American troops "were essentially prisoners, and received very little help from the army or the State Department. They had no patients to care for, and a very small active duty population to pretend to support. They were never given any reason for their extension."

Most of the Americans in Tehran had long since suggested to their superiors that the situation was becoming increasingly perilous. In October, for example, Gast had held a meeting one evening with three army colonels, an admiral, an army general and an air force general, and they had discussed the possibility of attacks against American targets. Yet Gast never laid down plans for self-defense, even at military headquarters. One of the American generals felt compelled to ask Gast, "How many Americans will have to die before we do anything?"[2]

The Pentagon became aware of the peril to which American soldiers were being exposed, but was slow to move, even after some fairly dramatic events. A high-ranking officer in the MAAG called Washington one night. He was lying on the floor of his unheated house, the shades drawn and a small kerosene stove flickering in the corner. There were some two hundred Iranians outside, screaming: "Death to the Americans!" and he wanted someone in Washington to know what was going on. On the night of January 28, Air Force Major Larry Davis was shot from behind while unlocking his front door. Fortunately, Davis had carried a pistol and was able to draw it and drive off his attacker, but the incident underlined the very real dangers the American servicemen faced even before Khomeini's return from Paris. And they were encouraged to walk around unarmed, thus increasing their anxieties.

The situation was so bad that one high-ranking officer who was in Tehran throughout the last winter recalls that "MAAG personnel were as close to mutiny as any I've ever seen."[3] When they finally got out of Iran, they did so under equally unnerving conditions. In the words of William Branigin of the Washington *Post:*

> As a result of Gast's attitude, the sources said, hundreds of U.S. military personnel and dependents who remained were forced into a hasty, unseemly, and often tumultuous evacuation after the February 1979 revolution, leaving behind vast quantities of classified records and equipment at U.S. military installations seized by the revolutionaries, as well as millions of dollars worth of other property.[4]

Brzezinski shared in this general refusal to take prudent measures against the whirlwind. Convinced as he was that Bakhtiar was succeeding, he was loath to do anything that suggested a lessening of American support. Throughout November and December Iran was failing to meet its payments. This was due to a variety of factors: with the oilfields shut down, there was less money available; the Azhari government had diverted considerable funds from military purchases to social programs; and revolutionaries in the banks were simply refusing to issue checks for purchases of American military equipment. In mid-December the Pentagon sent Erich von Marbod, the deputy director of the Defense Security Assistance Agency, to Tehran to see what could be done to get the bills paid. Instead of looking for financial solutions, Von Marbod acceded to the entreaties of the top Iranian generals and negotiated a memorandum of understanding that terminated programs amounting to more than $10 billion. It was a highly useful agreement, because it saved the Iranian government from having to default on its obligations, and also cleared away some potentially sticky debris for future relations between the two countries. Not least of all, it saved the American government both money and considerable paperwork; once Khomeini came in, the United States would have had to terminate the programs unilaterally. Nonetheless, Brzezinski was deeply concerned about the negotiations, and held up the agreement for about a week on the grounds that it might undercut the Iranian military. Thanks to strong advocacy from Defense Secretary Brown, the President finally approved the agreement at the eleventh hour, and it was signed on February 3, two days after Khomeini's return from France.

At the same time, a similar euphoria settled over those Americans who felt the shah had been the cause of the trouble all along. When it became clear that the Pahlavi dynasty would not survive the crisis, some of the State Department officials took pains to call attention to what they saw as positive developments. Thus, in mid-December, Henry Precht called the *New York Times* bureau in Washington to make sure that a *Times* correspondent in Paris would cover Khomeini's press conference the following day when, according to Precht, the ayatollah would make some positive remarks about the United States.

In short, the worse the situation became, the harder most Americans strove to convince themselves and others either that the situation was basically all right, or that the impending changes were actually desirable. Instead, what actually happened fulfilled the forecasts of Schlesinger, Sullivan, and Haig. The induced inertia plus the irresistible turmoil in the streets eventually produced the disintegration of the armed forces. SAVAK had been virtually nonexistent since the summer, and the regular forces dissolved in February. At a meeting of the Supreme Council of the Armed Forces on the morning of February 11, Gharabaghi, as the presiding officer, asked the twenty-six assembled generals to evaluate their options. There was little to be done; two days earlier the imperial guard had been routed by Khomeini's guerrillas at the Doshan Tappeh airbase in Tehran, exposing the weakness of what had always been considered the elite force of Iran. Without the slightest hint of activating the celebrated safety net, the generals issued a unanimous statement that "to avoid bloodshed and chaos the armed forces declare themselves neutral in this political conflict and order their troops to return to their barracks."

The Iranian generals had surrendered. Their opponents were too strong, and the Americans offered no eleventh-hour solution. In addition, the junior officers and rank-and-file had disintegrated— part of a process that reflected both the effective techniques of the Khomeini-led movement and the weaknesses of the shah's absolute control of the armed forces. Throughout the early stages of the crisis, top commanders were aware of the need to maintain discipline and morale among their troops. Training exercises were kept on schedule until well into the winter, with the imperial guard and the paratroop units under specially tight disciplinary control. These units, along with the air force, were considered the tough professional core of the shah's military establishment, and in a tight situation were expected to tip the balance in favor of the state.

Elsewhere the situation was more fluid. The overwhelming majority of the troops were "short-termers," with little dedication to the standards imposed upon them. Their educational level, like their salaries, was quite low, and they had few ties to their units or their unit commanders. There was a great resentment against the privileged officers, particularly as the calls of the mullahs started to gain a wider audience. Troop morale began to evaporate in the second half of 1978, when the soldiers' grievances merged with those of their civilian counterparts. By the end, the common soldier felt the same sense of alienation from the imperial system. The economic difficulties that afflicted the civilian population inevitably afflicted the enlisted men as well, since their families were suffering from the high costs of the failure of the shah's modernization programs. Furthermore, the revolutionary leaders used tactics similar to those used on American university campuses in the late 1960s and early 1970s:

soldiers were wooed, not confronted, their gun barrels filled with flowers, their ears with words of solidarity and calls to defect to the movement.

The collapse of the armed forces might conceivably have been slowed if unit commanders at the level of major and colonel had shown greater resolve. But such men were inclined toward caution rather than initiative, for the same motives that had deprived the generals of leadership qualities. Advancement through the military ranks was based on obedience, not independent judgment, and the shah had provided for an elaborate system of informers who watched carefully for any signs of overly autonomous behavior. The Palace was directly informed of activities of officers down to the rank of major, and most intermediate-level officers undoubtedly recognized that any independent activity on their part would be discovered by the shah's "moles" in the barracks. The shah had taken great precautions to avoid a military coup directed against his reign; but this meant he was unable to depend upon the spontaneous loyalty, fantasy, and courage of his officers when the crisis arrived. He had rendered the military totally dependent upon him, from top to bottom. When he failed, the iron fist could not fall.

The American military was little better when it came under direct attack. After the announcement of the "neutrality" of the Iranian military, the streets filled with joyous mobs, and thousands headed for the supreme commander's staff building in downtown Tehran, also the MAAG headquarters. Despite warnings from his junior officers, General Gast elected to keep his men at their posts, even after Admiral Richard Collins—just across the street—had evacuated the naval headquarters and sent his men back to the safety of the embassy compound.

By noon, there were barricades in the street, and when a curfew was declared at 4:30 in the afternoon, Gast found himself trapped in the building. All night long the revolutionaries fired into it, and Gast moved the guards up to his office, thus leaving his junior officers without protection on the lower floors. The following morning a few officers escaped during a lull in the shooting around 6:30, but Gast remained in his office. Later in the day, revolutionary guards took over, and led the Americans into what might be termed protective custody. Gast and the others returned to the embassy, where most of them would be captured again on the 14th. The general, however, escaped this second indignity by finding a safe haven in the communications vault when the attack took place.[5]

Of the group of Iranian generals who dealt regularly with Huyser and Gast, only five survived the revolution. Gharabaghi made an arrangement with the mullahs and was spared; Toufanian went underground, lived on rooftops and in friends' homes for nearly six months, and eventually reached the West; Oveissi, Habibollahi, and Azhari also went to the West. All the others were killed.

As for the Bakhtiar government, it failed to live up to Huyser's high expectations. Four days after his return, Khomeini appointed his own government under the premiership of Mehdi Bazargan. There were frenetic meetings between representatives of the two "governments," but it was simply a matter of time before Bakhtiar fell. He was not destined to have a long tenure in any event, but once again the leaky Washington bureaucracy speeded up the process. Just a couple of days before his fall, Marvin Kalb announced on CBS News that the American government was convinced Bakhtiar's days were numbered, and that he would go "within a day or two." The report was accurate, as was the prediction, and it created a furor in the White House. For one of the few times in his presidency Carter delivered himself of some angry words to his top advisers.

The formal act of resignation took place on February 11, along with the surrender of the armed forces. The mob was now in control of the country, and with the violently anti-American broadcasts from Radio Baku and rumors of an impending coup spreading through the streets of Tehran, the American Embassy came under siege on the 14th. According to some of those who lived through the day, the attack was well disciplined and carefully prepared (Sullivan believed some of the attackers wore scarves associated with the PFLP followers of George Habash). After hurried negotiations with the Ayatollah Beheshti, Sullivan managed to free the embassy, although the *Mujahidin* left an occupying force behind that remained until July, a symbol of the enmity toward the United States that would characterize the Khomeini regime.

The last bittersweet footnote to the failure of the Carter administration to shape an Iran policy during the crisis came early in the morning of the 12th. Sullivan—who had spent most of the night trying to get Gast and the others safely out of the SCS building—

was awakened by a telephone call from Washington. At Brzezinski's urging, either David Newsom or Warren Christopher (Sullivan cannot remember which) had called to activate the safety net. The White House had decided the moment for decisive action had come. But the iron fist was shattered, as Sullivan had long maintained. He cursed, and slammed down the phone.

SEVEN

The Ayatollah's Revenge

IT TOOK KHOMEINI about seven months to bring the country under his control, and from February to September 1979 he demonstrated a masterly tactical touch. Most experts were convinced that while Khomeini might well have had the charisma to become the symbol of a revolutionary movement, he was unlikely to have the political and administrative skills required to stem the whirlwind and govern the country. Many of those who admired the ayatollah expected he would be a brooding presence in the holy city of Qum rather than the creator of a new theocracy. Still others convinced themselves that he was a traditional social reformer with admirable religious convictions. All were proven wrong, although the myths live on in a variety of published and unpublished commentaries on the revolution.*

It might have been expected that Khomeini's impressive victory over his ancient enemy would have driven both American analysts of Iran and those involved in the revolution on behalf of moderate or even radical secular goals to a careful study of the ayatollah's

---

*As, for example, in the series of articles in *The New Yorker* (June 2, 9, and 16, 1980) devoted to David Newsom, in which the occupation of the American Embassy in October is attributed to Khomeini's desire to do something spectacular to save his position after seeing the revolution "fail." In truth, the theocratic revolution had only just entered its decisive phase, and the seizure of the embassy was a symbol of Khomeini's control over it.

world view. Instead, American academics and policymakers, as well as representatives of non-Islamic groups ranging from the National Front to the Tudeh Party and the Marxist guerrilla bands, continued to underestimate Khomeini's political skill and coherent vision. The American and Iranian misperceptions were sometimes linked. Since the National Fronters and their many American friends and supporters in the bureaucracy and the academy had expected Khomeini to abstain from political activity once the shah had been overthrown, they were systematically outmaneuvered, surprised, and finally humiliated by the ayatollah. True modernists all, they could not seriously entertain the notion that the Iranian "revolution" would prove to be a regression to a medieval model. Nor could they be expected to believe that a movement they had hailed as a liberation from the Pahlavis would turn out to be more intolerant, and more successful in mass mobilization, than the shah's regime. In short, they forgot that political enthusiasm—whether secular or religious —has often been successfully mobilized on behalf of fascistic regimes in this century.

The wry comments of Mehdi Bazargan may well stand as emblematic of a general failure of understanding:

> . . . something unforeseen and unforeseeable happened after the revolution. What happened was that the clergy supplanted us and succeeded in taking over the country. . . . If, instead of being distracted, we had behaved like a party then this mess wouldn't have occurred. . . . In that respect, all the political parties . . . went to sleep after the revolution. And that included the parties of the left, which have never been able to attract the masses in Iran and have always remained on the fringes of reality. Yes, it was the lack of initiative by the laity that permitted the takeover by the clergy.[1]

One can perhaps forgive a Bazargan, who had been mesmerized by Khomeini at close hand, and was successfully manipulated by him from February to September. It is more difficult to excuse the scores of others who simply refused to examine the evidence. Even before the seizure of power in February, a Revolutionary Council had been created, composed entirely of individuals loyal to Khomeini. The Council was in effect a shadow parliament, with the enormous advantage of operating in virtual secrecy yet wielding considerable power. With its deliberations carried out in an atmosphere free of public pressure and journalistic surveillance, the Revolutionary Council became Khomeini's state within the broken officialdom in February. And right until November, even leading Iranians outside the inner circle around Khomeini did not know how many members the Council had, how it reached its decisions, or how it implemented its will. Figures ranging from Shariatmadari to Sanjabi complained publicly that the official government was a vast Potemkin village, while real decisions rested with the Revolutionary Council. To take just one example among many, the Iranian ambassador to the United States, Shahryar Ruhani (Yazdi's son-in-law), took his instructions from, and reported to the Council, rather than the foreign ministry throughout the first months. The Revolutionary Council remained Khomeini's legislative body until he could purge the Majlis of all undesirable (that is, nonclerical) elements, at which time he began to transfer power to the parliament.

On February 13, Bazargan announced his cabinet, which contained a mix of religious figures and secular members of the revolutionary movement, including Karim Sanjabi as foreign minister and Dariush Forouhar as minister of labor and social affairs. Cabinet members made repeated announcements of policy, only to find that Khomeini had a different view. The latter always prevailed. On February 18, for example, Bazargan announced that all political parties would be free to operate openly. A few hours later he was forced to amend his policy, following Khomeini's flat statement that Communist activity was illegal. The minister of defense fired the commander of the military police in early July following his public attacks on the government's policies. Khomeini challenged the action, whereupon the defense minister reversed himself and plaintively remarked that "the decision of Imam Khomeini is above that of myself and the government."[2]

Khomeini's policies served several purposes. First, he undoubtedly knew that the early days and weeks after the overthrow of a regime are terribly untidy, characterized by all manner of excess. No leader wishes to be tarnished by responsibility for such actions, and Khomeini neatly made Bazargan theoretically responsible for all activities in this period. Second, with the collapse of the shah's regime, it would be impossible for the government apparatus to function satisfactorily for some time. Here again, the blame fell on Bazargan and the other ministers, while Khomeini could complain that his will was not being carried out. Yet at the same time that he had maneuvered Bazargan and the other National Fronters into an exposed position, Khomeini had managed to retain real power in the various organs of the revolution: council, guards, and courts, plus the ubiquitous komitehs—the local collectives that seized administrative and executive powers throughout the country. Not only did Bazargan have to pay the full price of unpopularity for inefficiency, but he was unable to take any meaningful action. The official government, in Bazargan's bitter expression, was a "knife without a blade."

It is always difficult to identify a person's intentions, and it can legitimately be argued—as the luckless Bazargan did—that Khomeini simply seized his opportunities. Yet one must then explain away the singular correspondence between Khomeini's writings and the Islamic state he created. While men like Bazargan and Sanjabi were earnestly reassuring themselves that the ayatollah agreed with their goals of a modern, social-democratic society, Khomeini himself was ensuring that Iran return to a more ancient code of harsh and summary justice, ruthlessly enforced and irresistibly supported by the religious enthusiasm of the masses.

By the time the Bazargan cabinet was sworn in, the country was effectively in the hands of the revolutionary organs. There were well over one thousand komitehs, almost always headed by a mullah or ayatollah, with little in the way of coordination among themselves, but apparently under at least a modicum of central control from the Revolutionary Council. The komitehs "for a time virtually ran the country."[3] They had been crucial in organizing the paralyzing strikes during the shah's last months, and continued by taking matters into their own hands during the first months of the new order. If the government appointed persons who did not meet with the approval of the komitehs, they were simply removed from their offices. If there was resistance, the komitehs could call upon their paramilitary arm, the revolutionary guards. The guards were the vigilantes of the Iranian revolution, relentlessly searching out enemies of the ayatollah, shutting down government buildings or Tehran Airport when it suited their purposes, and demonstrating that Bazargan and his associates were unable to control them. The guards—probably organized around the remnants of the old Islamic *Feday'i* by the Ayatollah Khalkhali—became the shock troops of the regime in dealing later in the year with efforts by ethnic groups like the Kurds, the

Baluchis, and the Turkomans to achieve some degree of autonomy.

Finally, there were the dreaded revolutionary courts, directly under Khalkhali. By the end of 1979, this singular personage was known by two nicknames: "the cat-killer" and "the butcher of Kurdistan." The first label came from stories according to which Khalkhali had served time in a mental institution because of his habit of compulsively strangling and dismembering cats; the second derived from his activities during the campaign against the Kurds in the summer of 1979, when he sentenced several hundred of them to death before firing squads. Although Bazargan was the prime minister, Khalkhali had by far the greater influence over events; despite numerous protests from the cabinet, the revolutionary courts continued their grim work. In an interview in early summer 1980, Khalkhali estimated he had ordered the execution of four or five hundred sinners.[4]

Taken together, the revolutionary institutions represented a formidable apparat. And the toll of victims was impressive; according to a conservative estimate, the first seven months of the ayatollah's reign saw more than six hundred people die at the hands of Khalkhali's tribunals, not to mention the hundreds more who fell victim to the often spontaneous outbursts in the streets. Among the victims were former SAVAK chiefs, former Prime Minister Hoveida, dozens of leading military officers, and other members of the shah's government. Nor was the killing solely on one side; several leading mullahs were murdered by a shadowy organization known as "Forqan," which had attracted some attention in the last years of the shah. Ostensibly an anarchistic Shi'ite movement that held Khomeini unworthy to lead a true Islamic revolution, most observers believed Forqan to have been the creature of SAVAK. But then, after a few months of Khomeini, every unpleasantry in Iran was held to be the creature of some malign foreign power, the Soviet Union, the United States, Great Britain, or Israel being the favorite devils. Agents of the CIA, the KGB, and Zionism were purportedly omnipresent in Iran, slowing oil production, frustrating efforts to distribute the vast quantities of imported food for the poor (which did not include frozen meat, because Khomeini believed it to be part of a conspiracy to trick Iranians into eating cadavers), and spreading disorder. Such paranoia was not unknown to Persia—the shah had always explained trouble by alluding darkly to Communist plots—but the intensity and quantity of Khomeini's warnings about "satanic agents" were extraordinary.

Alongside the systematic weakening of the moderates and the mobilization of the masses on behalf of extreme Islamic fundamentalism, Khomeini adopted two other techniques to guarantee his success: careful attention to the most immediate needs of the very poor, and unrelenting war on anything that smacked of the West. The first was relatively elementary. Despite some loss of capacity, Iranian oil production continued to bring money into the country. This was redistributed in ways calculated to help the new regime. Over Bazargan's protests, Khomeini announced that the poor would not have to pay taxes or fees for public transportation; in September the exemption was extended to basic utilities. Moreover, to keep the oil moving, the government sharply raised the salaries of the workers in the oilfields. Such measures, combined with the seizure of houses and lands of the former elite and then turning them over to the poor, sufficed to keep Khomeini's popularity high among the lower classes.

To be sure, the official statistics on the Iranian economy were grim. Unemployment was at a staggering 35 percent by May 1979, industrial production was at a standstill, and within the first year the value of Iranian currency dropped by 50 percent compared with the dollar. But this did not have the consequences for Khomeini that far milder forms of economic dislocation had had for Mohammed Reza, partly because of a great disinterest in the industrial development of the country. Neither the ayatollah nor his leading advisers (such as Bani Sadr) believed that industrialization was desirable. There was no lack of money—oil, with prices rising more than 50 percent by the end of the year, took care of that—and Khomeini simply distributed the spoils in politically astute ways. A second reason for the lack of economically inspired opposition to the ayatollah was that the nation's difficulties paradoxically favored the traditional bazaaris. If the banking system was wrecked, that merely permitted them to charge higher interest rates (and exchange rates) than before for their own money; if imports on luxury items were terminated as part of the anti-Western campaign of the new regime, that made their own stocks more precious. And Khomeini carefully kept his vengeance far from the bazaars. Even though Khalkhali had carte blanche to try anyone he chose on charges of "corruption," this was rightly interpreted by the head of the revolutionary courts as license to purge the elite of the previous era, rather than an invitation to bring equity into the bazaaris' transactions.

The major long-term task that the ayatollah set for himself was the eradication of Western culture from Iranian mores and institutions. The most celebrated of the early measures was the ban on music, which attracted international attention, but the relentless extirpation of the achievements of the White Revolution was carried out in all fields. Western books were removed from the schools, and were sometimes burned. Western dress, above all for women, was once again pronounced provocative, and women were urged to wear the chador. As early as February 26, Khomeini had recommended a review of the 1975 Family Protection Act, which had permitted women to sue for divorce and restricted polygamy.

Henceforth, Iran was to be an "Islamic republic," by which Khomeini had always meant rule by the mullahs. The referendum of March 30–31, which officially sanctioned the new state, was explicitly taken to be a religious act. Those who voted against it were voting against Islam itself. And the ayatollah reserved his greatest scorn for those "Westernized intellectuals" who wanted a republic along Western lines. These were people who were contrary to the "spirit of Islam." Their protests against the wave of summary executions that washed over Iran were likewise held to be a violation of the very concept of the Islamic state; Khomeini demanded the elimination of "all European criteria built into the judicial system." There was to be no appeal from the decision of an Islamic judge: "every hearing must end in a final absolute decision in a single phase." Of all Khomeini's institutional changes, this was to be the most difficult, and the most significant, for if finally achieved (and in mid-1980 there were still some courts functioning along prerevolutionary lines), it would give full control over daily life into the hands of the clerics.

Thus, despite the considerable enthusiasm of his "progressive" supporters and allies, Khomeini made no effort to conceal his intentions once returned to Iran. If he can be accused of deception, it would be while still in Paris, for on January 11 he told reporters that neither he nor the other religious leaders would hold top positions in an Islamic republic. But by the end of February there was no mystery about his intentions to carry out the design spelled out in his writings.

A further indication of Khomeini's intentions—as well as an insight into the background of the revolution itself—occurred on February 17, when PLO chief Yassir Arafat arrived with thirty-one of his followers for a hero's tour of Iran. Arafat took over the building that had until recently housed the Israeli diplomatic delegation in Tehran—the PLO also set up an information office in Khuzistan—and in an emotional oration announced that many of the guerrillas who had fought for Khomeini in the streets of Iran (including those who had organized the seizure of the American Embassy three days earlier) had been trained by the PLO. The street on which the new headquarters was found was renamed "Palestine Street," and Khomeini and Arafat pledged mutual support. The Iranian government broke all relations with Israel.

While there was considerable ideological affinity between Khomeini and Arafat, the ayatollah does not appear to have made a major contribution to PLO activities since the revolution. Despite spectacular claims by PLO leaders and Iranian spokesmen that Iran would give the PLO one dollar for every barrel of oil sold, Khomeini stuck to his main tasks, although "Jerusalem Day" was added to the revolutionary calendar, and the destruction of Zionism was made an obligation of all Muslims.

THE FIRST TO WASH his hands of the enterprise was Foreign Minister Sanjabi, one of the original middle-class intellectuals who had given Khomeini his support the previous year. Announcing "the absolute breakup of the armed forces, the distribution of weapons amongst incompetent individuals, confusion in all social and economic affairs, and the failure of the government to establish executive authority,"[5] Sanjabi resigned his post. His complaints were constantly echoed by Bazargan—and subsequently picked up by the many émigrés from among the ranks of the Westernized intellectuals who left Iran as the nature of the Islamic republic became evident —but with no effect. For just as the middle-class reformers had been compelled to make their peace with the ayatollah during the challenge to the shah, so they were without sufficient troops to fight Khomeini for control of the state. Bazargan repeatedly attempted to resign, first on March 15, then on July 1, and again on August 31. On each occasion Khomeini imperiously required that he remain in office. In the fullness of time, when the theocratic coup of August and September had been achieved, Bazargan was permitted to step down on November 6, two days after the seizure of the American Embassy and the majority of its staff of seventy. The National Front and Bazargan's movement, having served the ayatollah's purpose, returned to the salons.

The lay intellectuals like Bazargan and Sanjabi never challenged Khomeini, but rather hoped either to win him over or to outlast him. Such was not the case with the more aggressive secular reformers and radicals, who soon broke with the ayatollah and tried to take charge of the revolution. These ranged from some Communists of the Tudeh Party—who on the eve of the revolution replaced their leaders with a radical mullah, the better to blend in with the rest of the anti-shah movement—to some of the more determined National Fronters, the Marxist guerrillas, and some of the hundreds of thousands of recent university graduates and students. On March 6 Hedayatollah Matin Daftari, the grandson of Mossadeq, announced the creation of the National Democratic Front. Claiming that Sanjabi had effectively abdicated leadership of the National Front, Daftari proposed to combat "ideological and religious fanaticism." This was a rather more serious threat to Khomeini, and was one of the targets of the ayatollah's constant attacks on the pro-Western intellectuals. "They want to make a Western country for you in which you will be free, you will be independent, but in which there is no God." Such a democracy, Khomeini warned, "would lead to our destruction."[6]

The challenge of these lay politicians could have been treated in one of two ways: an immediate, frontal reply, based on a conviction that the masses were solidly under clerical control; or a more subtle, long-term strategy designed to isolate the lay politicians at the same time as Khomeini gained control not only of the masses but also of the remaining power centers of the old regime. Foremost amongst these centers was the armed forces.

Khomeini evidently planned to take his time, for his steps toward the creation of the first Shi'ite theocracy in history were relatively cautious, and he showed an uncharacteristic willingness to compromise in the early stages. By mid-June, he came forward with a draft for the new constitution, prepared by him and the Revolutionary Council. The draft was strikingly similar to the 1906 Constitution, for it provided for a chief executive, elected by direct vote, who would have most of the autocratic powers previously held by the shah. There was no requirement that the president be a cleric, although like the earlier constitution, Khomeini's draft contained a proviso for a Supervisory Council, to be composed mostly of mullahs, to guarantee that the government would act in accordance with Islamic precepts.

Some aspects of the draft constitution were challenged by other religious leaders, such as Shariatmadari, and Khomeini was extremely forthcoming, modifying certain articles and agreeing to have the final draft prepared by a "Council of Experts" that would itself be elected by popular vote.* The elections for the Council of Experts were held on August 3 amidst the most intense criticism of Khomeini since the beginning of the revolutionary movement. Attacked by the ethnic minorities because of his refusal to grant them any meaningful form of autonomy, by the secular parties because of their opposition to the blatantly undemocratic nature of the proposed Islamic republic, and by the followers of Ayatollah Shariatmadari both because of Khomeini's arrogant assumption of the role of *marja'e taqlid* ("source of imitation") and because they feared that Khomeini was moving too fast (thus jeopardizing the projected Islamic republic), Khomeini once again carried the field. Of seventy-three "Experts" elected, sixty-one were either clerics favorable to Khomeini's positions or lay Islamic fundamentalists. On the 19th, the Council met for the first time, and elected two of Khomeini's closest colleagues as its vice-chairmen: the Ayatollahs Beheshti and Hussein Ali Montazeri, Khomeini's closest disciple and probable successor as leader of the Islamic republic.

With the drafting of the constitution now solidly in his own hands, Khomeini quickly moved to consolidate his physical control over the nation. In previous months he had approved purges of the *Mujahidin* and the komitehs, the institution of a rudimentary press censorship ("The press must write what the nation wants," he said in mid-May; "The nation wants newspapers which conform with its views.'"), and limited military actions against the belligerent ethnic autonomists, whether Kurdish, Arab, Turkoman, or Baluchi. But in August, fol-

---

*Even the popular vote, however, had its ominous side since special polling places were reserved for Jews, Zoroastrians, and Christians—evidently as a means of checking on their loyalty during the voting.

lowing his electoral coup, Khomeini was directly challenged in the streets of Tehran by the radical Left and the generally more moderate followers of the National Democratic Front. At first there were protests of alleged voting fraud, and by the 12th and 13th tens of thousands of leftist demonstrators were out in the streets of Tehran, protesting the "strangulation and suppression of freedom." There were banners denouncing the limitations on the press, and even some calling for an end to Khomeini's "fascism."

This forced the ayatollah into action. But whereas the shah had dealt with similar demonstrations a year before by one burst of fire in Jaleh Square, and then come forward with a mixture of rhetorical violence and actual appeasement, Khomeini took the opportunity to move against all his enemies. His techniques are familiar to students of the practice of mass mobilization. First the declaration of a national emergency; then the identification of internal forces as one of the principal causes of the crisis; and finally the purge of the internal elements and the mobilization of the armed forces for combat against external enemies.

The national emergency was declared on August 13, when Khomeini banned public demonstrations. It was the initial move against the political parties (already termed "a fatal poison" by the ayatollah a month earlier). Next came the newspapers: the most objectionable were simply shut down by the revolutionary guards, or by small bands of irate citizens stirred up by the mullahs during their Friday sermons. The pretexts varied, but for the most part journalists and editors were accused of collaboration with foreign enemies. In late August and early September, some forty newspapers were silenced. And while some resumed publication later in the fall and winter, they were notably more cautious.

The foreign press was similarly instructed, with those who continued to file unfavorable stories summarily shown to the airport. Correspondents from the Los Angeles *Times*, *The New York Times*, the *Financial Times* (London), and *L'Express* of Paris were expelled. In a further move to conceal the developments in Iran from world public opinion, foreign correspondents were required to obtain permission from the government to conduct any interviews, and then only in the presence of a representative of the newly renamed Ministry of National Guidance (formerly the Ministry of Information).

At the same time, Khomeini turned his attention to the Communists. On August 20 Tudeh headquarters, along with those of the Marxist *Feday'i*, were occupied by the revolutionary guards, the Communist newspaper *Mardom* shut down, and the Communists labeled "sons of Satin, atheists, the evil of the earth." The Communists were not only attacked for their ideas; they were linked to the ethnic disturbances that threatened the unity of the country: "Now we understand that they were taking advantage of our tolerance to sabotage us, that they did not want freedom but the license to subvert and we decided to stop them."[8]

The charge of subverting the country by instigating ethnic disturbances was followed two days later by Khomeini's assumption of the post of commander-in-chief of the armed forces, and a general mobilization of the military for an all-out campaign against the Kurds. The status of the Kurds had been on the agenda for many years. Prior to the Algiers Treaty, the shah had given sanctuary and arms to the Iraqi Kurds in order to harass his Iraqi opponents. The program of assistance to the Kurds had been supported by the United States, which was then forced by the shah to cease its pro-Kurdish activities in 1975, since the Algiers Treaty required that the shah terminate the program. The Kurdish leaders were enraged at what they viewed as the shah's (and the Americans') treachery, and the Iranian Kurds began to call for increased autonomy—and to receive Soviet support.

The movement became extremely active in January 1979, when the central government ceased to exist, and the leaders of the Kurdish Democratic Party held marathon talks with Khomeini's representatives in the winter and spring. The ayatollah's spokesmen promised some support for the Kurds' demands, but by July it was clear that this was a deception. Armed clashes occurred with increasing frequency, then in late August Khomeini attacked. Scores of Kurds were executed by Khalkhali's courts, the Kurdish Democratic Party was outlawed as an "enemy of Islam," held to be "directly dependent on the U.S. and Israel," and the full force of the regular army brought to bear on Kurdistan. On September 3 the city of Mahabad was seized by government forces following an intense bombardment of the city and the evacuation of 100,000 persons. By this time, Khomeini had changed his line, and the invasion of Kurdistan was justified by the claim that the Kurds were under Communist control. As will be seen, government officials were urgently seeking American weapons for the Kurdish campaign, and Khomeini's sudden switch may have been due at least in part to his desire to send a conciliatory signal to the Americans.

The Kurdish campaign marked the first occasion on which the ayatollah used the regular armed forces rather than the revolutionary guards, and thus showed his growing confidence. Moreover, it was undertaken in concert with other moves against his secular opponents that would leave him astride the country's institutions. On September 12 the Council of Experts issued new articles for the constitution that adhered closely to Khomeini's long-held vision of a theocratic Iranian state. In particular, the Council announced that the clerics would hold ultimate authority. And, according to Article 5, "In the absence of the hidden Imam, guardianship of the affairs and leadership of the nation rests in the hands of the honest, efficient, and aware theologian whose leadership has been accepted and recognized by the majority of the people. . . ."[9] No longer would power reside in a popularly elected president. Henceforth it would rest in the hands of the ayatollah, his own legitimacy growing out of the consensus of the masses. This was theocracy, to be sure, but not of the sort envisaged by the Islamic sages. In their traditional vision, the *marja'e taqlid* would be chosen by the ayatollahs themselves. But Khomeini did not wish to rest his authority on the fickle alliances of his fellow clerics; instead, he stood upon the base of mass allegiance. This was the Iranian version of the Hitlerian *Führerprinzip* elaborated earlier in the century in the satanic West.

There was one other element in Khomeini's program that bore a striking resemblance to those of earlier dictators: his conviction that the revolution had to be exported. Khomeini's original vision was of a revolution that began in Iran and then spread throughout the Islamic world, a vindication of Shi'ite doctrine at the expense of the Sunnis, and a revolutionary *jihad* or holy war that would drive all vestiges of Western culture out of the Muslim world. Calls for the export of the revolution were heard repeatedly from February on, directed variously against such moderate Middle Eastern countries as Egypt, Saudi Arabia, and Bahrain. Moreover, Khalkhali came up with a novel twist on the theory when he called upon volunteers to assassinate family members and leaders of the shah's government abroad, from Princess Ashraf to Ambassador Zahedi. Even if the assassins were apprehended, Khalkhali announced, they would be granted diplomatic immunity because they would be recognized as representatives of a revolutionary government in Iran. Thus the revolution may have begun in Tehran, but its field of action was to be the entire world.

THE FIRST MAJOR CRISIS faced by the Carter administration had led to the fall of an ally to forces ostentatiously hostile to the United States; the supply of precious petroleum to the industrialized West had been thrown into question; the stability of the Persian Gulf and perhaps the entire Middle East was uncertain; the weakness of the central government in Tehran might offer the Russians an irresistible opportunity for expansion; and American resolve and capability had received a damaging blow. In addition, there were many matters of a more strictly technical nature: Thousands of Americans were trapped in a suddenly hostile country, victims of their own illusions and those of the U.S. government; highly secret military weapons, as well as the invaluable electronic surveillance apparatus at two different locations, were suddenly in danger of falling into enemy hands; and the embassy staff itself had to be provided for. In a few weeks there would be the additional difficulty of an exodus of frightened Iranians reaching substantial dimensions.

The President and his advisers closed ranks and marched to a single refrain: We could live with Khomeini. The United States would embark upon a policy of accommodation to the revolution, try to convince Khomeini and his associates that their best interests lay in cooperation with America, and see what could be salvaged out of the ruins of the special relationship with the shah. For many of the President's advisers, a policy of accommodation or even support for the revolution was the course they had preferred all along. For these advocates of a "progressive" solution to the Iranian crisis, the fall of the shah was a major accomplishment; now the United States would not have to bear the onus of supporting a right-wing dictatorship in Tehran. They were certain that with time the ayatollah would realize that the Carter administration had made no attempt to destroy his movement, and that the President and his advisers genuinely wanted good relations with the new Iran. In some quarters there was growing enthusiasm at the thought that if Khomeini were successful, his brand of revolutionary Islam might spread throughout the Middle

East. If America could have good relations with the ayatollah, it might demonstrate the strategic superiority of U.S. support of progressive regimes, as Khomeini's still inchoate Islamic republic was taken to be.

At the other end of the foreign policy establishment, Brzezinski once again shifted his affections. After arguing for months that the fall of the shah would be a disaster, only to find brief enthusiasm for the evanescent Bakhtiar, the national security adviser now threw himself headlong into the courtship of the ayatollah. As usual, Brzezinski had a persuasive philosophical theory to justify his appeal, arguing that the spread of radical Islamic regimes could counteract Soviet expansionism, and quite possibly feed the Islamic revolution within the Soviet empire. Members of the NSC staff were accordingly put to work preparing special studies and briefing memoranda on such subjects as the role of Shi'ism in Southwest Asia; basic precepts of Shi'ism, including its theoretical underpinnings; the likelihood that religious fundamentalism could serve as the vehicle for other revolutions in the Muslim world; the Muslims of the Soviet Union; and the role of Islam as a barrier to communism.

Those who had favored the fall of the shah and many who had wanted to defend Mohammed Reza now backed a policy of accommodation. In due course, there was some support for the policy even among those who had regarded the shah's fall as a disaster. As one senior official put it, "we became convinced that the system of theocratic government espoused by Khomeini augured well for American interests in the region."[10] Among high levels of the policymaking establishment, it became generally accepted that Khomeini's brand of radical Islam was simply a mirror image of the ingrained Iranian sense of national identity and national pride. Khomeini did not wish to rule Iran, but only to reign in the name of Allah. In short order, he would turn over the reins of power to those suited for political power: the "moderates" and "social democrats" of the National Front and other secular organizations, with the odd mullah included for the sake of religious correctness. Like the followers of Bazargan in Tehran, many Americans remained convinced that the revolution would inevitably turn toward democratic populism. Incredibly, some American officials even spoke of Khomeini's theocracy as an Iranian version of the New England town hall meetings during the American Revolution.

These optimistic assessments were buttressed by the writings of academic experts, most of whom were enthusiastic about Khomeini even when they held the United States responsible for the "evils" against which the revolution was carried out. The mood of the enthusiasts can be sensed in the Spring 1979 issue of *Foreign Policy* magazine.* The editors invited various American experts to comment on the revolution. Not surprisingly, only the anti-shah experts contributed, while those who had been associated with American support for the monarch decided to wait a while. The latter were clearly in no mood to defend support of a shah who had so totally collapsed, and the editors announced: "Alas, all who we had supposed would defend past conduct declined our invitation." The published pieces from American academics were highly critical of past American policies.† The most pessimistic assessment came from Professor Richard Cottam, already noted for his early contact with Khomeini, his admiration for the ayatollah's humanism, and his emergence as a possible replacement for Ambassador Sullivan. For Cottam, the shah had fallen because the Iranians had become convinced—with some reason—that their country had suffered from "a rapacious American policy implemented by a puppet shah." Khomeini's movement was simply "a continuation of the movement for fundamental change that has been developing for over a century . . . to bring Iran genuine independence, free institutions, and a revival of Islamic and Iranian cultural values." Cottam argued that the shah could perhaps have saved himself by throwing out the Americans in 1955, and forging a coalition with Mossadeq's followers. Failing that, the shah had sealed his own fate by 1960, by which time "he had become the symbol of American domination of Iran."

Was there anything the United States could do? Cottam believed the only chance was to disengage from traditional alliances, on the grounds that "any regime considered by its attentive public to be an American creation, or at least dependency, will be fundamentally fragile." Hence the United States should develop "a dissociation strategy, conducted in a period of domestic stability that is designed

---

*Assistant Secretary of State Richard Holbrooke was the former editor, and Leslie Gelb, Anthony Lake, and other high-level officials had written fairly regularly for the magazine.
†Interestingly, an article by an Iranian living in London referred to the ayatollah's view that the shah had been "sponsored by outside powers" as "absurdly simplistic." The Americans tended to accept it.

to counter perceptions of American control." In other words, any American alliance was intrinsically destabilizing for Third World countries, and therefore potential allies should be saved from themselves by the American government via the simple expedient of denying them full support.

Compared with this gloomy view, the article by Professor Richard Falk of Princeton was upbeat. Echoing Cottam's conviction that the United States had erred in supporting the shah (and lamenting that America had been consistently counterrevolutionary ever since the days of the French Revolution), Falk wrote that Khomeini's new Islamic republic "need not necessarily be inherently anti-American, let alone a fanatical theocracy." Citing the presence of Bazargan, Sanjabi, and Forouhar as evidence of the commitment of the new regime to a "democratic constitutional order," Falk went on to describe Shi'ism as "entirely different from the harsher Sunni variety" dominant in other Middle Eastern countries. Under the circumstances, he advised the United States to maintain a low profile, do nothing to heighten Iranian suspicions that the Americans were still trying to save the shah's dynasty, and hope for the best. In an article for *The New York Times* written in February, Falk commented: "Despite the turbulence, many nonreligious Iranians talk of this period as 'Islam's finest hour.' Having created a new model of popular revolution based, for the most part, on nonviolent tactics, Iran may yet provide us with a desperately needed model of humane governance for a third-world country. . . ."[11]

There were similarly optimistic views from Professor James Bill of the University of Texas, and from several members of the Center for Contemporary Arab Studies at Georgetown University. Under normal circumstances, university professors have limited influence on American policy, but in the confusion of the winter and early spring of 1979, such ideas were seized upon by administration officials who had no reliable ideological compass to guide their moves.

Of the leading policymakers, Andrew Young was the most forthright in his enthusiasm. Speaking in Washington, Young suggested that Khomeini's movement was simply the result of the American educational system. Young claimed that the Iranian revolution had been inspired and led by the 25,000 to 50,000 students who had imbibed American notions about democracy and representative government while attending universities and colleges in this country.

"We should not be afraid when people begin to feel a sense of their own power," he said, and suggested that the purposes and goals of the Iranian revolutionaries were essentially those of the American civil rights movement. When the revolution was complete, Young added, Khomeini would be recognized as "some kind of saint."

It was hard to find an accurate assessment from the academy in that early period, although one had been delivered orally in mid-December by Professor Marvin Zonis of the University of Chicago. He had talked with Khomeini in Paris and had found the ayatollah highly irrational. In response to Zonis's observation that Khomeini and his followers could expect to find considerable opposition among the Iranian military, the ayatollah blandly commented that they had nothing to fear from the soldiers, since "no Moslem would kill another Moslem." And when Zonis objected that Khomeini himself deplored the many killings allegedly being carried out by the shah and his associates, the ayatollah said that this was not the work of Iranians but of Israeli troops who had moved into the country. Zonis was thoroughly debriefed by American officials.

Similarly prescient testimony was delivered to the Joint Economic Committee of the U.S. Senate in March by Professor Leonard Binder, also of Chicago. Binder considered various scenarios for Iran, and his prediction of one possible outcome—a theocratic regime under Khomeini's leadership—was deadly accurate:

> The essence of the struggle to create an Islamic state is, of course, militance, preaching, teaching, organizing, mobilizing and repressing anti-Islamic elements. The target groups against which such activities would be carried out would be the very same bourgeois intellectuals, and leftist allies of the clergy. In order to succeed in this effort a new organizational and bureaucratic instrument would be needed, and one is inclined to think of precedents such as the "cultural revolution" in which students, workers, and soldiers were encouraged to bring pressure to bear on bureaucrats, professors, and military administrators. It is unlikely that the successful mobilization of such a mass movement in Iran could be stopped short of the use of military force and perhaps even short of Iran's international boundaries.[12]

But voices like Binder's and Zonis's were lost in the chorus of those who either admired Khomeini or felt that the United States could make a successful accommodation with his regime. To have taken the warnings of such critics seriously would have entailed facing the full extent of the American debacle in Iran, and this the President and his advisers were unwilling to do. Indeed, through one of those psychological adjustments celebrated in the nineteenth-century German schoolboy's rhyme—"For, he argued razor-witted, That can't be, which is not permitted"—the foreign policy establishment simply denied that there had been any American failure in Iran. Had America not honored its pledge to avoid interference in the internal affairs of other countries? Had America not refused to support a military solution on behalf of its ally? And had America not thereby demonstrated that it would no longer consider itself bound by the rules of the old cold war? If there were any remaining doubts, America would now proceed to establish good relations with the new regime, thereby demonstrating that the apparent setback was really a success.

It might have been more difficult to pursue the policy of accommodation if the true nature of the new order had been generally recognized, but the government was no better than the scholars in this regard. The policymakers were pleased to see several familiar names at high levels of the new government: Bazargan himself, with whom the United States had carried on contacts over the years; Yazdi, the deputy to Khomeini in charge of "revolutionary affairs," with whom Warren Zimmerman had maintained a consistent relationship in Paris on behalf of the American government; Sanjabi and Forouhar, well-known National Fronters; and Rear Admiral Ahmad Madani, the minister of national defense, a man with friends at high levels in Washington. Given the presence of these reassuring faces, how bad could the new regime be?

One unnerving response came from William Sullivan, who had lived through some difficult days since the fall of the shah. In mid-February he observed in a cable that "we no longer have a military establishment integrated and responsive to our influence and interests . . . and those with guns are anti-American, because we encouraged military resistance rather than collaboration." Moreover, for those concerned with the safety of American diplomatic personnel, the chancery in Tehran was a shambles and "dependent on a group trained to assassinate us." This last reference was to the *Mujahidin,* who continued to roam the compound until July with their machine guns. For the most part they concerned themselves with looting the embassy commissary and offices, the better to participate in the flourishing black market in Tehran, but they also threatened embassy staff (particularly women), and generally kept an eye on things.*

Moreover, Sullivan stressed that the country was in a state of chaos, and that one could not exclude a repetition of the events of the 14th. He hardly needed to remind his interlocutors in Washington that American Ambassador Adolph Dubs had been murdered that same day in Kabul, and that Carter had decided as a result to reduce the American diplomatic presence in Afghanistan.

It was important to the President that relations with Iran be good, and he was not about to take any provocative actions in the first days of the revolution. However, in an effort to decrease the risk of injury to Americans, an airlift was organized on the 16th to carry out civilian personnel, and this was followed by the evacuation of most officials. The embassy staff was cut down from more than 1,000 to 40 over the next couple of months (later raised to 70 in time for the November assault).

Some of the technical problems were actually resolved with a minimum of friction. Despite great concern, American personnel at the top-secret observation posts were quietly spirited out of the country with the cooperation of Iranian armed forces, with no loss of vital classified material. And the three different defense ministers of the period all expressed a desire to continue to purchase spare parts for the American equipment in the country. Moreover, there were reassuring gestures from Yazdi and some of the ayatollahs (like Beheshti, to whom Sullivan had spoken prior to the revolution in his efforts to broker a compromise), leading to the departure of most of the guerrillas from the embassy compound.

These few straws in the wind were sufficient to convince American officials that the United States should try to work things out with the Iranians, and this conviction underlay the two major decisions taken in the first three months of the postrevolutionary regime. One concerned American diplomatic representation in Iran; the other was the question of granting sanctuary to the shah. In November, the two decisions became inextricably linked.

---

*Those who were present on February 14 recall that the assault team was obsessed with the idea that SAVAK officials or documents were in the embassy, probably the result of the Radio Baku broadcast that day.

SULLIVAN HAD OUTLIVED his usefulness, both in Tehran and Washington. Having worked closely with the shah, he was discredited in the eyes of the new regime. His ability to serve effectively under revolutionary conditions was in serious doubt, and Richard Falk was correct in suggesting that he should be replaced by someone with credentials more acceptable to the revolutionaries. At the same time, Sullivan had fallen into disfavor in Washington. Always suspected of "Kissingerian" loyalties, Sullivan had committed three sins during the shah's long agony. He had first permitted himself to be "scooped" by other governments in predicting the shah's downfall; then he had brought bad news to his own government for five months; and third, this bad news turned out to be true. The White House could not abide him because he had exposed the folly of the Huyser mission; the State Department did not wish to be represented in Tehran by a man out of favor with the President; and no one in a position to do so felt like protecting him. He was recalled in early April 1979, and left the foreign service.

Sullivan's departure from the front ranks of American diplomacy was only one of many such cases. Indeed, those who accurately called the shots during the Iranian crisis frequently found themselves on the periphery of the foreign policy establishment: some went on sabbaticals, others were given the opportunity to take year-long seminars, still others took early retirement. Those who pushed for the shah's ouster, however, and believed that Khomeini would turn out to be a positive element in international affairs, were generally promoted, along with those who simply gave poor advice or misunderstood the course of events. The two most notable cases are those of Gast (promoted) and Huyser (promoted and given an extra year on active duty). Nor does there seem to have been any recognition at the highest levels in Washington that such people had badly misunderstood some of the principal ingredients in the Iranian crisis. In late February, for example, Huyser was asked to attend a Special Coordinating Committee meeting in Washington, along with embassy officials who had flown in from Tehran. Huyser sat impassively, "like a wooden Indian," in the words of one participant, while the fall of Bakhtiar and the disintegration of the Iranian military were reviewed by the senior officials. Yet no one tried to discover how he could have been so completely misled and misleading about events in Iran. The administration's anger was rather directed at Sullivan.

The mood in the White House can be gauged from the behavior of Vice President Mondale at the SCC meeting. After hearing about the events during the revolution, Mondale came up to a top CIA official just in from Tehran, extended his hand, and said: "I'm Fritz Mondale. When are you going back?" The official replied that he had no intention of returning. Mondale had sat through a detailed discussion of the February events without realizing that Tehran had become a very dangerous place for representatives of the American government, let alone CIA officials who had had contacts with the previous regime. The Vice President was simply looking forward to resuming normal relations with, and activities in, Iran.

On one point the foreign policy establishment seems to have been agreed: it was dangerous to let the shah come to the United States. Given the super-sensitivity of the Iranians to the movements of the fallen monarch, to permit the shah entry would suggest a continuation of the close links between America and Mohammed Reza Pahlavi, and make it far more difficult to win the confidence of the Iranian government. On the other hand, if the shah were to remain in the Middle East (especially in pro-Western countries like Egypt or Morocco), the Iranians would fear that a coup was imminent. Was there some other solution?

After Kissinger's and Nelson Rockefeller's arrangement for sanctuary at Walter Annenberg's estate in Palm Springs, the shah was left with the clear impression that he could come to the United States if he so desired. From Egypt, he soon flew to Morocco to stay with King Hassan. Like others of the world's few surviving absolute monarchs, and in keeping with Islamic principles, Hassan felt he could not fail to offer hospitality to another king *in extremis* (especially a Muslim friend of long standing), and he told the shah and the Iranian royal family they could stay in Morocco as long as they liked. The visit to Morocco was not as tranquil as the shah would have liked. For one thing, his pilot defected to Tehran with the shah's 707, to the cheers of the revolutionaries. (It was later learned that the man's parents had been taken hostage, and he had been given an ultimatum. Upon his return, the revolutionaries broke both his hands, ensuring that the flight from Marrakech to Tehran was the last he was capable of making.) And a few weeks later the shah was informed by a Western intelligence official that a group of international terrorists had targeted members of Hassan's family for kidnapping; the king's relatives would be held for exchange with the shah and his family.

While Hassan had given no hint to Mohammed Reza that he was aware of the report, the shah did not wish to place his friend at such risk, and he accordingly began to explore other possibilities. These soon proved to be extremely limited, as those Western leaders who had heretofore spared no effort to ingratiate themselves with the shah told him in only slightly embarrassed tones that it would now be inconvenient to have him come to their countries. The shah had resisted suggestions that he go to the United States because of his conviction that the Americans had abandoned him in his hour of need, but at this point he asked Washington whether the offer of sanctuary still applied. He learned that it did not.

So began the abandonment of the shah. The lack of American support for his regime had already sent chills through the pro-Western rulers of the Middle East. What can be said about the refusal of the United States to provide its old friend and ally with a haven in his hour of need? In a sense, this was a greater blow to American national prestige than the failure to develop an effective policy during the crisis. For while nations often act foolishly, the abandonment of the shah after he left Iran indicated to the world that no friend of the United States could depend upon American assistance if he lost his position. Rarely has an ally performed so many services for the United States as the shah, and rarely has an old friend been so shabbily treated.

The American failure to grant Mohammed Reza a visa was not only deplorable on moral grounds—this has always been a country that prides itself on offering sanctuary to political exiles—but a serious error on geopolitical grounds as well. If foreign leaders are to be willing to take risks on behalf of American interests, they need some assurance that America will help defend them in turn. The ideal arrangement, as has been argued earlier, is to have allies who are confident that American power will come to their aid if they are challenged in their own countries; but if that cannot be provided, there must be at least the security that the United States will give them a place to live. The moral failure over the shah was thus compounded by political shortsightedness; in Montesquieu's phrase, "It is worse than a crime, it is a mistake."

The ostensible reason for refusing to grant sanctuary to the shah was that it was feared his arrival in America might provoke another attack against the Tehran embassy. But this was a flimsy argument, for in neighboring Afghanistan where the ambassador had been assassinated, the United States had cut back to a skeleton staff, tightened security, and conducted business without a replacement. There never was a serious approach to security in Iran, despite repeated attacks against the Tehran embassy itself and against American personnel. Moreover, the United States accepted assurances of security from an Iranian government manifestly unable to guarantee order in its own buildings, let alone the American compound. These were not indications of a government profoundly concerned about the well-being of its citizens; on the contrary, they suggest that the self-deceptive euphoria of the winter season had carried over into the new year. The American government insisted upon pretending that Iranian-American relations were good, that its diplomats were not virtual hostages to the anti-American mob at Khomeini's beck and call, and that the United States had to bend over backwards to maintain a good working relationship. The shah was kept adrift purely and simply for political purposes: Carter wanted to ally himself with the revolution in Iran and its supporters in the United States.

The shah therefore became, in Kissinger's phrase, a Flying Dutchman, searching the world for a friendly port. The President cannot have felt comfortable with this cynical decision, for he had made much of the moral basis of his foreign policy. He cannot have failed to recognize that the refusal to admit the shah was an act of accommodation to the vengeful desires of the Iranian revolutionaries. Once started on the path of conditioning American policy to the passions of Khomeini, there was no convenient escape.

Not only was the shah not granted a visa, but the American government refused to take any action to find him another haven. Instead, administration leaders turned to Henry Kissinger and the Rockefeller family to bail the country out of its dilemma. First Kissinger and David Rockefeller were asked by State Department officials to convince the shah that he should not apply for a visa to the United States; both refused. When it became clear that the Carter

administration would not budge, and other formerly friendly countries would not grant the shah asylum, Rockefeller arranged for a
brief stay in the Bahamas; then Kissinger negotiated a more permanent sanctuary in Mexico. Once settled there, the shah was able to
count on his two old friends for other forms of help, ranging from
finding schools for his children, haggling with the State Department
over visas, locating experts to check on security (on at least one
occasion Kissinger's own security chief, Walter Bothe, talked with
the shah about the problem), and generally providing human
companionship.

Kissinger was enraged by what he considered American appeasement of Khomeini, and he would become angrier still after the
seizure of the American hostages in November, when the White
House staff and people like George Ball accused him of having
brought "obnoxious pressure" on the President to let the shah come
into the country for cancer surgery in late October. In reality there
had been little direct pressure from Kissinger on the administration
—a total of five approaches in all between April and July—but there
had been a considerable amount of ire in the White House at Kissinger's highly effective private campaign. Kissinger left no opportunity unexploited to tell listeners that the United States was giving
Iran a veto over who would be permitted to enter the country as a
private citizen. Journalists, members of Congress, national and international business leaders, were daily reminded that Carter would not
let the shah come to America. And Kissinger also pointed out that
when President López Portillo of Mexico accepted the shah, he did
so with the observation that "Mexico was being asked to run risks
on behalf of a friend of the United States that we were not willing
to assume ourselves."

The point of López Portillo's barbed observation was that the
United States was behaving like a frightened nation, not a superpower. Furthermore, the constant refrain from Washington in that
period was that the President was concerned about the safety of
American diplomats and businessmen in Iran, and the repetition of
those words may well have encouraged the Iranians to believe that
the seizure of Americans would be a highly effective weapon against
the Carter administration. Jimmy Carter, in short, was beginning to
behave the way the shah had done in the final months of his reign.
For just as Mohammed Reza had permitted former prime ministers,

counsellors, and generals to be arrested in a vain attempt to appease the Ayatollah Khomeini and his followers, the American President forced the shah to search for sanctuary so that Carter could try to ingratiate himself with the ayatollah's regime. And just as the shah kept his armed forces under wraps, so Carter took no steps to defend American diplomats in Tehran against the widely rumored attack that eventually overwhelmed the building.

The shah's deteriorating health made the situation more tragic, for he was not only forced to wander about looking for a safe haven but compelled to fly doctors great distances to treat his advancing cancer. Yet at no time did Carter speak with the shah about his plight, nor did he offer any sort of assistance. Indeed, the shah's request that he be permitted to come to New York for surgery in October caused a mini-crisis. As if to underline American courtship of the ayatollah, U.S. representatives in Tehran were dispatched to ask Bazargan and Yazdi whether the safety of the embassy could be guaranteed if the shah were admitted to an American hospital. The response was guardedly positive, even though chargé d'affaires L. Bruce Laingen had earlier warned the State Department of the consequences, and the decision to permit the shah to come to New York was made by Carter and Vance. The State Department wanted "independent" doctors to check on the diagnosis in Mexico, even though two French physicians and a distinguished New York City expert in tropical diseases had been sent to Mexico by David Rockefeller to examine the shah. And even after the shah had been admitted to New York Hospital, the State Department was still trying to work out an arrangement by which Iranian physicians could either examine the shah or confer with his American doctors. Mohammed Reza understandably vetoed the first proposal, and the American doctors—sensitive to the privileged doctor-patient relationship—rejected the second. The shah arrived on October 22. In the following days, despite the growingly vituperative rhetoric from the ayatollah, no measures were taken to protect American diplomatic personnel in Tehran, nor was anything done to destroy the vast quantities of highly sensitive documents in embassy files. Some of these documents evidently contained details regarding diplomatic "cover" given to American intelligence officials in the embassy. If so, failure to destroy them must be considered a major dereliction of duty.

The period from October 22 to November 4 recalls the days im-

mediately before the revolution in February. Even though there was
abundant evidence of Iranian hostility, and every reason to expect
violence directed against any American in Iran, the government was
reluctant to do anything significant to bolster the capacity for self-
defense on American soil at the compound. The number of Marine
guards was increased from eight to thirteen, and some new steel
doors were installed at the chancery, but that was all, though it had
been demonstrated twice before that the well-directed Tehran mob
was quite capable of overwhelming the Americans. The events of
February were a sort of dry run, and the Americans had been tested
again on May 25-26, when 100,000 demonstrators attacked the compound, broke through the defenses, and tore down the flag. This time
there had been a response, however. The flag was tied off 20 feet from
the top, and the pole covered with pig grease to discourage climbers.
There was every reason for the attackers to believe they could take
the compound whenever they wished. And by late October and early
November there were many developments to spur them on.

WITH THE DEPARTURE of Sullivan in April, the time seemed to be
right for a new *démarche*. The perpetuation of full diplomatic and
military ties was seen in some quarters of the administration as a way
of extending the American government's recognition to the revolution and according it a degree of "legitimacy." American diplomatic
and military representatives diligently strove for close ties with officials within the Bazargan government. Even when the nomination
of Walter Cutler as Sullivan's replacement was rejected by Iran (on
the grounds that Cutler had been ambassador to Zaire when the
United States "interfered" in that country's internal affairs), a new
chargé d'affaires—L. Bruce Laingen—was appointed in the hopes
that this gesture might facilitate better relations.

The Americans were resolutely insensitive to the barbarisms of the
new regime, silently acquiescing in human rights violations that
would have been grounds for angry protests if they had been committed under the shah's regime. There was far more toleration of "revolutionary" violence than there had been for the institutionalized
violence of the shah's regime, and the mass murders and summary
executions were explained away as excesses of the revolutionary
process. At no point was there any serious consideration of the

possibility that the new regime embodied an unalterably anti-American clerical fascism.

The U.S. Senate had a clearer view of the realities, and passed a resolution in May urging the government of Iran to moderate its behavior. Khomeini replied with an attack against westernized intellectuals: ". . . sectors that oppose Islam should take our guidance, otherwise they will be destroyed by the same fist that destroyed the shah. Their ideas and speeches should be in keeping with the masses, or else they should go."[13]

By June, when Cutler's nomination was rejected by the Iranians, it should have been appreciated in Washington that hatred of the West—and especially the United States—was the focus for the political enthusiasm that lay at the heart of the new order in Iran. This would have made it possible for Carter to have conducted the sort of prudent policy one designs for a hostile country in the throes of a mass movement: careful diplomacy, full security for diplomatic personnel, contingency plans for actions designed to encourage forces more favorable to the United States, and so forth. But the President and his advisers were by now committed to full diplomatic and military relations between the two countries, and hence prudent measures to protect Americans in Tehran were rejected. Just as Carter and his advisers had deceived themselves in January, when they maintained that Bakhtiar had an excellent chance to survive, so they deceived themselves again in the summer and fall, when they believed that things were going well with the government of Iran.

There was, accordingly, a failure to appreciate the depth of the anti-Americanism of the Khomeini-led masses, and of the methods by which the ayatollah wished to destroy all remnants of Western culture in Iran. For such a man, any hint that the United States was attempting to restore the previous relationship (which in Khomeini's mind was one of virtually total domination of Iran by the United States) would set off an alarm, with unforeseeable consequences. Yet this is precisely what the Americans did.

Laingen arrived in June, and after a series of courtesy calls on Iranian leaders, he returned to Washington to report that the situation in Tehran was "improving." In the next five months, Laingen, along with Gast and those in Washington concerned with Iranian affairs, preached this sermon to all audiences. Businessmen were encouraged to invest and work in Iran; members of Congress were urged to withhold remarks critical of the new regime; and the top policymakers were implored to continue toward full government-to-government relations.

So eager were the Iranian hands in the government to have close working relations with the Khomeini regime that in the first week of October, Laingen, along with Henry Precht, held a breakfast briefing in Washington for a selected number of correspondents. Laingen's message was that relations with Tehran were much improved, that there were many American businessmen working successfully with the new situation, that the chaos, brutality, and anti-Americanism of the government and people had been very much exaggerated, and that the time had come for the United States to find an ambassador acceptable to the Iranians, so that full diplomatic ties could exist. Laingen asked the journalists to be less critical of the situation in Iran, both because he felt the press was exaggerating the difficulties in the country, and because articles critical of Khomeini in the American media made his life more difficult.* Some of the journalists felt Laingen was making a strong pitch to become ambassador himself, but the conviction with which he spoke about improving relations with Iran impressed them, especially because they were receiving quite a different story from other sources.

Laingen was supported by Precht and by General Gast, ever convinced that the United States should maintain a military "presence" in Iran. All three pushed hard for "a resumption of the U.S. military supply relationship with Iran, including the dispatch of U.S. technicians and spare parts to the country." Indeed, the military supply question was the one that most encouraged the Americans to believe that a major breakthrough was close at hand in October.

The new government had always been interested in maintaining a certain level of military power, and while numerous contracts with the United States were canceled in the first few months after the revolution, military commanders and officials of the Ministry of National Defense insisted that the United States continue to provide them with spare parts for the equipment already in the field. They

---

*Such articles sometimes led to the execution of Iranian citizens, if the source could be identified. On one occasion the female director of a hospital in south Kurdistan was executed for "spreading inflammatory and counterrevolutionary appeals in the foreign press." Her sin had been to tell a team from *L'Express* about the genocidal policies of the Khomeini government in Kurdistan.

were particularly concerned about keeping their fighter planes, helicopter warships, and transport vehicles, whether trucks or boats, in working order to deal with the ethnic separatists who threatened the unity of the country. The United States had no objection to the selling of this equipment to Iran, so long as it was properly paid for. But just as the shah's generals had found it impossible to settle their bills in the end because of the sabotage by bank employees, so the revolutionaries were confronted with the same problem. Employees of the Central Bank of Iran refused to issue checks for American equipment.

This impasse was solved in an ingenious manner: Since the fleeing Americans had left behind great quantities of personal effects, household goods, and other items during the forced exodus of late winter and early spring, the American government was prepared to pay for transportation costs. It was therefore possible to hire Iranian pilots —generally American-trained—to fly American goods from Tehran to the United States (McGuire Air Force Base was the favorite location, because so many of the spare parts were warehoused there), where they would be issued a credit for moving the Americans' property. The credit was then applied against the cost of the spare parts, and the Iranians could load their planes and return to Tehran with their cargo.

While the method was clever, the quantities did not satisfy the Iranians, who were planning throughout the summer for a major campaign against the Kurds. Iranian interest was sufficient to justify a request by Gast in mid-July for a visit to Tehran by a Pentagon team. From the standpoint of the two chief American representatives in Iran—Gast and Laingen—a hint of a major breakthrough came at the end of the month. In a distinctly upbeat cable to the State Department dated July 30, Laingen reported that Gast had just received a call from Colonel Kamkar, the deputy minister of national defense, on behalf of the minister, General Riahi. The minister asked the Americans to speed up handling of the Iranian request for additional military material: "We can only speculate that Riahi's sense of urgency is associated with mounting problems in the West and Northwest. In any event, it is an indicator of their growing need for assistance and represents a direct request for U.S. favorable response. Mission supports strongly a favorable response."[14] In fact, there was considerable information to support the "speculation" that the Iranians wanted the spare parts to smash the Kurds, for Gast had cabled Washington that the commander of the ground forces logistics command had also solicited spare parts, and the general had noted: "we see [the commander's] call immediately after his return from Kurdistan as an indication of the high priority . . . on getting the spare parts pipeline operating again."

So there was little ambiguity about the operation. Khomeini's military commanders needed spare parts for a successful campaign in Kurdistan. The question was whether the U.S. government was prepared to send weapons to the ayatollah to wage war on the Kurds. It was not the first time the United States had been involved in this question; in 1975, the shah had asked Ford and Kissinger to cease support of the anti-Iraqi Kurdish groups. They acquiesced, but American officials admitted privately that the abandonment of the Kurds had been one of the most distasteful events in that period. However, this was a case in which a close American ally—the shah —had made a decision and asked the United States to go along with it. The Kurds had previously been supported by the shah, and he wanted good relations with Iraq; America concurred.

The Carter problem was quite different. Iran was no longer an allied country, nor could it be considered friendly. The Senate had condemned the Iranian government for its repeated violations of human rights, and Tehran had replied by threatening to eliminate westernized intellectuals. Now that same government was menaced by centrifugal forces in Iran, the most important of which was the Kurdish autonomist movement. Should America actively cooperate in providing the weapons with which the ayatollah could consolidate his own power in Iran and attempt the liquidation of the Kurds?

The response from the White House—as from every element of the bureaucracy—was enthusiastically positive. The Pentagon was ordered to unblock the pipeline and work out the details with the Iranians as quickly as possible. By August, the United States was supplying spare parts to the Iranian armed forces and discussing the possibility of brand-new contracts in the amount of $5 or $6 million. All of this was going on despite a considerable body of information demonstrating that there was widespread resentment among the rank-and-file of the armed forces. The pilots who flew missions against the Kurds, for example, knew that their families were being held hostage by the revolutionary forces, and that failure to perform assignments could lead to the execution of their relatives.

There was no American security interest at stake in the campaign against the Kurds; indeed, it may be argued that a proper appreciation of U.S. interests required support of the Kurds against Khomeini, a point that was made by several American allies in the Middle East and western Europe. But determined as they were to make the romance with the ayatollah succeed, Carter and his advisers went ahead with the military supply program, hoping that this would open the way to an expanded relationship between the two governments.

A series of secret meetings held in October well illustrates the state of mind of the administration. There were three meetings in all, two in New York and one in Tehran, each dealing with the general question of improved relations between Iran and the United States, and with the more specific matter of providing weapons to the Iranian armed forces.

The first took place on October 4 between Yazdi and his aides, on the one side, and Precht, Lucy Benson, David McGiffert (head of the Pentagon's International Security Agency), and General Frank Graves (director of the Military Security Assistance Agency) on the other. Precht's account of the meeting, in a cable sent two days later, reflects the atmosphere:

> Meeting was characterized by frank, sometimes bluntly-stated Iranian questions or objections. While the air was thick with suspicion there was little acrimony. U.S. side was extraordinarily patient and understanding, repeatedly indicating willingness to review issues on their merits and to provide additional information where feasible. . . .
> Undersecretary Benson opened by indicating our willingness to cooperate with and assist Iran on defense matters where that was desired by both sides and feasible. She reaffirmed U.S. interest in Iran's independence, territorial integrity, and security. . . .[15]

The picture is one of American representatives striving to make a good impression, even though there were evidently moments when they wanted to use stronger language (as Precht did in a celebrated meeting with Iranian representatives after the hostages were taken). The official version of the meeting was that it had been productive, and that everything seemed to be developing nicely, despite the thick suspicions and the "bluntly-stated Iranian questions or objections."

In any event, things had gone well enough to progress to the next stage: a conference between Yazdi and a top-level American delegation consisting of Vance, Newsom, Harold Saunders, and United Nations Ambassador Donald McHenry two days later. By all accounts, the meeting was a blow to American expectations. Yazdi bluntly announced his conviction that the United States had not yet accepted the revolution, and asked for concrete steps to demonstrate such acceptance. Vance replied that the U.S. government had showed its acceptance through a number of public statements. This was not enough, however, and Yazdi indicated that his government wanted the extradition of Iranian "criminals" who had fled to the United States after the revolution, and also favorable disposition of the military contracts that had been signed by the shah. Yazdi further made it clear that he would brook no interference from the Americans, especially on the subject of human rights. The Iranian revolution, he said, was "the cleanest in world history."

This was not what Vance had expected, and the meeting with Yazdi was a minor setback to the campaign for normalization of relations. Yet once again it seemed almost impossible for the American diplomats to recognize Iranian hostility for what it was:

> Newsom felt, after seeing Yazdi, that the Iranian suspicions of us were only natural in the post-revolutionary situation but that after a transition period common interests could provide a basis for future cooperation—"not on the scale of before but sufficient to demonstrate that Iran has not been 'lost' to us and to the West."[16]

Newsom's remark about "losing" Iran was highly revealing, because it showed how determined the Americans were to believe that Iran had not been lost after all. It also pointed to one of the major rationalizations for American accommodation toward Khomeini: "better Khomeini than the Communists."

A week later—just three weeks before the storming of the embassy —Gast met with the deputy minister of national defense once again. Colonel Kamkar had spoken with the new defense minister, Ali Chamran, and was happy to discuss the prospect of obtaining additional spare parts for the Cobra helicopter gunships for the campaign against the Kurds. Despite the strained atmosphere at the high-level meeting in New York, Gast pushed ahead with an ambitious proposal: Why didn't the Iranians set up a full-scale purchasing mission in Washington? This would permit them to make up an extensive shopping list, and negotiate their purchases directly with the Pentagon and other American agencies and departments on the spot. Kamkar was interested, and told Gast he would be pleased to have "any ideas based on similar missions now operated by Israel, the Federal Republic of Germany and others in the U.S." Gast commented laconically in the cable that he did not think it would be wise to give Iranians detailed information about the Israeli mission in the United States. Other than that, there was no hint that anything untoward had occurred.

On October 20—just two weeks before the storming of the embassy—Precht arrived in Tehran to take matters even further. According to Washington *Post* correspondent William Branigin, Precht's trip was viewed by some other Western diplomats in Iran as "a bullish effort by Washington to resume its old relationship with Iran," and Branigin added that "Precht offered Iranian officials in Tehran further American help in equipping their armed forces." A State Department official told the *Post* that Precht's trip had no "special design or purpose" other than to "acquire first-hand impressions" of revolutionary Iran. There are several administration officials who support Branigin's account, which fits neatly into the pattern of American-Iranian discussions on military matters. In any event, whether Precht actually made additional offers to the Iranians during his later October trip to Tehran is of only marginal importance. The policy was already firmly established, and his trip— during which he encountered leading mullahs, government officials (including Yazdi), and other figures among the religious, political, and intellectual groups—was part of a visible effort to raise the level of contacts between the two governments. To the suspicious leaders of the Islamic republic of Iran, it looked as if the Americans were up to their old tricks.[17]

Having convinced themselves that all was going well, the Americans acted as if the Iranian government was much like any other. Despite all indications to the contrary, they pretended that the leader of Iran was Bazargan, and that since Bazargan was a reasonable man, one could deal reasonably with his government. This attitude was widespread by the summer of 1979, promoting Assistant Secretary of State Harold Saunders to tell a congressional subcommittee in July: "I don't sense [a strong anti-American feeling amongst the leadership in Iran]. I don't sense it as something that makes the relationship unworkable among much of the leadership. I think it is fair to say that the intensity of anti-American feeling in the streets has diminished recently. There is, of course, a latent resentment. . . ."[18]

This was the official view. And while there was considerable concern that by admitting the shah to New York Hospital, the American government might have put its diplomats in Iran at risk, there does not seem to have been any parallel concern that the stepped-up level of official activity with governmental officials might enrage the ayatollah and his followers. (And, after all, the shah had already been to four different countries before arriving in New York, and no action had been taken against the diplomats of those countries.) Throughout the period from the revolution to November 4, there was no direct contact with Khomeini; but a casual reading of the Iranian press in October would have revealed a state of high alarm about the activities of the "great satan" Carter and the "American devils." Weeks before the shah went to New York, Islamic militants were calling for action against the United States.

If one is to believe the few "students" interviewed by a correspondent from the Los Angeles *Times* in December 1979, the plan to attack the embassy predated the shah's trip by several weeks. The original idea was to invade the compound in order to seize documents, the better to demonstrate the presumed nefarious activities of the Americans. But the shah's arrival in New York suggested that taking Americans prisoners could conceivably lead to a swap of bodies: fifty-three Americans for one shah.

Again, the particulars are of marginal significance, for the ayatollah's policies were clearly established. Throughout October he inveighed against the Americans, and late in the month he called upon the "dear students" to teach the Americans a lesson, and save Iran from the infidels' schemes.

Carter and his colleagues pursued their Persian dream with mounting euphoria, ignoring all the warning signals. On November 1, Brzezinski was in Algiers for the celebrations of the twenty-fifth anniversary of the Algerian struggle for independence. He took the opportunity—presumably scheduled in advance—to meet with Yazdi and Bazargan. The national security adviser reiterated the points that had been made so often in the recent past: the United States recognized the revolution, had no intention of helping the shah recover his throne, hoped that Bazargan and his colleagues would successfully create a stable political structure for Iran, and encouraged full government-to-government relations. Brzezinski reported that the meeting was highly successful, but in Tehran there was considerable anxiety. Many newspapers saw the encounter as another round in the American effort to destroy the foundations of the revolution.

In fact, Bazargan had little more than a week before his calvary as prime minister came to an end, and Brzezinski was talking to a figurehead with limited power. Even though Yazdi and Bazargan had taken precautions to assuage the fears of the mullahs (the day before the meetings with Brzezinski, Iran had abrogated the 1959 Mutual Assistance Pact between the two countries), the only practical consequence of the Algiers meeting was to raise the anti-American fever in Iran. On the night of November 3–4, the State Department operations center—the vital communications nexus for alerting the President and his senior aides to looming crisis situations—was not operating at full personnel capacity, and there was no Iranian specialist on duty to respond to the first signals from the embassy. Official Washington required twenty-four hours to digest the information from Tehran and to comprehend that it had once again badly misjudged the situation in Iran.

CONCLUSION

The Future of Foreign Policy

THE DEBACLE IN IRAN is destined to become one of the most passionately discussed issues of recent American history, and properly so. The fall of the shah marked the collapse of an American Persian Gulf strategy that was based on Saudi Arabian economic and political power, and Iranian political and military strength. With the removal of the Iranian "pillar," this strategy could no longer function.

In addition, Jimmy Carter's inability to define policy goals during the first major crisis of his administration inevitably altered the perception of the United States by friend and foe alike. When it was realized that the American government had not formulated a policy, established objectives, or designed tactics to protect the vital American interests in Iran, leaders and analysts were forced to reevaluate their view of the effective value of American guarantees. If the Americans would not act to support the shah, under what circumstances could they be expected to move? If the Carter administration did not judge Iran to be a vital interest of the United States, what ally could consider itself truly secure?

Finally, there was widespread conviction that the American government was not only ineffective and timorous but also hypocritical, particularly in its treatment of the shah himself. The failure to grant sanctuary to the shah had considerable psychological impact, above all among foreign leaders who could well imagine themselves in similar straits. This disappointing moral performance was perhaps best exemplified in a speech by Deputy Secretary of State Warren Christopher to the Los Angeles Bar Association on November 6, 1979, devoted to the subject of "political asylum." Coming as it did just two days after the capture of the American diplomats in Tehran, the speech had considerable importance. Christopher began by observing:

> For a nation like ours, the decision to grant or deny asylum in a particular case cannot turn on a cool calculation of the international pros and cons. Because of our historical role as a country of refuge for the oppressed, because of our firm commitment to human rights, we must insure that our actions in such cases comport not only with the law but also with the dictates of conscience.

There was no hint that the administration Christopher served had denied asylum to Mohammed Reza Pahlavi for eight months precisely because of a cynical "cool calculation of the international pros and cons." Indeed, Christopher permitted himself a highly self-congratulatory observation: "For us in the United States, these requests for refuge may create temporary abrasions and difficulties. But they are a tribute to our way of life—and to the values we represent in the world. They are also a challenge to our support for human rights."[1]

The hypocrisy in Christopher's words was underlined a few days later when the Carter administration drove the former shah from his New York hospital toward another temporary haven outside the United States. This occurred when it became evident that the government would not be able to secure the release of its diplomats without surrendering the shah to the Khomeini regime. Since such a concession went beyond the bounds of surrender that the American people were prepared to contemplate, the opportune "solution" was to send the shah elsewhere, hoping that the problem would find some other resolution.

The wandering shah was symbolic of the lack of clear direction from Washington that characterized the entire American debacle in Iran, for Carter's inability to deal with the problem of the shah's presence in the United States was the continuation of his failure to shape American foreign policy throughout the crisis. Just as he had been unable to define coherent action when Mohammed Reza was on the throne, so he attempted to ignore his difficulties with the deposed shah, hoping for the best and getting the worst once again. This continuity of behavior suggests that the American failure in Iran was not simply the result of specific and limited errors, but was rather the outcome of more systematic shortcomings in the American government. Are there, then, some general lessons to be learned from the Iranian debacle?

IN ORDER TO MAKE effective policy, the President and his advisers needed to realize the nature of the shah's opponents, and of the shah himself. But by and large, top American officials believed that Khomeini was a social democrat in priest's clothing, and that the shah was a tough guy. Given those perceptions, there were persuasive reasons for a "wait and see" attitude. The shah could be expected to act, and the triumph of the ayatollah—in Stansfield Turner's words—was "something we could live with." Indeed, Andrew Young welcomed the revolution, as did many other leading advisers. Thus there are two intelligence failures: no one knew that the shah had cancer—and remembered the basic facts about his personality —and no one read Khomeini's books. The first was perhaps unavoidable. Princess Ashraf, the shah's twin sister, has claimed that she herself was unaware of her brother's condition. But the second failure was easily avoided; one had only to go to the library and read. Or, lacking that, one had only to listen carefully to Khomeini inside his villa in Paris. American officials listened—electronically—but the evidence was not believed. Instead, they accepted the wishful thinking of the National Fronters and the deceptions of some of Khomeini's supporters. Was this failure of perception a one-time affair, or does it point to a structural problem? In other words, if future American governments had to face similar crises, would they do any better than the Carter administration in the Iranian case? We are not optimistic.

THE FAILURE IN IRAN was basically the result of the absence of clear goals. The administration did not know what it wanted to happen in Iran, and therefore was unable to bring the instruments of foreign policy to work for an acceptable outcome. This failure, which is basic to the story we have told, must be laid directly at the feet of the President himself. Only the chief executive can provide the kind of overall guidance that the foreign policy establishment requires for the effective conduct of policy. Had the President made his objectives clear to the National Security Council and the departments of State and Defense, most of the functionaries in the government would have worked to support him. Iran was not Vietnam; there would not have been the substantial mutiny that afflicted Johnson, Nixon, and Ford in their efforts to shape American policy toward Southeast Asia. Nor would there have been the public outcry that finally altered the nature of American policy in Vietnam.

This is not to say that the President would have had an easy time of it, but presidents are elected to defend the interests of the country, not simply to take the politically opportunistic course. Carter will be judged harshly for his inability to define national objectives during the Iranian crisis.

This criticism does not solely concern Carter's failure to insist upon the use of force in the last two to three months of the crisis. For he had a chance to pursue his own self-proclaimed principles earlier, and failed to do so. Despite all the talk about human rights, there was never any systematic effort to induce the shah to create new political structures in Iran. Indeed, Carter and his associates— like their predecessors under Nixon and Ford—did not even demand an end to the illegal activities of SAVAK in the United States. Thus, there was a double failure: Carter did not insist upon the moderniza- tion of political structures in Iran when that would have defused the revolutionary explosion; and he then failed to insist upon adequate defense of American interests—and long-term prospects for democ- racy in Iran—when the explosion took place.

The President must be judged a failure on every count, for he did not pursue any coherent strategy at all. If Carter had concluded that the "shah was the problem," then he should have taken steps to remove Mohammed Reza as quickly as possible and replace him with something more to his liking. But there was no such plan. The embrace of the Bakhtiar "solution" was not a policy decision as such; it was simply hoping for the best.

We are not convinced by former Ambassador Sullivan, who argued in *Foreign Policy* magazine that the situation could have been saved if only the American government had supported his suggestion to back a government headed by Mehdi Bazargan in late December 1978. There seems no good reason to believe that Bazargan had any greater popular base than Bakhtiar, and in fact Bazargan was already in league with Khomeini in Paris, while Bakhtiar remained independent. Both the Bazargan and Bakhtiar "solutions" beg the central issue: Could the military remain intact once the shah had left the country, and without the possibility of fighting for their own cause? Haig and Schlesinger did not believe it possible. Brzezinski permitted himself to be tempted by the evanescent promise of a Bakhtiar government, while Sullivan proclaimed Bakhtiar a lost cause and held out for Bazargan. But all of the "solutions" offered by the top administration officials (with the exception of Schlesinger and Haig) involved the departure of the shah. There was never any real chance that the President would permit a clear message to go to Mohammed Reza, saying: "Things are serious, you must now establish order. Do what needs to be done."

In their heart of hearts, American policymakers wanted the shah to use the military, even if they could not say so either to the American people or to the shah himself. And, as has been argued, they fully expected the shah to do so. But they would not urge the President to make this clear to the shah, because they did not wish to be accused of encouraging "another Pinochet" in Iran. One may sympathize with their desire to retire with reputations as men and women of peace, but such feelings are no substitute for the defense of American interests. The stakes in Iran were very high, and required decisive action from the President and his advisers. None was forthcoming.

The shah's posture was a mirror image of the American President's. Just as Carter awaited decisive action from the shah, so the shah waited for Carter to unveil his grand design. Like Carter, the shah wished to avoid responsibility for ordering the use of force; like Carter, he had convinced himself that the military would inevitably be used, and that it was not necessary for him to give the orders. He may also have believed that, just as in 1953–54, the Americans had planned a dramatic covert operation that would restore him to his throne. He did not realize how much things had changed.

It will be said that Carter was an amateur in foreign policy, and that he should have received better guidance from his top advisers, who had devoted their lives to the study of international affairs. Many of the articles devoted to this subject have stressed the "Vance-Brzezinski conflict" as if the divided counsel that the President received accounted for the lack of an American policy. This, however, is not an explanation at all, but a further indictment of the Carter administration. Had the President's advisers spoken to him with a single voice, it would have been said that the foreign policy establishment had failed to present him with a range of options. Any President should desire conflicting opinions, with the widest possible range of alternatives, and to judge by the passions surrounding the disagreements between the Secretary of State and the national security adviser, Carter was given diverging views. The real embarrassment in the Iranian case is that the opinions were not well judged. We agree with Schlesinger and Brzezinski that Iran was of vital importance to the United States (and to the entire West), and that the American government should have taken strong action. We also suspect that Schlesinger's proposal of a special emissary to the shah was the only effective course of action, particularly if it had been combined with the projection of American military power into the Persian Gulf. But Brzezinski was not an effective policymaker; his instincts were perhaps healthier than some others in high places in Washington, but his attention span was short, his bureaucratic weight quite low, and his powers of persuasion minimal. He seems to have assumed that once a theoretical position had been formulated, the conduct of policy would take care of itself. Even when he was accurate in his assessments, Brzezinski failed to translate his insights into policy.

Vance, on the other hand, was more effective in controlling the implementation of policy at the same time that he was far less perceptive in analysis. The resignation of the Secretary of State in 1980 suggested that he was strongly committed to the avoidance of the use of military power by the United States. This visceral reaction could be seen during the shah's time of troubles, when Vance tended to support the human rights theme, insisted that Sullivan remind the shah about the American position on political repression even when the existence of the monarchy was at stake, and strongly objected to Brzezinski's desire to organize a military coup in the final weeks. To be sure, Vance was flexible: he finally ordered the release of the tear gas canisters for crowd control after the shah had waited nearly a year for them. But the secretary wanted to leave office with clean hands. Having been subjected to public vilification for his earlier role as one of the participants in the Vietnam war, he seems to have decided to oppose any similar action in the future, as did Defense Secretary Brown.

With the exception of Schlesinger, none of the top advisers to the President put the Iranian crisis in a global geopolitical context and attempted to design an effective policy on that basis (Brzezinski understood the geopolitical importance of the crisis but failed to implement his insights). Most of those who participated in the Iranian debacle treated the shah's crisis as a self-contained problem, and failed to place it in the wider context dictated by American national interests. Even Ambassador Sullivan, who was one of the more imaginative and active performers in the piece, defined American interests in Iran in quite narrow terms: protecting the integrity of Iran, and preserving it from undue Soviet influence and control. It is difficult to find a leading American official who foresaw the grave international consequences that would follow the fall of the shah and his replacement by forces hostile to the West. In part, this was due to the misperception of Khomeini; but there were broader ideological and political reasons for the singular lack of geopolitical concern in Washington.

Carter, Brzezinski, Brown, Turner, and Vance wished to distinguish themselves and their policies from those of the recent past, and especially from those associated with Kissinger. Whatever else this implied, it required that the President wrap his foreign policy initiatives in a moral blanket, and not present his ideas on the basis of pure *realpolitik*. All these men wanted to be perceived as supporting "progressive" goals, both at home and abroad, and they consequently desired to see America on the side of those movements that were considered progressive. The role of Andrew Young in shaping and supporting this attitude was undoubtedly important, and it is not an exaggeration to suggest that a good deal of Carter's policy was based on the model of the American civil rights movement. The administration would not wish to be identified with governments or movements that could be defined as conservative, repressive, colonial, or racist. The President wanted to be seen in tandem with governments and movements that were considered progressive, revolutionary, black, anticolonial, and democratic. This was an admirable ambition, but in their enthusiasm for the moralization of American foreign policy, Carter and his advisers often forgot that words do not always have the same meaning in different cultures and contexts. And one of the most seductive words during the Iranian crisis was "religious." Once the ayatollah had been identified as a religious leader, it was difficult for the President to think of him as an enemy. Carter's own religious experiences led him to feel that an ayatollah was a kindred spirit. Young's conviction that Khomeini was saintly undoubtedly came from a similarly uncritical outlook. Thus the intelligence failure on Khomeini was to at least some degree a by-product of the subjective attitudes of the President and his leading associates.

The same applies to the administration's handling of the shah. In their desire to be "progressive," the Carter officials failed to make some of the elementary distinctions that are required to analyze the contemporary world. Foremost amongst these is the difference between totalitarian and authoritarian regimes: The first are not only repressive but create political structures that eliminate all possibilities for the development of freedom. The second are often heavily repressive, but are designed to perpetuate the rule of a single individual or group, rather than to establish a durable *system* that will withstand any and all initiatives for change. The difference can readily be perceived when one considers what happens after the death of the ruler in the two cases: When an authoritarian ruler like Franco or Salazar dies, the entire structure of the government is thrown into question. When a Stalin dies, the only question is the identity of the successor, not the survival of the system itself. There are therefore significant differences between dictatorships; and while Americans properly deplore all dictatorships, it is necessary to distinguish between those that are totalitarian, and hence highly immune to change, and those that are authoritarian, and hence likely to be relatively short-lived. To take the case under discussion, one could conceive of successfully modernizing the Iranian government under the shah, even though he was a dictator. One cannot easily imagine structural reforms in the Soviet Union, China, Cuba, or Vietnam without violent revolution or military defeat. These distinctions were not made by Carter or his top officials, with the result that the U.S. human rights policy eventually bore fruit in countries that cared about American opinions, and were capable of making at least some internal adjustments. Unfortunately, most of these countries were friends or allies, and often risked their internal stability to curry favor in Washington. One may applaud such changes, provided that they do not produce damaging shifts in the overall security of the United States. One cannot ask of an ally that it commit suicide in the name of human rights.

If one distinguishes properly between authoritarian and totalitarian regimes, then American criticism of the practices of other countries will concentrate on the latter instead of being limited to the former. The human rights theme is entirely appropriate to American traditions and aspirations, and should be an integral part of the nation's foreign policy. But it should not be a policy of masochism masquerading as a civilizing mission.

This leads to another broad consideration that can only be touched upon here: the question of cultural differences. Americans are often seduced by the form of things, and the words given to various institutions and practices. In Iran, the process of "Westernization" or "industrialization" was given the same significance that it had in western Europe and the United States, with the result that American analysts tended to think of Iranian classes, institutions, and processes in much the same way they thought about their American equivalents. This was a grievous error, for in many non-Western countries —including Iran—much of "Westernization" is a myth, and the tools with which a society is supposedly being "modernized" are actually used as weapons by local elites for attaining and maintaining power. In Iran, the shah exploited modernization to concentrate power in his own hands.

Thus the mere establishment of Western-seeming institutions does not automatically create the same kind of social and cultural changes that were brought about in the West. This was often forgotten, especially in the case of the religious caste. It is a commonplace in the literature on modernization that as a society takes on the forms of Western countries, religion becomes less important, and religious leaders lose power. This is no doubt true in the long run, but it is not a reliable guide to policy in the shorter term. Both the Americans and the shah forgot that classes that are losing power are nonetheless capable of remarkable signs of life. Yet the shah wrote in his autobiography that if the White Revolution had been permitted to function for just three more years, the people would no longer have listened to the mullahs, and the Americans did not grasp the true nature of the Iranian revolution until very late in the day. One needed to be more empirical about Iran, and less taken with models of socio-cultural development. As usual, the finest instrument of analysis is the nose; those analysts who got it right were those who spent a lot of time in Iran, immersed themselves in the popular culture, and sensed the mood of the country.

The failure to diagnose the true nature of the Khomeini movement also stems in part from the debasement of political language in the United States. The term "fascist" had been used so often in recent years—against local police forces, petty dictators, and even American government officials—that the true meaning of the word had been forgotten. Hardly anyone recognized the genuine article when it appeared, and more often than not scholars and officials alike spoke of a "religious protest" movement, or even demands for civil rights.

Yet the ideology and the sociological composition of the movement had all the marks of the fascist revolution. Both the emerging and sinking components of the lower middle classes were threatened, and were mobilized into a hyper-nationalistic movement that was organized around a charismatic leader, exploiting mass rituals and religious symbolism.

Good intelligence requires good intelligence collectors and analysts, who will generally have to be out on the job rather than in offices in Washington. Critics of the CIA's performance in Iran have fairly stressed the low level of contacts with the opposition, yet this criticism is slightly exaggerated on two counts. First, American personnel *had* contacts with the opposition, both in Iran and elsewhere. There might well have been more, but this was not central to the understanding of the Iranian crisis; there was no lack of information, whether in human or printed form. The real issue was the dynamics in the street, the attitudes of the people, the low esteem of the monarchy—and, of course, the shah himself.

There is an agency in Washington that is supposed to provide an "institutional memory" for the President when he has to make a decision: the Department of State. The archives of the department ought to have been full of information on religious leaders, and on the shah of Iran. There should have been area specialists capable of explaining to the President the dynamics of Khomeini's movement, and of charting the shah's psychological decline. No such expert seems to have existed. Why?

The American bureaucracy does not reward specialists, but instead insists on the development of well-grounded generalists. The system of incentive and rewards is geared to the foreign service officer who can do many things well, has a passing acquaintance with several countries and cultures, and facility in several languages. It is far harder—if not impossible—to advance speedily as an expert in a restricted area. While this system guarantees versatility among State Department officials, it makes the continuity of understanding among regional experts very difficult. It is rare indeed that anyone spends more than three to four years working on a particular country before moving on to a different area, and possibly a different focus of interest altogether.

The intelligence community is not much better. By the time of the Iranian crisis, there was only one CIA analyst who had spent the bulk of his professional career working on Iranian questions. And, as has been seen, when it was deemed necessary to create a special task force, the CIA appointed as its chief an expert on the Arab Gulf states. Once again, there was limited institutional memory.

If America is to conduct a first-class foreign policy, it needs the kind of expertise that can only come from a person who has devoted his or her life to the detailed study of a limited subject. To be sure, there are scholars in the academic community who do just that, but they are often unfamiliar with diplomatic or strategic problems, and with the delicate secret information that only a government collects. Both the State Department and the intelligence community should provide for the creation of regional bureaus manned at least in part by career specialists, thus guaranteeing that the government will have long-term continuity at a fairly high bureaucratic level.

THE UNITED STATES currently suffers from the worst sin in the diplomatic bible: lack of clarity. Neither allies nor enemies know what the nation desires. The Iranian debacle is one of the clearest cases of recent disarray in Washington, but it is easy to name other examples—the confusion over the neutron bomb, the proposed cuts in American strength in South Korea, and the ambitious program for a comprehensive Middle East peace settlement, for instance. When

American goals are unclear, no effective alliance policies can be formulated, and American allies are tempted to strike out on their own. So a U.S. President must specify the national goals.

We do not presume to suggest the full range of American objectives, but it is surely time to stop trying to shape foreign policy to the requirements of an abstract standard of human rights. The overriding requirement for American foreign policy—as for that of any other country in any time or place—is national security. And since the United States has global commitments, it must conduct a global policy that will pursue working arrangements with all manner of foreign governments. The United States wishes to see its friends— and others—move toward democracy, and when the opportunity presents itself, Americans should be prepared to exert considerable pressure toward that goal. But when the United States is faced with a choice between a productive alliance with a dictator, or loss of security by destabilizing another government, it should be mature enough to accept temporarily the former, with all its obvious discomfort.

From time to time Americans will have to remind themselves that the world is not always amenable to their national standards, and that American policies must be accommodated to the unpleasant realities of different cultures and different political systems. At the same time, this is no reason to abandon America's own revolutionary values, or to lose faith in its mission. The ideological struggle may well prove decisive, and this consideration suggests a long-term policy of exporting the democratic revolution.

It is also necessary to admit that the United States has enemies. Not all problems in the world are the result of misunderstandings or American failures; there are many who wish the nation ill, as the Khomeini regime in Iran has richly demonstrated. In retrospect, it is plain that Khomeini had a better appreciation of the strategic importance of Iran in the Middle Eastern equation than did President Carter. America failed to perceive that Iran was a potentially weak link in its international security system, but Khomeini saw this quite clearly. His success in Tehran was only the initial stage in a revolutionary wave that he hoped would sweep through the entire region. Carter and his advisers saw the Khomeini phenomenon solely in its national context. It is now realized that countries from Egypt and Israel to Saudi Arabia, Iraq, and the Emirates of the Persian Gulf must deal with the consequences of the Iranian revolution.

So the United States must return to the basic principles upon which all successful foreign policy is based: sufficient military power to deter potential enemies (or to win a military conflict), stable alliances to enhance national security, and, above all, clarity and coherence in the pursuit of objectives. It does not seem beyond American capabilities; yet it has been some time since the nation has been blessed with leaders able to meet these reasonable standards.

If the United States finally embraces a more reasonable and realistic approach to world affairs, it will need to have all the traditional weapons of foreign policy at its disposal. But some of these are currently in short supply. The intelligence community is not what it should be, and the armed forces are distinctly inferior to the demands of the situation. The defense of American interests requires more power than at any previous moment in the country's history, yet that power is not currently available.

This is not an entirely new story, for the democracies of the West have always been slow to recognize their peril and have arrived late at their most important appointments. Nearly thirty years ago, Walter Lippmann implored his countrymen to alter their course:

> We must take the manly view, which is that the failure of the Western democracies during this catastrophic half of the twentieth century is due to the failings of the democratic peoples. They have been attacked and brought down from their preeminence because they have lacked the clarity of purpose and the resolution of mind and of heart to cope with the accumulating disasters and disorders. They have lacked the clarity of purpose and the resolution of mind and of heart to prevent the wars that have ruined the West, to prepare for those wars they could not prevent, and, having won them at last after exorbitant sacrifice and at a ruinous cost, to settle those wars and to restore law and order upon the face of the globe.[2]

America will soon discover whether it is capable of acquiring "the clarity of purpose and the resolution of mind and of heart" to lead the Western democracies out of their current predicament.

Notes

ONE The King of Kings

1. Robert Graham, *Iran: The Illusion of Power* (New York: St. Martin's Press, 1979), p. 53.
2. Arthur Arnold, *Through Persia by Caravan* (London: Tinsley Bros., 1877), p. 179.
3. Shaul Bakhash, "The Iranian Revolution," *New York Review of Books,* June 26, 1980, p. 23.
4. Graham, *Iran,* p. 57.
5. Ernest R. Oney, *The Revolution in Iran: Religion and Politics in a Traditional Society,* International Association of Chiefs of Police, 1980, pp. 9–11.
6. This, along with much of the information in this book, comes from diplomatic cables, made available to us on a confidential basis.
7. Diplomatic cable.
8. Official text of John F. Kennedy's toast at a dinner in the State Dining Room at the White House, April 11, 1962.
9. Diplomatic cable.
10. Nikki R. Keddie, "The Iranian Power Structure and Social Change 1800–1969," *International Journal for Middle East Studies* 2, no. 1 (January 1971): 17.
11. Manfred Halpern, "The Revolution of Modernization" (draft ms., Princeton University, April 24, 1964).
12. Diplomatic cable.
13. Mohammed Reza Shah Pahlavi, *Mission for My Country* (London: Hutchinson, 1974), p. 321.
14. Diplomatic cable.
15. Yair P. Hirschfeld, "Decline and Fall of the Pahlavis," *Jerusalem Quarterly,* Summer 1979, p. 27.
16. George Lenczowski, "Iran: the Awful Truth," *American Spectator,* December 1979, p. 2.

Two   The Washington-Tehran Axis

1. Graham, *Iran,* p. 66.
2. Robert Pranger and Dale Tahtinen, *United States Policy in the Persian Gulf* (Washington, D.C.: American Enterprise Institute, 1979), p. 7.
3. Roland A. Paul, *American Military Commitments Abroad* (New Brunswick, N.J.: Rutgers University Press, 1973), pp. 27–28.
4. Pranger and Tahtinen, *U.S. Policy,* p. 9.
5. Diplomatic cable.
6. Stanley Hoffmann, *Primacy or World Order* (New York: McGraw-Hill, 1978), p. 47.
7. U.S. Congress, Senate Subcommittee on Foreign Assistance, "U.S. Military Sales to Iran," July 1976, p. xi.
8. Ibid., p. 32.
9. Ibid., p. 32.

Three   Carter and Iran

1. Unpublished ms. by a member of the Human Rights Bureau.
2. Richard Sale, "Carter and Iran: From Idealism to Disaster," *Washington Quarterly,* Autumn 1980, p. 80.
3. U.S. Department of State, *Bulletin,* November 9, 1977.

Four   The Crisis, I

1. David Menashri, "Iran" in Colin Legum and Haim Shaked, eds., *Middle East Contemporary Survey,* vol. 3 (1978–79) (New York and London: Holmes and Meir, 1980). Since we worked from galley proofs of Menashri's article, we cannot cite a printed page number.
2. Confidential interview shortly after the shah's departure from Iran.
3. Cf. Michael Ledeen, "Khomeini's Theocratic Vision," *Wall Street Journal,* January 5, 1979. For an example of the reaction from Khomeini's supporters in the United States, see the letter to the *Wall Street Journal* from Mahmoud Rashdan, the Secretary General of the Muslim Students Association of the U.S. and Canada, January 22, 1979.
4. Joseph Alpher, "The Khomeini International," *Washington Quarterly,* Autumn 1980, p. 61.
5. The most careful analysis of the phenomenon is found in Ervand Abrahamman, "The Guerrilla Movement in Iran, 1963–1977," *Merip Reports,* no. 86 (March–April 1980).
6. Oney, *Revolution in Iran,* and Robert Moss, "How Russia Plots Against the Shah," *Sunday Telegraph* (London), November 5, 1978.
7. Michael Ledeen, "The KGB Radio Hour," *American Spectator,* February 1980.
8. Stansfield Turner on ABC's "Issues and Answers," February 4, 1979.
9. Mohammed Reza Shah Pahlavi, "How the Americans Overthrew Me," *Now!,* December 7, 1979, p. 33.
10. U.S. Congress, House Permanent Select Committee on Intelligence, "Iran: evaluation of U.S. intelligence performance prior to November 1978," staff report, pp. 4 ff.
11. *Washington Post,* November 20, 1978.

12. Joseph Kraft, "Letter from Iran," *New Yorker,* December 18, 1978, p. 159.
13. Text of President Carter's press conference, November 13, 1978.
14. *Newsweek,* March 5, 1979, p. 43.
15. *U.S. News and World Report,* May 7, 1979, p. 32.

FIVE   The Crisis, II

1. Robert Moss, "Who Burned the Rex Cinema?" *Daily Telegraph* (London), November 6, 1978.
2. David Menashri, "Iran," in Colin Legum and Haim Shakhed, eds., *Middle East Contemporary Survey,* vol. 2 (1977–78), p. 483.
3. Kraft, "Letter from Iran," p. 162.
4. Sharif Arani, "Iran from the Shah's Dictatorship to Khomeini's Demagogic Theocracy," *Dissent,* Winter 1980, pp. 17–18.
5. Herman Nickel in *Fortune,* March 12, 1979, p. 98.
6. Cited in Menashri, "Iran," vol. 3.
7. Arani, "Iran," p. 14.
8. Robert Shaplen, series on Newsom, *New Yorker,* June 2, 9, and 16, 1979.
9. See George Ball's interview in *Politique Internationale,* Autumn, 1979.
10. Washington *Post*, November 19, 1978.
11. Washington *Post*, November 20, 1978.
12. Official text of President Carter's press conference, December 7, 1978.
13. Arani, "Iran," p. 19.

SIX   The Revolution

1. Kraft, "Letter from Iran," p. 168.
2. Confidential interviews.
3. Confidential interviews.
4. Washington *Post*, June 18, 1980.
5. Confidential interviews.

SEVEN   The Ayatollah's Revenge

1. See Bazargan's interview with Oriana Fallaci, *New York Times Magazine,* October 28, 1979.
2. *Kayhan International,* July 10, 1979.
3. Menashri, "Iran," vol. 3.
4. *L'Express,* June 21, 1980. For some excerpts in English, see Michael Ledeen, "Presswatch," *American Spectator,* August 1980.
5. Cited in Congressional Research Service chronology prepared by Clyde R. Mark and by members of the Iran Task Force.
6. BBC broadcast September 11, 1979, and *Ettela'at,* May 24, 1979.
7. *Ettela'at* and *Kayhan,* May 16, 1979.
8. Radio Tehran broadcasts, September 6 and 7, 1979. See also *International Herald Tribune,* October 15, 1979, and Menashri, "Iran," vol. 3.

9. *The Guardian,* September 14, 1979.
10. Confidential interview.
11. *New York Times,* Jan. 28, 1979.
12. Leonard Binder, special presentation to Senator Lloyd Bentsen and the U.S. Senate Joint Economic Committee, March 1979.
13. Congressional Research Service chronology.
14. Diplomatic cable.
15. Diplomatic cable.
16. Shaplen, Newsom series, II.
17. Washington *Post*, June 18, 1980.
18. U.S. Congress, Senate Committee on Foreign Affairs, Subcommittee on Europe and the Middle East, July 26, 1979.

CONCLUSION   The Future of Foreign Policy

1. U.S. Department of State, *Bulletin,* November 16, 1979.
2. Walter Lippmann, "The Shortage of Education," *Atlantic Monthly,* May 1954.

Index

ABOUT THE AUTHORS

MICHAEL LEDEEN became special adviser to the secretary of state in the summer of 1981. He was executive editor of the *Washington Quarterly* from 1977–81. He was educated at Pomona College and the University of Wisconsin, receiving his Ph.D. in 1969. He taught at Washington University from 1967 to 1974, and is the author of five books on Italian politics and history. He has contributed articles to the *New Republic*, *Commentary*, *Harper's*, the *American Spectator*, and other publications.

WILLIAM LEWIS is professor of political science at the Institute for Sino-Soviet Studies, George Washington University. He studied at Oxford University and Johns Hopkins University and received his Ph.D. from American University. He has worked in the State Department's Bureau of Political and Military Affairs and has been a senior fellow at the Brookings Institution. He has written several books on African and Middle-Eastern affairs.